Developing Brazil

DEVELOPING
BRAZIL

Overcoming the Failure
of the Washington Consensus

Luiz Carlos Bresser-Pereira

LYNNE
RIENNER
PUBLISHERS

BOULDER
LONDON

Published in the United States of America in 2009 by
Lynne Rienner Publishers, Inc.
1800 30th Street, Boulder, Colorado 80301
www.rienner.com

and in the United Kingdom by
Lynne Rienner Publishers, Inc.
3 Henrietta Street, Covent Garden, London WC2E 8LU

Library of Congress Cataloging-in-Publication Data
Pereira, Luiz Carlos Bresser.
    Developing Brazil : overcoming the failure of the Washington consensus /
Luiz Carlos Bresser-Pereira.
        p.   cm.
    Includes bibliographical references and index.
    ISBN 978-1-58826-624-8 (hardcover : alk. paper)
    1. Brazil—Economic policy. 2. Brazil—Economic conditions—1985–
3. Macroeconomics—Brazil. I. Title.
HC187.P392212 2009
338.981—dc22

                                                            2008048410

British Cataloguing in Publication Data
A Cataloguing in Publication record for this book
is available from the British Library.

Printed and bound in the United States of America

        The paper used in this publication meets the requirements
 ∞   of the American National Standard for Permanence of
        Paper for Printed Library Materials Z39.48-1992.

    5 4 3 2 1

Contents

Preface

This book is a discussion of why the Brazilian economy performed so poorly after the 1994 price stabilization and, more generally, a critique of the Washington Consensus—the conventional orthodoxy—that has presided over economic policy in Brazil since the early 1990s. It is also an analysis of the national development strategy that is gradually being defined in Brazil—an approach that I call new developmentalism—which is an alternative to the strategy that caused high rates of growth in Brazil between 1930 and 1980 (i.e., national developmentalism) and to conventional orthodoxy.

I know that in the North today conventional economists and journalists regularly praise Brazil's economic performance and moderate international policies. Such positive assessment reminds me of the way that Argentina and Russia were presented in the 1990s, although President Lula is no Carlos Menem or Boris Yeltsin. Yet, since 1980, when the debt crisis began, or even since 1994, when the Real Plan stabilized high inflation, Brazil's growth has been much smaller than what its natural resources and its relatively cheap labor would predict. I will present data to demonstrate that the economic performance of Brazil is much worse than that of China and India since 1980 and worse than Russia's since the late 1990s—three countries that usually are cited together with Brazil as the BRIC countries (Brazil, Russia, India, and China).

The Washington Consensus demonstrably failed to promote growth and redistribution in the countries that adopted it, whereas the countries that didn't adopt it, but instead updated their development strategies, continue to grow steadily. Brazil falls into the former category, the dynamic Asian countries into the latter. There is also a third category of countries that, like Argentina and Russia, adopted the conventional orthodoxy promoted by the Washington Consensus and suffered major crises, but that learned their lessons, changed their macroeconomic policies, and experienced high growth rates. Nevertheless, in many countries, including Brazil and Mexico, the conventional orthodoxy continues to dominate economic policies. I argue in the pages that follow that Brazil and many other developing countries can achieve substantially higher rates of growth and be successful in catching up with the income levels of advanced countries if they adopt specific national growth strategies instead of simply abiding by an economic ideology that reflects rich countries' recommendations and pressures. In doing so, I use theories and models, but keep them simple, believing that good economics, like any good theory, can almost always be explained in simple terms. My subject matter is Brazil's economy, but my analysis is intended to have a broader application to other developing countries.

I have been critical of the Washington Consensus and of the macroeconomics of stagnation that it implies ever since it became dominant in Latin America (Bresser-Pereira 1991a [1990]). My criticism, however, gained a new dimension beginning in the first quarter of 1999, by which time I had been for several years a member of the Cardoso administration.[1] That administration's economic policies, after the successful and innovative Real Plan of 1994, became fully orthodox and led the country to two balance-of-payment crises. From 1999 to 2001, Yoshiaki Nakano, my constant companion on this intellectual journey, and I embarked on a systematic critique of the conventional orthodoxy based on our shared structuralist and Keynesian views of economics (see Bresser-Pereira 2001a [1999]; Bresser-Pereira and Nakano 2002, 2003). Our criticism showed that the conventional proposals, albeit inclusive of certain necessary policies and reforms, did not, in fact, promote a country's development, but instead kept it semistagnant, incapable of competing with wealthier countries, and easy prey to a form of economic populism, namely, foreign exchange populism. Our alternative economic strategy—new developmentalism—was innovative in that it acknowledged a series of historical facts that implied a need to review the national development strategy. New developmentalism is both a "third discourse" between old developmentalism and conventional orthodoxy and a national development strategy that attributes a smaller role to the state and to industrial policy while emphasizing macroeconomic stability and sustainable development. It may be viewed as an updated developmentalist strategy applied to countries that have risen to become middle-income countries. It is also a strategy that responds to the new realities of global capitalism. I am not proposing to return to the "developmental state" that Chalmers Johnson (1982) identified in Japan, but to look to the state that in a middle-income country in the twenty-first century effectively complements markets in the coordination of the economy and the promotion of economic, social, and sustainable development.[2]

An earlier version of this book was published in Portuguese in Brazil (Bresser-Pereira 2007); the present edition is not, however, simply a translation, but an updated, improved work. In writing the book I relied on the collaboration of a group of macroeconomists who have been colleagues in criticizing the prevailing system and who read the manuscript and offered suggestions: Yoshiaki Nakano, Fernando Ferrari Filho, Gilberto Tadeu Lima, José Luís Oreiro, Luiz Fernando de Paula, Matias Vernengo, and Paulo Gala. I am also grateful for the assistance of several economists and political scientists who provided me with data or with whom I discussed topics in the book: Alexandre De Zagottis, Antônio Carlos Macedo e Silva, Arício Xavier de Oliveira, Arthur Barrionuevo Filho, Cícero Araújo, Fábio Giambiagi, Fernando Dall'Acqua, Gilberto Dupas, Gildo Marçal Brandão, Hélcio Tokeshi, João Sicsú, José Márcio Rego, José Roberto Afonso, Lauro Gonzalez, Lílian Furquim, Luiz Antônio Oliveira Lima, Márcio Holland, Miguel Bruno, Nelson Marconi, Ricardo Carneiro, Rodrigo Bresser Pereira, Paulo Nogueira Batista Jr., and Rogério Mori.

Cleomar Gomes dos Santos was involved in writing the chapter on inflation-targeting policy and Paulo Gala the chapter on the critique of growth with foreign savings. Help from Carmen Augusta Varela was crucial to my research, and I am indebted to her and to Cecília Heise for their meticulous review of my manuscript. I am especially indebted to Alexandra Strommer de Godoi for reviewing the manuscript and making several useful comments. During the writing of the book I had support from G. V. Pesquisa at the São Paulo School of Business Administration of the Getúlio Vargas Foundation. My final thanks go to Lynne Rienner, an old friend and publisher of several of my books in the United States, who showed interest in also publishing this one and who stimulated me to improve it. My permanent interlocutor throughout this effort was my lifelong wife, Vera Cecília. I dedicate this book to my five children and ten grandchildren, who stand to gain the most if any of the ideas proposed and discussed here take hold.

Notes

1. From 1995 to 1999 I was a member of the Fernando Henrique Cardoso administration—as minister of federal administration and reform of the state—

and throughout that period I personally made clear to the president my disagreement with the economic policies that his economic team was pursuing.

2. Other classical analyses of the developmental state include those by Alice Amsden (1989) on Korea and Robert Wade (1990) on Taiwan. For a more recent treatment, see Woo-Cummings (1999). These works deal with Asian countries, but between the 1930s and the 1980s, Brazil was also a developmental state (see Bresser-Pereira 1977).

Introduction

Brazil in the early twenty-first century is experiencing a time of uncertainty and self-questioning. The country attained democracy in 1985 and has been making a great effort to reduce the radical inequalities that mark its society, but the economy has been nearly stagnant since 1980; although the huge increase in commodity prices has improved growth rates in the early years of the century, overappreciation of the domestic currency makes the future uncertain and optimism unwise. The core political goals of modern societies are security, freedom, well-being, social justice, and protection of the environment, but we do not know how to achieve them. Capitalism is victorious and organizes the surface of the earth with nation-states that compete through their firms, but many forms of capitalism exist, all more or less dynamic, more or less assuring of freedom, more or less fair, and none has a monopoly on the one true path. The hegemonic power, the United States, which at one time—the early 1990s—thought it knew what this true path might be, turned it into the Washington Consensus and into an economic "conventional orthodoxy" that failed to convince a number of Asian countries; those that it did convince lagged behind economically. This is one of the reasons why such hegemony has, since the turn of the century, been experiencing a very deep crisis.

My goal in this book is to better understand the perverse economic reasoning that, inspired by the conventional orthodoxy, prevails in Brazil, notwithstanding that high inflation rates were tamed in 1994 and despite a favorable international economic scenario. My goal is to develop a political argument and a macroeconomic argument to criticize a strategy that rich countries seek to sell to developing countries or (if they get duly indebted) to impose on them using the International Monetary Fund (IMF), the World Bank, and the international financial system as tools. To this end, I attempt to determine why Brazil has not yet attained macroeconomic stability despite the economic policy framework put in place on its behalf. I attempt to determine the coalition of social and political forces that has led Brazilian governments to ignore the Dutch disease (see Chapter 6 for a complete definition) and to accept the policy of growth with foreign savings and other recommendations from the North. And, finally, I propose to lay out the general outlines of a prudent and viable alternative to the macroeconomic policy in place—a new policy that preserves price stability, attains true macroeconomic stability, and enables development to resume—as well as to show the falsehood of the conventional discourse that maintains that the only alternative to the orthodoxy is economic populism: Brazil has shown in the past, and other nations, Asian ones in particular, are showing now, that an alternative does exist. The argument is complex, both politically and macroeconomically, but, if I had to offer an explanation for the quasi stagnation since the early 1980s, I would summarize the political argument as the loss of the idea of nation and the macroeconomic argument as the loss of control over the exchange rate. If I and many others argued in the 1980s that the great problems the country faced were a fiscal crisis of the state coupled with a foreign debt crisis, I now claim that the main political obstacle the country faces is the weakening of the Brazilian nation and that the main economic hurdle is the acceptance of the conventional orthodoxy as the country's macroeconomic policy.

Every power system has its own logic, which becomes more sophisticated as societies progress. Old imperial systems relied on the force of arms; modern ones, such as those represented by advanced countries in the age of global capitalism, prefer ideological hegemony as a means to affirm their interests and to neutralize the competitiveness of middle-income countries such as Brazil.[1] Old empires merely bought the collaboration of subjugated elites in order to exercise imperial domination; modern, and relatively weaker, imperial systems resort to the ideological co-optation of local elites but, to this end, require complex ideological systems such as hegemonic thinking and its application to developing countries: the Washington Consensus and its conventional orthodoxy. To criticize hegemonic thinking, even if limited to the conventional orthodoxy, is by no means a trivial republican endeavor. The rhetoric of hegemonic thinking is always that of perfect rationality, of the identification of its postulates and conclusions with common sense, scientific objectivity, and morality of the day; it is the rhetoric of the sole legitimate option. Hegemonic thinking sees itself as perfect because it finds legitimacy in the economics developed by the world's best universities—its own—and because every empire sees itself as the bringer of enlightenment and civilization, of peace and progress, of freedom and democracy. No matter that all the evidence shows that, on the contrary, the most successful developing countries have accomplished their capitalist revolutions by following a different path; it is irrelevant that those countries that accept hegemonic thinking with docility almost invariably go into a state of quasi stagnation. Although force is always to hand, it is far more important for hegemonic power to impose conventional knowledge or an orthodoxy on the dominated. J. K. Galbraith (1958) coined the term *conventional wisdom,* which has now become part of the English lexicon as a synonym for accepted—and mistaken—truths. This is the kind of truth that the empire transfers to its periphery through the "soft power" of hegemony—a kind of power that many progressive Americans believe superior to the "hard power" of their hawkish peers, heedless of the fact that, right though they may be, this shows that the alternative of not exercising power simply does not exist for the hegemonic power.[2] Words such as *nationalism, developmentalism,* and *capital controls* enter the index of forbidden words (after all, it is not only Catholic orthodoxy that had its *Index Librorum Prohibitorum*), and those who embrace such ideas are termed "outdated" or "populists." This kind of thinking, or language, is presented as naturally as possible, but, according to Edward Said (2003 [1978], p. 321), who criticized hegemonic domination by the West of the Eastern peoples, it is a mythical language. "Mythical language is a discourse and, therefore, cannot help but be systematic; no one discourses freely, no one makes statements without first belonging—in certain cases unconsciously, but always involuntarily—to the ideology and institutions that assure one's existence. The latter are invariably the institutions of an advanced culture dealing with less developed societies, a strong culture encountering a weak one."

The opponent, therefore, is powerful, but this is not to say that developing countries are condemned to eternal subordination. Hegemonic idea systems follow a cyclic pattern of an increasingly short duration. British hegemony lasted a little more than a century, ending in World War I. US hegemony established itself after World War II, reaching its acme in 1989 with the collapse of the Soviet Union, but in 1995—the start of the period analyzed in this book—the neoliberal and globalist wave through which this hegemony expressed itself was already facing internal problems; in the 2000s it is in deep crisis. Hegemonic power is by definition strong but is offset by the real interests of peripheral societies, whose elites often refuse subordination, whether because of patriotic feelings of belonging, or because their real interests lie in their own country, or because only in their own country can they rely on the state as an instrument of collective action, as the states of developed countries are in their own nations. Although hegemonic thinking has encountered substantial hurdles since it assumed a neoliberal form and managed to impose itself on the world circa 1990, it remains dominant in a large number of developing countries. The following years have been marked by deep financial crises affecting "emerging markets" in the 1990s, by the brutal crisis in Argentina in 2001, and by the disaster that was the invasion of Iraq—years that indicate the hegemony's clear decline. As a result, even the traditionally more dependent Latin American countries, which more easily accepted the recommendations of the conventional orthodoxy and suffered the most, have now begun to appreciate the decline of hegemonic thinking and the opportunity this decline affords them to reorganize and formulate national development strategies. Around the world, the North's neoliberal and conservative hegemony is being challenged; the Washington Consensus is contested and severely criticized.

This book, by focusing on Brazil and the period during which conventional orthodoxy was prevalent there (1995–2006), seeks, on the one hand, to contribute to changing the country's economic policy and, on the other, to stand as a critique of the set of diagnoses and policies by means of which the North's hegemony is exercised. Criticism of imperial systems has always been fundamental in late countries' efforts to attain higher levels, to catch up. In the nineteenth century the English hegemony did not prevent France, the United States, Germany, and Japan from developing. The Great Depression of the 1930s created an opportunity for Latin American countries, and particularly Brazil, to find a path to industrialization and development. The end of colonialism after World War II created the opportunity for Asian countries such as South Korea, Taiwan, Thailand, Malaysia, and, later on, China and India to attain high economic growth rates.[3] In Latin America, the great foreign debt crisis of the 1980s disorganized the region's nations, cut short their national revolutions, and led them, beginning in 1990, to surrender to the conventional orthodoxy. As a consequence, countries lost importance and contented themselves with much lower growth rates. In Brazil, after 1995 the conventional orthodoxy implemented a macroeconomic policy based on soft fiscal policy, high interest rates, and a noncompetitive exchange rate;[4] this would be an orthodox policy. Meanwhile the dynamic

Asian countries adopted the opposite policy, namely, the macroeconomic tripod that I understand to characterize new developmentalism: hard fiscal adjustment, moderate interest rates, and competitive exchange rates. If we leave aside the claim that in practical terms the conventional orthodoxy is soft in fiscal terms (I discuss this in Chapter 4), the strange thing is that the high interest rates–noncompetitive exchange rate binomial is the opposite not only of new developmentalism but also of the good, "orthodox" practices of rich countries' central banks and finance ministries; macroeconomic orthodoxy in rich countries is one thing, in developing countries, another. This fact, besides showing the difference between using a national development strategy and using an imported strategy, also shows a well-known imperial use: "make what I say, not what I do." The failure of the conventional orthodoxy's policies and the success of Asian national strategies, however, have created a new opportunity for Latin American countries, especially Brazil: an opportunity to rebuild themselves as nations and to resume formulating a national development strategy, that is, new developmentalism. This book is essentially about Brazil, but it includes the dynamic Asian countries because it makes repeated reference to their new developmentalism. On the other hand, I believe that the ideas discussed in this book will be helpful to many other developing countries that, like Brazil, were unable to frame a serious and workable alternative to the conventional orthodoxy—the alternative that I call new developmentalism.

Method

In this book I employ the historical-deductive method, which takes an observation of an economic reality and, based on the determination of patterns and trends, attempts to generalize from it and build a theoretical model. This was the method that Adam Smith and Karl Marx used to understand the fundamental economic transformation that was the capitalist revolution and that John Maynard Keynes adopted for the world economy after World War I to formulate the first macroeconomic monetary economy model. The assumption is that the purpose of economics is not merely to provide a toolbox but to formulate models for concrete economic systems. When the great classical economists analyzed the capitalist revolution, the economic system they sought to model was exceedingly broad; when Keynes and Michael Kalecki originally formulated macroeconomics, their subject was more restricted, but still broad; when I, in this book, attempt to understand the macroeconomics of stagnation that has prevailed in Brazil since 1995, I am focusing on a more constrained economic system, but since I am simultaneously analyzing and criticizing the reasoning of the conventional orthodoxy in terms of macroeconomics, the scope again expands.

Macroeconomics lies at the heart of economics; it is the branch of economics that shows how economic systems work based on the behavior of the fundamental economic aggregates—income or product, investment, savings, consumption, public revenues and expenditures, or domestic revenues and expenditures—plus the five macroeconomic prices: profit rate, wage rate, inflation rate, interest rate, and exchange rate. Macroeconomics, therefore, is an empirical science with a historically observable subject, so that the appropriate method for approaching it is the historical-deductive method. This method differs from the hypothetical-deductive method used by neoclassical economists and used fundamentally in microeconomics, although the neoclassical authors tirelessly attempt to apply it to substantive areas of economics such as macroeconomics and the theory of economic development. The hypothetical-deductive method, based as it is on a hypothetical *homo economicus,* facilitates making economics more "accurate"—as accurate, in extremis, as mathematics, which, as a methodological rather than a substantive science, legitimately uses the method. Thus developed, microeconomics is useful if treated as a methodological aspect of economics, as is the case with game theory or econometrics. Analysis of concrete economic systems, however, can be performed only with the historical-deductive method, which does use hypothetical-deductive tools, but only to arrive at models for the system under examination (Bresser-Pereira 2005d). Making economic theory means developing models for real economic systems and then testing them, insofar as it is possible, through empirical, econometric research. The models thus obtained are open-ended ones that provide a modest description of open systems such as real economic systems. Mathematics, a methodological science devoid of subject and based purely on logical assumptions, may have closed models; substantive sciences, working as they do with empirical subjects, may develop simple models of great explanatory power, but such models will necessarily be open-ended and, therefore, modest about their claims to truth.

Adopting this method clearly frames me as a Keynesian rather than a neoclassical economist. And what kind of Keynesian economist am I? Post-Keynesian, neo-Keynesian, new Keynesian? I choose not to tie myself to this or that thread, as the reality to hand—the Brazilian economy—is very different from that with which these schools concern themselves. What matters is to believe that all of macroeconomics will be forever Keynesian, because it was founded by Keynes; but no form of macroeconomics can be Keynesian alone, because it is a historical discipline that, faced with new facts or with ever-present structural or institutional changes, must be constantly updated, revised, rethought. Adopting an empirical-deductive, rather than hypothetical-deductive, method implies that the truth criterion for economics is not mainly logical consistency (this is the criterion that applies to the methodological sciences), but empirical verification. Still, as such verification is not always easy or feasible, and as the ultimate goal of science is to guide human action, a second criterion of validity for economics is the pragmatic forecasting ability of its models. If, for example, a model showing that an economic policy based on loose fiscal adjustment, high interest rates, and volatile exchange rates tends to produce low economic growth is confirmed in practice—as has been the case in Brazil—such a model will be correct. Another example: if the same model predicts that inflation will not spin out of control if interest rates drop to civilized levels, and such a prediction is borne out when rates are lowered, the model will be likewise confirmed. A final example: when, based on the theory of inflation inertia, we argued that a stabilization plan as powerful as was the Collor Plan in fiscal and monetary terms would be unable to eliminate inflation because it failed to adopt a strategy to neutralize inflation inertia, and this forecast was borne out—then the theory of inertial inflation is confirmed as true.[5] For all this, I reject the "consistentialism" implied in neoclassical economics and its attempt to reduce macroeconomics to a closed system by assuming rational expectations. Since economics is the science of markets, the two central laws according to which markets operate—the law of supply and demand and the tendency of profit rates to equalize when relative prices are in equilibrium—must never be cast aside in the name of the voluntarism arising from the role in which statists cast planning or, as neoclassical economists put it, of expectations and "credibility."

Neoclassical macroeconomics often exaggerates the role of expectations, accusing them of running against the second law in particular. A good example lies in the disastrous attempts to stabilize inflation by coordinating expectations, as was tried in the Southern Cone of Latin America at the turn of the 1970s and into the 1980s, using the exchange rate as a coordination instrument (Diaz-Alejandro 1991 [1981]). Another example can be found in neoclassical economists' and the conventional orthodoxy's insistence on explaining high inflation as simply an expectations-related problem that could be overcome by means of the government's commitment to strict monetary and fiscal policies, instead of understanding that inflation inertia was characterized by a permanent distributive conflict due to lagging price adjustments on the part of actors who were therefore constantly pushing relative prices into and out of equilibrium.[6] The radical use of the "rational expectations" assumption and of the concept of "credibility" lies at the root of serious mistakes in macroeconomic theory and policy. Expectations and credibility are crucial to markets' behavior, and there is always rationality in them, but the expectations of economic actors are not so rational as to "correspond to the true model," as intended by the radical theory of rational expectations. For economic and social life to flourish and for economic policymakers to be effective, trust must be omnipresent. This trust, however, springs not from an acknowledgment of the appropriate model and the strict observance of rules, but from the mutual understanding of all—an understanding that requires theorists and policymakers to be prudent and modest, as well as able to discern what is new—to understand the structural change that institutional change and, therefore, economic policy change requires.[7]

The economic system I analyze here is well defined. It is the macroeconomic system that has prevailed in Brazil since the Real Plan of 1994 achieved price stability. An economic system is defined not only by its capitalist nature or its openness to international competition within the framework of globalization, not only by the ratios of wages, profits, and interest through which income is distributed, and not only by the technological variables that condition growth and distribution; it is also defined by the institutions and economic policies it may adopt: by its degree of capital account openness, that is, by whether it accepts involvement in financial globalization (not to be confused with trade globalization); by whether the selected fiscal regime is loose; by its short-term interest rates and foreign exchange policies, which it may seek to manage or to leave to the devices of the markets; and by the political coalitions that support this or that policy. The economic system addressed here is that of countries, such as Brazil, that compete within the framework of global capitalism and, notwithstanding, adopt the recommendations of, or yield to the pressures that come from, the North—the conventional orthodoxy—thereby adopting the competition's advice. Contrasted to them are the dynamic economic systems of Asian countries that follow their own economic policy counsel. The economic system I examine here, therefore, is not an abstraction but a concrete economic, social, and political reality that demands definition in terms of a specific model.

This book is on the area of *development macroeconomics* because its basic tenets are employment and growth, and the basic variables and policies it discusses are macroeconomic ones. I will be using this latter term synonymously with *economic development*—that is, a process of structural transformations in economy and society that lead to better standards of living through the accumulation of capital and the incorporation of technical progress in production—and reserve the term *development,* on its own, to signify the end result of economic, social, political, and environmental development, that is, development as regards the four major objectives of modern societies: well-being, social justice, freedom, and environmental protection. Income growth in a country that finds oil reserves and remains dependent on this product is neither growth nor economic development because its structures, cultures, and institutions—the three dimensions on which a society can be analyzed—remain almost unchanged. Economic development, however, is not always just, does not always take place democratically, and does not always preserve the environment. For equal opportunities, freedom, and respect of nature to be present, there must be social development, political development, and sustainable development.

The Conventional Orthodoxy and New Developmentalism

This book springs from a basic question: why has neither the price stability attained in 1994 nor world prosperity in recent years been enough to lead Brazil to macroeconomic stability and resumed economic growth? Since 1980, Brazil's economy has remained macroeconomically unstable, with low growth and high unemployment. The growth rate of income per capita, which was 4 percent a year between 1950 and 1980, fell to less than 1 percent at one point. In 1994 the Real Plan finally overcame the high inflation that had ravaged the country for 14 years, but the long-awaited resumption of development never came. After 2002, a structural external shock, caused by growing worldwide prosperity, added to two large devaluations of the Brazilian currency and doubled Brazil's exports, but even so, the country failed to show satisfactory growth. This prolonged quasi stagnation of the Brazilian economy led me to write this book. If the Brazilian economy were healthy—if the main macroeconomic indicators pointed toward stability and if the economy were growing at a reasonable pace—we might concern ourselves with long-term reforms capable of contributing to gradually making Brazil a more prosperous, just, and, perhaps, happier society. Alas, this is not the case. Although no country grew as fast as Brazil between 1930 and 1980, since 1980, or since 1994, it has been among the slowest growing of countries.[8]

In this book I offer an explanation of the chronic quasi stagnation of the Brazilian economy. The Brazilian economy fails to grow because it is caught in a trap of high interest rates and an uncompetitive exchange rate that keeps savings and investment rates depressed—a trap that economic policy reinforces instead of identifying and overcoming. Why do these mistakes occur? Naturally, there is an issue of incompetence, there are obstacles to true fiscal adjustment, and there are domestic vested interests in maintaining a high interest rate and an uncompetitive exchange rate, but the main reason is that, in 1995, after 15 years of crisis and no national development strategy, the country's macroeconomic policy was fully subordinated to the dictums of the Washington Consensus: the country's economic "strategy" came to be determined abroad. Never have Brazil's economic policymakers received as many compliments from Washington and New York as they have since 1995. The underlying rationale of the conventional orthodoxy, however, is not resumed development, nor even macroeconomic stability, but serving the commercial and financial interests of advanced countries and, therefore, neutralizing the capacity of middle-income countries such as Brazil, which are regarded as competitors and a threat because of their cheap labor. I will probably be called a "conspiracy theorist" or an "outdated nationalist" for this statement, but it stems from the very nature of globalization, characterized by generalized economic competition between nation-states. In this ever fiercer competition, middle-income countries pose an objective threat to advanced countries, owing mainly to their cheap labor. The threat hangs mainly over the working class and the middle class (whether professional, or wage-earning, or business), who are directly affected by competition from developing countries; this is why US workers opposed the admission of Mexico into the North American Free Trade Agreement (NAFTA); on the other hand, the interests of large multinationals and their executives and shareholders are not so clear, because some stand to gain while others may lose. Since, however, these countries are democracies and politicians play a strategic role, hegemonic thinking and the policies it generates represent the average of national interests; it is this thinking, expressed in the conventional orthodoxy, that regards middle-income countries such as Brazil as threats.[9] In the medium term this is a mistake, as advanced countries will end up benefiting from the greater economic development of all countries;

but, in the short term, the stagnation of wages in rich countries is related to the growing competition from countries with cheap labor.

In accordance with a pattern common to many developing countries, after 1990 the Brazilian economic authorities—with a brief interregnum during the Itamar Franco administration, which included the formulation of the Real Plan—adopted the reforms prescribed by the Washington Consensus and the accompanying monetary policy—one based on high interest rates and an appreciated exchange rate. The same happened in every Latin American country that, having accepted the recommendations of the conventional orthodoxy, relinquished control over its exchange rate by accepting the policy of open foreign accounts and the growth with foreign savings put forward by Washington and New York. The sole exception was Chile, which did the right thing by liberalizing its economy and turning toward exports but also imposed controls on capitals inflows and was thereby able to manage its exchange rate. Not by chance, Chile was the only Latin American country to report satisfactory growth. The orthodoxy's inadequacy as regards resuming economic development, however, soon made itself felt. The second country to adopt it—Mexico—faced a balance-of-payments crisis as early as 1994, and, as the country most committed to the conventional orthodoxy, remains semistagnant to this day. Later, in 1998, Brazil's number came up. But the crisis that indelibly marked the failure of the Washington Consensus was Argentina's, where President Carlos Menem had fully adopted every recommendation—and been commended for it. Like Argentina, Brazil is an example of the disaster of mindless adoption of the conventional orthodoxy by a developing country. Asian countries brought about their capitalist revolutions without implementing certain key conventional orthodoxy recommendations—particularly those regarding open capital accounts and the policy of growth with foreign savings—whereas Brazil, like almost all Latin American countries, subordinated itself to the orthodoxy and to the local interests of nonproductive, or rentier, capital, lagging behind the massive international competition that characterizes today's global capitalism. Several studies show the baleful outcome of the application of the Washington Consensus to Latin America. A recent one (Berr and Combarnous 2007, pp. 536–537) uses factor analysis to examine the impact of these reforms on 23 Latin American and Caribbean countries from 1990 to 2003 and concludes that "an engagement in the process of reforms is not accompanied by significantly stronger growth or a significantly reduced poverty or inequality." In addition, "the 'good students' failed to reach better results than the rest in terms of economic growth." In Asia, several countries that held their ground in the face of the conventional orthodoxy, such as South Korea, Thailand, Indonesia, and Malaysia, also made the same mistake in the early 1990s and endured the crisis of 1997, whereas at the same time, and faced with the same constraints, other countries in Eastern Asia, particularly China, India, and Taiwan, retained control over their exchange rates, preventing them from appreciating, and continued to grow. In more general terms, at the level of reform, while Latin American countries indiscriminately accepted every liberalizing reform, interrupting their national revolutions, letting their nations became disorganized, and losing cohesion and autonomy, Asian countries were more prudent: they accepted certain reforms that were compatible with the higher income levels they had attained but preserved their national autonomy—their national development strategies.

After all the crises, one Latin American country seems to have learned its lesson. The case in point is Argentina, which since 2003 has attained economic growth rates almost on a par with China's. The policy that has been in place since the crisis of 2001, with controlled public accounts, low interest rates, and a managed exchange rate (thanks to those interest rates and to the taxation of commodity exports that, by exploiting abundant natural resources, can cause malignant exchange appreciation), indicates that Argentina is treading a new-developmentalist path. It is still too soon to be sure of its success. Inflation rates close to 12 percent a year in 2006 are a problem whose solution—price controls—is not sustainable in the medium run. The Argentine authorities, however, have been fiscally responsible and are putting up a strong resistance to the pressures of the International Monetary Fund—and, therefore, of the conventional orthodoxy—to appreciate the exchange rate and thereby control inflation. This control will have to be achieved by other means, through a temporarily higher interest rate and more stringent fiscal adjustment—measures compatible with new developmentalism.

Developmentalism was the name given to the national strategy that Latin American countries in general and Brazil in particular adopted between 1930 and 1980. In this period, and especially between 1930 and 1960, many Latin Americans were firmly set on nation building and on finally endowing their formally independent states with national societies equipped with basic solidarity when it came to international competition. But the weakening caused by the crisis of the 1980s, combined with the hegemonic force of the ideological wave that began in the United States in the 1970s and with the internal prevalence of an ideological cycle that I call the Democracy and Justice Cycle, brought the national revolution in Latin American countries to a halt or to a new dependency.

Local elites, who stopped thinking with their own heads, took the advice of, and yielded to the pressures from, the North, and their countries, deprived of their national development strategies, saw development stop in its tracks. The conventional orthodoxy, which replaced national developmentalism, had not been internally formulated and failed to reflect national concerns and interests, but instead reflected the vision and objectives of rich countries. Furthermore, as is typical of neoliberal ideology, it assumed that the market could coordinate everything automatically and proposed that the state should dispense with the economic role it had always played in developed countries: that of supplementing the market's coordination in order to promote economic development and equity. I have been a systematic critic of the macroeconomics of stagnation that the conventional orthodoxy proposes because it is based on a mistaken agenda—it still regards inflation as the main problem in the Brazilian economy—and, mainly, because it fails to produce the macroeconomic stability that is expected of it. Instead, because of the high interest rates and the appreciated exchange rate, the conventional orthodoxy keeps the country in permanent semistagnation, besides rendering it prone to recurring balance-of-payments crises such as those that occurred in 1998 and 2002 and that will occur again in time, depending on what happens to the world's economy, as a result of the brutal appreciation of the real in recent years. I have also criticized the loss of a sense of nationhood and the lack of a national development strategy. But my criticism is aimed not just at the prevailing conventional wisdom but especially at the prevailing conventional wisdom that complains of excessive fiscal adjustment, suggests that the country should again turn to its domestic market, advocates higher public spending to foster effective demand, and irresponsibly proposes "renegotiating" domestic and foreign debt. The national macroeconomic stabilization and development strategy I advance in this book—the new-developmentalist strategy—involves, first, more—not less—stringent fiscal adjustment, has as its main goal lower short-term interest rates (today's real disease in the Brazilian economy), and advocates managing the exchange rate in such a manner as to keep inflation under control and sustain the Brazilian economy's competitiveness. New developmentalism is a national development strategy that has been gradually defining itself in Latin America as the region's countries see the failure of the Washington Consensus to promote growth and its socially inequitable nature, which favors only the wealthy and the more educated strata of professional middle classes while imposing losses on middle-class business owners, professionals, and the poor. New developmentalism replaces its forerunner—a national development strategy that was enormously successful in promoting Brazil's economic development between 1930 and 1980 and then fell into a severe crisis in the midst of which it degenerated into economic populism.[10] New developmentalism, as a reflection of the much more advanced condition of the Brazilian economy today as compared with the 1930s, is not protectionist but export-led, and, although it stresses the importance of industrial policy, sees more relevance in macroeconomic policy and does not cast the state in an important role as a producer of goods and services.

As we will see throughout this book, however, the differences that truly matter today are those between the prevalent Washington Consensus and the emerging new developmentalism. In a nutshell, whereas the conventional orthodoxy proposes growth with foreign savings and open capital accounts, new developmentalism advocates financing investment with domestic savings and maintaining control over the exchange rate to prevent artificial wage gains (foreign exchange populism); whereas the conventional orthodoxy loosely defines fiscal adjustment in terms of a greater primary surplus, new developmentalism defines it more strictly in terms of lower public deficits and bigger public savings; whereas the conventional orthodoxy understands that the exchange rate is nonmanageable and imposes strict limitations on the management of the only instrument it deems to have available—the short-term interest rate— new developmentalism embraces the possibility of and the need for managing both rates as much as possible; whereas the conventional orthodoxy sees the lack of market-oriented reforms as the root cause of Brazil's quasi stagnation (when it even concedes the existence of such a stagnation), new developmentalism, although in favor of reforms to strengthen the state and the market, argues that the main cause of this quasi stagnation is today's macroeconomic policy. This policy, based on a high interest rate and on an appreciated exchange rate, fails to create the necessary demand for the capital accumulation rate to attain the levels needed to resume economic development. If we bear in mind that aggregate demand is essentially dependent on investment, the high interest rate, mistakenly justified as a requirement to keep inflation under control, in addition to imposing high financial costs on the state, hampers both private and public investment; an appreciated exchange rate, on the other hand, arising as it does from the government's inability to neutralize the Dutch disease[11] and from its acceptance of the policy of growth with foreign savings, discourages exports of goods with high per capita value added and, therefore, investment.

Brazil's economic development is now essentially dependent on the demand for investment, not on the supply of skilled labor. Even though education and scientific and technological development remain as national priorities on the supply side, the fact of the matter is that Brazil has vast idle human resources. The high unemployment rates and the mass migration of middle-class Brazilians to wealthy countries are evidence of this. Brazil's economic development depends, in the short and medium run, on a lower interest rate and a competitive exchange rate capable of stimulating investment. Demand is ensured, essentially, by investment or capital accumulation, which, in addition to expanding worker productivity on the supply side, is, on the demand side, the determinant of employment levels. This is why a satisfactory difference between the expected profit rate and the market interest rate—the determinant of growth—is so important to the growth process. Demand, however, is further determined by consumption, which depends mainly on wages, and on exports, which vary based mainly on the exchange rate. This is why the wage rate or average wage, whose growth is the manifestation of economic development on the supply side, is also important on the demand side. And this is why the exchange rate is a central macroeconomic price in the historic development process.[12]

My alternative to the orthodox and conventional economic policy is not the equally conventional Keynesianism that proposes increasing public expenditures and thereby fostering aggregate demand. There is certainly a need to stimulate aggregate demand through export-oriented investment, which will eventually stimulate foreign trade–oriented investment. The policy of stimulating demand through public or budget deficits makes sense only in a non-full-employment economy whose public sector is in fiscal equilibrium. Otherwise, such a move would be easily confused with fiscal populism; if a government with high indebtedness levels becomes involved in an expansive fiscal policy, the economic players' expectations of a potential failure of the state would make the investments promoted by public spending uneconomic. Likewise, with a highly indebted public sector, an indiscriminate rise of the interest rates does not contribute to lowering inflation, as rational economic actors foreseeing a state failure caused by interest (it was caused by expenditures in the former case) protect themselves by not reducing their margins.

In the 1990s, Brazilian society, convinced as it was of being in the less-than-zero-sum game of high inflation, managed to rally and developed a strategy to fight high and inertial inflation; it now needs a similar strategy to counter the trap of high interest rates and uncompetitive exchange rates. To do this, however, Brazil will need to be able to again rely on a nation, and this nation must use the state as its instrument par excellence for collective action and, thus, to formulate a national development strategy—an international competition strategy; only then will the Brazilian economy be able to increase public expenditures and private investments and, through growth greater than that of advanced countries, converge toward their development levels.

The Conventional Orthodoxy Defined

Brazil's inability to attain macroeconomic stability and resume growth is related to the capture of the state by a powerful political coalition that is not truly interested in the country's economic development: a coalition that coexists with government's fiscal populism and in practical terms supports foreign exchange populism because it has an interest in a relatively appreciated exchange rate. This coalition is made up of rentiers and the financial system that benefit from high interest rates and of multinational enterprises and rich countries' interests represented by the multilateral agencies that benefit from an overvalued local currency; the neoliberal discourse that it uses materializes in the stabilization and growth strategy that I call the "conventional orthodoxy." I have repeatedly made reference to this strategy—or more precisely, "anti-strategy"; the time has come to define it. The conventional orthodoxy is the set of diagnoses and recommendations emanating from Washington—more specifically, from the US Treasury, from the International Monetary Fund, and from the World Bank—and directed to developing countries. In its current guise, it has manifested itself since the 1980s through what has become known as the Consensus of Washington. This consensus, as expressed by John Williamson (1990), consisted of a series of principles that preached fiscal adjustment and market-oriented reforms or what was also referred to as "structural adjustment." In some chapters, I draw a distinction between the First and Second Consensuses of Washington to highlight the fact that the former is chiefly concerned with the current account and the fiscal adjustment that became necessary as a result of the great foreign debt crisis of the 1980s; the latter, which has been prevalent since the early 1990s, supports open capital accounts and growth with foreign savings, which implies a disregard of current account adjustment. Although the term *Consensus of Washington* remains in use and today has a clear meaning related to the neoliberal ideology, I also speak of the "conventional orthodoxy" because it is a more general expression and also because its failure to bring about growth made the relative "consensus" that existed in the 1990s disappear.

The ten reforms Williamson originally enumerated did not necessarily imply neoliberalism. It is quite possible to favor fiscal adjustment, or trade openness, or the privatization of competitive industries without aiming to reduce the state to a minimum. But in the form in which it was practiced around the world, it was certainly neoliberal and globalist—and this is precisely the ideological definition of the conventional orthodoxy. It is neoliberal insofar as it has a clear pro-market bias that weakens the state apparatus and preaches that most developing countries could benefit from fiscal adjustment and market-oriented reforms, especially greater trade and financial openness. It is globalist because it assumes that increased interdependency among nation-states implies a loss of their relevance: a thesis of particular interest to advanced countries, whose citizens are inevitably nationalist—so uniformly nationalistic that they do not need the adjective to define themselves. It is globalist because, within the generalized competition framework that defines globalized capitalism, the conventional orthodoxy ignores the fact that a country will be hard put to grow unless it can rely on a national development strategy: each nation-state must not allow its nation and its state to weaken, under penalty of paralyzed development. It is based on neoclassical economics but is not to be confused with it because it is not theoretical, but overtly ideological and oriented toward institutional reforms and economic policies. Although the dominant neoclassical economics is based in universities, particularly US ones, the conventional orthodoxy has its roots mainly in Washington, home to the US Treasury and the two supposedly international agencies that are in fact subordinate to the US Treasury, namely, the International Monetary Fund and the World Bank, the former concerned with macroeconomic policy, the latter with development. Its secondary wellspring is New York, the headquarters or center of major international banks and multinational companies. This is why we can say that the conventional orthodoxy is the set of diagnoses and policies meant for developing countries and originating in Washington and New York. The conventional orthodoxy changes over time, but, since the United States became hegemonic, it has expressed its ideological hegemony over the rest of the world at the level of economic ideas. This hegemony represents itself as "benevolent" when it is in fact the arm and mouth of neoimperialism—the imperialism without (formal) colonies that established itself under the aegis of the United States and other rich countries following the end of the classic colonial system, immediately after World War II.

The conventional orthodoxy, as it has been applied in Brazil since the 1990s, says four different things: first, that the country's major problem is the lack of microeconomic reforms to allow the market to freely operate; second, that even after the end of high and inertial inflation in 1994, controlling inflation continues to be the main economic policy objective; third, that in order to exert this control, interest rates will inevitably remain high owing to sovereign risk and to fiscal issues; fourth, that "development is a competition among countries for foreign savings" and that the implicit current account deficits and the appreciation of the exchange rate caused by capital inflows are no cause for concern.

Usually the adjective "orthodox" is applied to macroeconomic policies: orthodox policies usually have a neoclassical foundation and are opposed either to Keynesian macroeconomics or to populist policies. If we ignore the latter, a macroeconomic policy is orthodox if it gives full priority to the control of inflation; it is Keynesian if it combines the control of inflation with economic growth. Both approaches, however, know that moderate interest rates and a competitive exchange rate are also objectives to be achieved. Perhaps the orthodox are less adamant than the Keynesians in this matter, but, for instance, during the times of high growth in Japan, we had a classical combination of an orthodox finance ministry with a developmentalist Ministry of International Trade and Industry (MITI), in which the orthodox macroeconomic policy was based on fiscal adjustment, moderate interest rates, and a competitive exchange rate. The "conventional orthodoxy" that is being adopted by many developing countries, including Brazil, however, is orthodox only because of the priority given to the control of inflation. In the three other variables, it adopts the opposite values: soft fiscal adjustment, high interest rates, and an uncompetitive exchange rate. Thus, the conventional orthodoxy is *an orthodoxy for developing countries.* We can discuss whether it is really soft or not in terms of fiscal policy, because the economists involved maintain a strong rhetoric of austerity, whereas Keynesians admit budget deficits in special circumstances. I discuss this matter in Chapter 4. There is no doubt, however, about the macroeconomic trap: high interest rates and an uncompetitive exchange rate. There is no doubt, either, as to the other two issues that I will discuss in this book and that are related to the uncompetitive exchange rate: the conventional orthodoxy proposes a policy of growth with foreign savings that usually does not increase the investment and the growth rates, but appreciates the currency and increases domestic consumption besides increasing the foreign debt, and ignores the Dutch disease that makes the national currency overvalued and uncompetitive. I discuss the latter two issues in Chapter 5. Besides a chronic macroeconomic instability, the consequences are insufficient effective demand, lack of export-oriented investment opportunities, and a low investment rate, which prevent developing countries from *catching up*—from gradually achieving the income levels of the rich countries.

The conventional orthodoxy has dominated the country since the early 1990s but has not led to resumed growth. It is uninterested in solving either the problem of the high real short-term interest rate or that of the overvalued exchange rate and ties everything to fiscal adjustment or to overcoming the structural fiscal imbalance, heedless of the fact that a major cause of this maladjustment lies in the absurdly high interest rates themselves and that the problem can be faced only with a simultaneous attack on the interest disease and on fiscal imbalance. As for the interest rate, it confuses short term and long term and understands that the short-term interest rate is endogenous, defined by the market, and, as a result, it feels comfortable accepting stratospheric rates. As for the exchange rate, it understands that it, too, is endogenous and, consistent with its convenient belief that a middle-income country such as Brazil can grow only with foreign savings, accepts that it should remain relatively appreciated. The appreciated exchange rate policy that the conventional orthodoxy adopts is interesting, first, to rich countries fearful of the competition of countries with relatively cheap labor, such as Brazil, and second, to multinationals, which can then transfer more strong currency for the same profits made in reals in the country. The interest rate policy is interesting for domestic and foreign rentiers who live on interest and for the financial industry that collects commissions from rentiers. The disaster that the orthodoxy implied in terms of balance-of-payment crises and low growth for the Latin American countries that adopted it after the late 1980s is now notorious (Frenkel 2003).

Nation and Globalization

New developmentalism, like the national developmentalism of the 1950s, at once assumes the existence and implies the formation of a true nation capable of formulating an informal, open-ended national development strategy, as is typical of democratic societies whose economies are coordinated by the market. A nation is a society of individuals or households that share a common political fate and organize as a state with sovereignty over a certain territory. A nation, therefore, like the modern state makes sense only within the framework of the nation-state that arises with capitalism. For a nation to share a common political fate, it must, in addition to having a state, strike solidarity bonds among its members and have shared objectives, chief among which, historically, is development. Other objectives, such as freedom and social justice, are also crucially important to nations, but nations arise, like the state and capitalism, with economic development as an intrinsic part of their logic, of their very being. Nations, nation-states, capitalism, and economic development are simultaneous and intrinsically correlated historical phenomena. In its more advanced form—today's globalization—the constitutive economic units of capitalism are not just firms operating internationally, but also, if not chiefly, nation-states or national states. It is not just firms that compete on worldwide markets, as conventional economics would have it; nation-states, too, are key competitors. The main criterion for success for the political rulers of every modern national state is high economic growth relative to that of other countries. Globalization is the stage of capitalism where, for the first time, nation-states span the entire globe and compete economically among themselves through their firms. With globalization, nation-states became more interdependent, but, for this precise reason, more strategic. In order to be able to compete (for competition is the essential relationship that makes them interdependent), they must also cooperate in the construction of an international system of institutions to set the rules of the game nations play. In the competitive process as well as in the cooperative one, each nation-state has a dramatic need for autonomy—an autonomy that hegemony attempts to constrain in order to impose and exert its own domination. Globalization occurs in every realm: commercial, direct investment, financial, technological, and cultural. The commercial globalization derived from trade openness is a competitive opportunity for Brazil given its relatively cheap labor; on the other hand, financial globalization, defined by financial or capital account openness, is not interesting to developing countries because it denies them control over the exchange rate and, therefore, their own national development process.[13]

A nation involves a basic agreement among classes when it comes to competing internationally. Businesspeople, workers, and the professional middle class (including state bureaucrats and intellectuals) may struggle with one another but know that their fate lies in competitive involvement in the world of nation-states. It involves, therefore, a national agreement—a nationalist agreement. A national agreement is the basic social contract that gives rise to a nation and keeps it strong and cohesive; it is the great accord among the social classes of a modern society that enables such a society to become a true nation, that is, a society equipped with a state capable for formulating a national development strategy. The great national agreement, or pact, made in Brazil after 1930 joined together the newborn national industrial bourgeoisie and the bureaucracy, or the new state technicians; these were joined by urban workers and the old oligarchy sectors more attuned to the domestic market, such as the very ranchers from whom Getúlio Vargas sprang. The adversaries were imperialism, represented mainly by British and US interests, and the associated agricultural-exporter oligarchy. The most strategic agreement that can be made in a modern capitalist society is that struck between industrial businesspeople and the state's bureaucracy, including politicians, but such an agreement also involves workers and the middle classes. There will always be domestic opposition, somehow identified with imperialism, or with today's colony-free neoimperialism, and with local collaborator or globalist groups. In globalized capitalism, the latter are the rentiers, who live on high interest rates, and the financial sector, which collects commissions from the rentiers.

A nation is inevitably nationalist, insofar as nationalism is the ideology of the formation of the national state and its permanent reinforcement or consolidation. Nationalism may also be defined, as Ernest Gellner does, as an ideology that pursues the correspondence of nation and state, that is, that wants a state for each nation.[14] This is a good definition, too, but typical of a thinker from Central Europe; it is a definition that exhausts itself as soon as the nation-state forms—when nation and state first coincide on a given territory, formally establishing a "sovereign state." Therefore, it disregards Ernest Renan's celebrated 1882 aphorism: "a nation is an everyday plebiscite."[15] It fails to explain how a nation-state may formally exist without a true nation, as is the case with Latin American countries, which, in the early nineteenth century, were endowed with states owing not only to the patriotic efforts of nationalist groups but also to the good services of Britain with its maneuvers to drive Spain and Portugal out of the region. As a result, these countries saw themselves equipped with states (i.e., with a national law system and an organization to guarantee such system) in the absence of true nations, as they stopped being colonies to become dependent on Britain, France, and, later, the United States. For a nation to truly exist, it is a requirement that the various social classes, notwithstanding the conflicts that set them apart, be joined in national solidarity when it comes to international competition and that they use national criteria to make policy decisions, especially concerning economic policy and institutional reform. In other words, rulers must think with their own minds, instead of dedicating themselves to confidence building, that is, the construction of foreign credibility at the expense of national interests, and all of society must be capable of formulating a national development strategy.

New developmentalism is a manifestation of a moderate nationalism that is reemerging in Brazil after the exhaustion of the society's cycle that I call the Democracy and Justice Cycle (1964–) and also after the failure of the conventional orthodoxy to promote economic growth. This was the case in Brazil between 1930 and 1960, under the leadership of Brazil's twentieth-century statesman, Getúlio Vargas. In this period, Brazilian society took national decisions on its own behalf and formulated a successful national development strategy. In those 30 years (or 50 if we count the military regime, which, despite a political alliance with the United States against communism, remained nationalist), Brazil changed: from an agricultural country, becoming industrial, moving from a mercantilist to a fully capitalist social formation, transitioning from a semicolonial status to that of a nation. Developmentalism was the name given to the national development strategy and the ideology that drove it. Therefore, the current process of defining new developmentalism is also a resumption of the concept of nation in Brazil and other Latin American countries. This implies a nationalist perspective in the sense that economic policies and institutions are formulated and implemented with national interest as a main driver and with each country's citizens as authors. This nationalism is not meant to endow a nation with a state, but to make the existing state into an effective instrument for collective action by the nation, an instrument that allows modern nations in the early twenty-first century to consistently pursue their political objectives of economic development, social justice, and freedom, in an international framework of peace and collaboration among nations. It implies, therefore, that this nationalism should be liberal, social, and republican, that is, that it should embody the values of modern industrial societies. Unlike liberalism and socialism, with their universal aspirations, nationalism, as Paulo Nogueira Batista Jr. (2006, p. 3) points out, "is not humanism . . . nationalism is a historical phenomenon and not a universal, timeless value."[16] Nationalism is an ideology of national unification and consolidation. It is always a reaction against the empire. Nothing, however, prevents nationalism from being liberal and social, as long as it is each of the two in moderate measure. And nothing prevents it from making a contribution to the ideals of universal peace and solidarity, as nation-states are the political organization principle of the world society; they are entities that compete among themselves, but, for this very reason, must act collectively to establish the institutions charged with regulating this competition.

Society's Cycles and State Cycles

Although this book is concerned with economic and political developments in Brazil after it was able to end high and inertial inflation in 1994, before ending this Introduction I permit myself to offer a broad view of Brazil in the twentieth century. To better understand the obstacles ahead and the complex relationships between the Brazilian nation and its state as an instrument for collective action, one must focus on the cycles that society and the state underwent in Brazil in the twentieth century— those of society preceding those of the state, the former creating social and ideological consensus, the latter leading to political pacts and control of the state. The model I summarize here is specific to Brazil, but I believe that, with the appropriate adjustments, it could apply to many Latin American countries. At the societal level, in the early twentieth century the Nation and Development Cycle begins with such imposing characters as Silvio Romero, Manoel Bonfim, and Euclides da Cunha; progresses to Alberto Torres, Monteiro Lobato, Oliveira Vianna, and Roberto Simonsen; attains classical status in the works of Gilberto Freyre, Sérgio Buarque de Holanda, Caio Prado Jr., and Barbosa Lima Sobrinho; and becomes fully defined in the 1950s in the thinking of great intellectuals such as Ignácio Rangel, Guerreiro Ramos, and Hélio Jaguaribe at the Instituto Superior de Estudos Brasileiros (Superior Institute of Brazilian Studies; ISEB) and Celso Furtado at the Economic Commission for Latin America and Caribe (ECLAC) of the United Nations.[17] In the early 1960s, with the military coup of 1964, whose roots lie in the increased Cold War tension in Latin America and in the consequent political radicalization brought about by the Cuban Revolution of 1959,[18] this nationalist cycle, which revolves around national identity and industrialization, collapses, as industrial businesspeople who were the "national bourgeoisie"—that is, a capitalist class committed to national interests—and the military, ever a pillar of Brazilian nationalism, afraid of the communist threat, associated themselves with the United States to establish a military regime in Brazil.

At the state level, which lags behind the societal level, the corresponding cycle is reflected in the National-Developmentalist Pact that begins with the *tenentista* movement (lieutenants' movement) and the revolution of 1930 and finds in Getúlio Vargas its main political actor. In this cycle the government successfully leads a national development strategy oriented toward import-substitution industrialization, and Brazil attains the world's highest growth rate. After redemocratization, in 1945, the National-Developmentalist Pact experiences a political crisis that culminates in 1954 with Vargas's suicide, reestablishes itself with the election of Juscelino Kubitschek, and faces a new crisis in 1961 that eventually resolves itself with the military coup of 1964. After that, the National-Developmentalist Pact, which includes industrialists, state bureaucrats, and organized workers, loses the last of these groups and turns into the Bureaucratic-Authoritarian Pact. Yet the national-developmentalist strategy is resumed and survives until the great foreign debt crisis of the 1980s.

This crisis arises at a time when the new social cycle, which I call the Democracy and Justice Cycle, has already taken large steps toward undermining the military regime. The cycle is born among left-wing intellectuals, usually associated with the São Paulo School of Sociology and the theory of associated dependency, who, after the coup of 1964, start leveling criticism at ISEB, which has diagnosed and supported the National-Developmentalist Pact, and rejecting its basic thesis—namely, that a great national accord led by the national bourgeoisie is giving rise to a Brazilian nation and to Brazil's industrial development. The theory of dependency, which becomes hegemonic in Latin America in the 1970s, originates from this rejection. If no national bourgeoisie exists, as the intellectuals mistakenly believe, then the concept of nation is unviable. In its stead, a new consensus forms, no longer based on the ideas of nation and economic development, but on the demand for democracy and social justice. Whereas the Nation and Development Cycle was born out of rejection of foreign dependency, the Democracy and Justice Cycle is based on acceptance of dependency as an inevitable sociological and economic fact. Whereas the nationalist cycle had economic development as its core goal, the new cycle, which corresponds to the theory of associated dependency, assumes that economic development is assured, be it as a result of the dynamic nature of capitalism or through the inflow of foreign capital. Since, according to the new consensual reasoning, continued industrialization is ensured, the two major problems Brazilian society still has to address are overcoming the military authoritarian regime and the country's pervasive and radical inequity.

This view of Brazil gradually becomes prevalent throughout society while the idea of a nation, identified as it is with the military and businesspeople, sinks into oblivion. Politically organized society fails to become a nation oriented toward national autonomy and development to become a civil society focused on the affirmation of civil, political, and social rights. Democracy becomes the core demand, social justice a requirement at once moral and political. After the "April package" of 1977,[19] the struggle for democracy, which has enjoyed the support of workers, the left wing, and important sectors of the middle classes since the coup, gains the additional support of businesspeople, no longer under the threat of communism.[20] A new government pact forms at the political level but remains outside the realm of the state: the 1977 Popular-Democratic Pact. From that year on, because of the bourgeoisie's negative response to President Ernesto Geisel's April package, the bourgeoisie's alliance with the military breaks down. The Democracy and Justice Cycle acquires momentum, becomes prevalent, and, with the "Diretas já" (the national movement demanding direct elections for the presidency), leads the country to democratic transition in 1985. Besides achieving democratic transition, its chief accomplishment is the constitution of 1988. But in the next year, amid the constitutional workings, the Popular-Democratic Pact collapses with the failure of the Cruzado Plan to control high inflation rates and with the ensuing economic crisis. Add to this the inability of the Partido do Movimento Democrático Brasileiro (Brazilian Democratic Movement Party, PMDB)—the political party that represented this pact—to face the crisis, and one can see why the Brazilian society will yield, from 1990 onward, to the neoliberal wave and to global modernity. The ideas of democracy and justice remain but are now joined by those of neoliberal, modernizing reforms. It is difficult to name the political pact that arises from this surrender of society and that controls the state after 1990, as it retains the notions of democracy and justice but adds to them the contradictory proposals of the conventional orthodoxy. I call it the Neoliberal-Dependent Pact, to emphasize its subordination to the North and its economic neoliberal or ultra-liberal character.[21]

The two parties that came to power after PMDB—Partido da Social Democracia Brasileira (Brazilian Social Democracy Party, PSDB) and Partido dos Trabalhadores (Labor Party, PT)—are also the fruit of the Democracy and Justice Cycle, and, therefore, of the waiver of a sense of nation. Democracy has been attained; the task at hand is to attain justice. But how? The three parties agree that it has to be through increased public spending in the social area. And so it is, as proven by the 9 percent increase of social expenditures as a share of gross domestic product (GDP) that occurs after redemocratization. The outcome of this great effort, however, is meager because its underlying assumption—that economic development is ensured—has proven false: growth has lasted for ten years; the economy has been in quasi stagnation since 1980.

Therefore, it is now increasingly clear that the Democracy and Justice Cycle has become exhausted. Its core goals—democracy and social justice—remain as valid and necessary as ever, but society is at a loss as to how to proceed given the lack of economic development and increased unemployment. A continued increase of the tax burden to fund social spending is evidently no longer a realistic option. The lackluster presidential elections of 2006 and the absence of genuine public debate are indications of this exhaustion: the political parties originating in the period have been unable to renew their vision for the country. Democracy has been attained, despite its current ethical crisis, but reduced inequality is still a distant prospect. Although income distribution data indicate gains in this area, they are misleading because they are incomplete. As 80 percent of the income that the surveys are based on is labor income, in a country where labor income is no more than a third of the national income, the survey underestimates capital income and, therefore, fails to take account of the fact that, in order to offset increased social expenditures, there has been a brutal increase in transfers in the form of interest from the state to rentiers, that is, to the unproductive members of the wealthy class. The strategy of redistribution via social spending was intrinsically limited. In addition to increased interest payments, it brought about an astronomical tax burden of 37 percent of GDP, and society is no longer willing to accept further tax hikes. It is now clearer than ever that inequality will subside only when economic development resumes and companies again absorb the unlimited supply of labor that characterizes Brazil's underdeveloped and dual economy. If the intellectuals of the Democracy and Justice Cycle were mistaken in their trust in the income-redistributing virtues of social spending, the ideologues of the conventional orthodoxy were even more seriously mistaken in assuming that development would resume as a result of the reforms and policies proposed by rich countries. Brazil must rethink its history during the past century, realizing that its objectives cannot be just democracy and the reduction of social inequality but economic development as well; otherwise it will never overcome its present quasi stagnation. After the two major cycles it has faced, society needs to find a new synthesis reconciling national development with social justice and democracy.

Notes

1. I refer only to middle-income countries because poor countries are incapable of competing with rich countries.

2. *Soft power* is an expression coined by the US "liberal"—that is, progressive—internationalist Joseph Nye (2002).

3. According to Claudia Trevisan (2006, p. 27), "vigorous growth, stability and national unity make up the tripod that drives the decisions of [China's] rulers, who continue to use state planning strictly, despite economic openness."

4. The conventional economists' tripod is fiscal adjustment, an inflation targeting policy, and a floating exchange rate. As we will see, however, what really characterizes the conventional orthodoxy's macroeconomic policy is high interest rates, an uncompetitive exchange rate, and, surprisingly, soft fiscal adjustment.

5. On the high and inertial inflation that prevailed in Brazil between 1980 and 1994, which is several times referred to in this book but will not be the object of specific analysis, see Bresser-Pereira and Nakano (1987 [1984]); on the several failed attempts to stabilize prices in Brazil, see Bresser-Pereira (1996b, ch. 14); on the 1994 Real Plan, which was successful because it adopted a strategy of inertia neutralization (the Real Value Unit [Unidade Real de Valor; URV), see Arida and Resende (1985 [1984]) and Bresser-Pereira (1994); on the intellectual origins of the theory, see Bresser-Pereira (1996a).

6. One of the most clear-cut cases of the application of rational expectations in connection with fiscal and monetary policy is the letter of intent to the IMF that Brazil signed in 1991, when Fernando Collor de Mello was president and Marcílio Marques Moreira his minister of finance. Inflation was then at 20 percent a month. For a year, very stringent fiscal and monetary policies were in place. The IMF expected that, by the end of 1992, inflation should be at 2 percent per month, but it remained at the same 20 percent.

7. This is how the more competent central bankers manage their countries' economic policies, as exemplified by Alan Blinder (1999), Blinder and Reis (2005), and Aglietta and Borgy (2005). See Le Heron (2003) and Le Heron and Carré (2006) for a theoretical analysis of the problem.

8. Brazil grew more quickly than any other country in gross terms; in per capita terms, Japan grew a little faster because its population was rising more slowly.

9. China and India, where labor is even cheaper, are naturally feared by rich countries, but so is Brazil. This is clearly depicted, for example, in a feature by the Washington correspondent to *Valor* newspaper (November 26, 2006) about the attitude of members of the US Congress toward Brazil. According to Ricardo Balthasar, "American politicians . . . who know something of Brazil regard it essentially as a competitor to be faced and as a threat to the well-being of American workers and farmers."

10. "Political populism"—the practice major political leaders adopt of striking up a direct relationship with the masses—was a permanent feature of old developmentalism. Getúlio Vargas, however, the main representative of this breed, never used "economic populism," that is, spending more than one's revenues, which, as we will see, can be either fiscal or foreign exchange related.

11. I define the Dutch disease in Chapter 6.

12. Oreiro, Nakabashi, and Lemos (2007) provided econometric proof of this thesis; according to their analysis, investments are constrained mainly by the exchange rate, which limits industrial exports.

13. Financial globalization relates to the "financialization" process, that is, the accumulation of financial resources by firms and governments, accompanied by high asset liquidity (Kregel 2004; Coutinho and Belluzzo 2004).

14. Gellner, a Czech philosopher who sought political asylum from communism in Britain, was probably the leading analyst of nationalism in the second half of the twentieth century (see Gellner 1983, 1996 [1993]).

15. Ernest Renan (1993 [1882], p. 55). In the immediately preceding text, Renan says: "A nation is therefore a large-scale solidarity, constituted by the feeling of the sacrifices that one has made in the past and of those that one is

prepared to make in the future. It presupposes a past; it is summarized, however, in the present by a tangible fact, namely, consent, the clearly expressed desire to continue a common life."

16. Batista then adds: "In its extreme form, nationalism is intrinsically adversarial towards the two other great political and economic ideologies of the 19th and 20th centuries: liberalism and socialism."

17. The ISEB was a think tank that existed between 1955 and 1964; it was formed by a group of major nationalist intellectuals that since the early 1950s had developed an original interpretation of Brazil and defined politically the strategy adopted by Getúlio Vargas, "national-developmentalism" (see Toledo, 2005). The beginning of ECLAC was the birth of the structuralist Latin American school that developed an economic rationale for industrialization and state intervention or, in other words, for the national-developmentalist strategy; it had in Raúl Presbisch and Celso Furtado its major intellectuals.

18. Concerning the new historical facts that determined the military coup and the end of Vargas's National-Developmentalist Pact, see chapter 4 of Bresser-Pereira (2003). This chapter has been part of the book since its first edition, published in 1968.

19. The "April package" was a set of measures taken by President Geisel that, for the first time, met with great opposition from sectors of the Brazilian bourgeoisie.

20. The main cause of the political crisis of the early 1960s, resulting in the alliance of industrial businesspeople and the military with the United States and in the coup of 1964, was the Cuban Revolution of 1959, which led to a great radicalization of politics on both the left and the right.

21. Note that I use the word *liberal* in the European and Latin American sense, as meaning, in economic terms, *laissez-faire,* not in the US sense, whereby *liberal* means *progressive.* To avoid confusion I use *neoliberal* instead of *liberal* whenever possible.

1
Low Growth

Since 1995 the two central characteristics of the Brazilian economy have been macroeconomic instability and low growth of income per inhabitant. Since 2004, growth rates, propelled by the high prices of the commodities exported and by the increase in domestic consumption, changed this picture somewhat. Given the strong appreciation of the real, however, this improved performance, besides continuing to trail the more dynamic developing countries, was far from being sustained. Since the international crisis of 1979, Brazilians have been strangers to fast economic development. There has been some growth of the economy, because per capita income has risen modestly. On the other hand, there has been political and social development because the transition to democracy has taken place and democracy has become consolidated and because massive investment in the social area has slightly alleviated poverty and reduced inequality. Still, for a significant group of families to go above the poverty line, economic development must be resumed and the surplus labor that still characterizes the Brazilian economy must be absorbed. The significant improvement in social indicators and inequality indexes came about as a result of greatly increased social spending by the state—an increase that was part of the Popular-Democratic Pact struck in the late 1970s, the political coalition that commanded the transition to democracy. Now, however, it has become impossible to increase the tax burden further in order to continue with this policy. The one solution available is to resume economic development, reduce the excess supply of labor that still exists in the dual society that is the Brazilian society, and thus allow wages to grow with increased productivity.

Low Growth Rates

Instead of economic development, however, what we have had in Brazil since 1980 are low growth rates. It is true that since 2004 the economic performance of Brazil has improved as the prices of commoditics have soared. Yet we cannot count on this to continue, because commodity prices are unstable and exchange rates tend to rise to dangerous levels. Taking a more long-term approach, what we see since 1980 is quasi stagnation, as Table 1.1 illustrates. Income per capita, which was growing at a brisk pace between the 1950s and 1970s, collapsed in the 1980s; the recovery of the 1990s was very modest, and in the early years of the new millennium, notwithstanding the great gains in exports, annual per capita income growth was small. As noted by the National Confederation of Industry (2006, p. 15), "in the past ten years Brazil's growth has been systematically lower than world average. At the last decade's average per capita income growth rate of 0.7 percent a year, it will take Brazil 100 years to double its income, that is, to attain the current per capita income of Portugal." The drop in per capita income in the 1980s was no surprise: after the stunning growth of the previous decade, distortions in the economic system were inevitable. Foreign indebtedness caused by the adoption of the policy of growth with foreign savings left the country internationally vulnerable. With the second oil shock in 1979 and the decision of the Federal Reserve Bank of sharply increasing the interest rates in the early 1980s, Brazil, along with many other developing countries, was plunged into a great foreign debt crisis.

This crisis soon became a fiscal crisis as well, whether because the dominant groups were able to transfer their obligations to the state or

Table 1.1 Comparative Per Capita GDP Growth Rates (annual averages as percentage)

	OECD Countries	Latin America	Brazil
1950–1979	3.3	2.3	3.9
1980–1989	2.3	–.3	1.0
1990–1999	3.04	1.34	.82
2000–2006	3.01	1.49	1.47

Sources: Economic Commission for Latin America and Caribe (ECLAC), available at www.eclac.org; Organization for Economic Cooperation and Development (OECD), available at www.oecd.org.

because the political crisis and democratic transition encouraged economic populism. The macroeconomic instability that then set in would be expressed in the high and inertial inflation that dominated the Brazilian economic environment between 1980 and 1994.

In the meantime, other countries developed. As can also be seen from Table 1.1, the Brazilian economy's growth since 1980, besides being lower than in the previous period, is also lower than that of wealthy Organization for Economic Cooperation and Development (OECD) countries. Between 1950 and 1979, Brazil grew faster than Latin America as a whole and OECD countries. After 1980 it grew much more slowly than rich countries, contrary to the economic theory that predicts a trend toward converging development levels; in 1990 it started growing more slowly than even the Latin American countries that had lagged behind Brazil in the past. In the 2000–2006 period, Brazil's growth became the same as Latin America's owing to the deep crisis in Argentina, but that country has already recovered and has been growing fast, whereas Brazil's growth rates remain unsatisfactory, despite the great increase in exports since 2002. Table 1.2, in turn, illustrates the average growth of per capita GDP in Brazil relative to selected larger countries from 1999 through 2006, and Brazil's rank among 25 developing countries. Brazil ranked twentieth in the 1999–2002 period, and twenty-fifth in the 2002–2006

Table 1.2 Country Ranking: Annual GDP Growth Rate (selected countries, 1999–2002 and 2002–2006)

Ranking, 1999–2002	GDP Growth, 1999–2002 (%)	Ranking 2002–2006	GDP Growth, 2002–2006 (%)
China (1)	8.22	1	9.87
Argentina (25)	−4.95	2	8.57
India (4)	5.14	3	7.72
Turkey	–	4	7.02
Russia (3)	4.88	5	6.72
Mexico (16)	2.77	24	3.02
Brazil (20)	2.09	25	2.79

Source: Gustavo Patu, "Brasil fica na lanterna entre emergentes," *Folha de S. Paulo,* September 3, 2006, based on IMF and *The Economist.* The 2006 data are based on an IMF forecast available at www.imf.org.

Note: The twenty-five countries considered comprise South Africa, Argentina, Brazil, Chile, China, Singapore, Colombia, South Korea, Egypt, Philippines, Hong Kong, Hungary, India, Indonesia, Israel, Malaysia, Mexico, Peru, Poland, Czech Republic, Russia, Thailand, Taiwan, Turkey, and Venezuela.

period. The rate of growth of Brazil increased in the second period (but the ranking deteriorated). Argentina changed dramatically for the better, as it emerged from a 2001 deep crisis. The data in these two tables clearly show that the Brazilian economy's low growth is a domestic problem, not a problem of the world economy or Latin America. In the 1980s, the crisis was Latin American and could be attributed to the foreign debt problem and high inflation, but since 1994, Brazil's semistagnation has been homegrown, the fruit of the country's inability to tackle the relevant macroeconomic disequilibria and set out a national development strategy.

As grave as it was, a crisis such as the one that started in Brazil in 1979–1980 with the second oil shock, the international interest rate hike, and the foreign debt crisis should have lasted for two or three years. But it has been going on for nearly three decades. Table 1.3 shows per capita GDP growth in Brazil since 1971. The figures are dismal. In the first seven years of the 2000s, income per capita increased by less than 2 percent a year.

After the 1980 crisis, a major event took place in 1994: the Real Plan succeeded in stabilizing the high and inertial inflation that for 14 years had been a curse for Brazil. That Brazil did not develop in this period is no mystery, although why it took so long to achieve price stabilization remains a puzzle. In 1995 a second period began—the one that is the subject of this book. This period should be subdivided to take account of the positive foreign shock represented by the extraordinary growth of Brazilian exports since 2002. Exports doubled from 2002 to 2007, but the effect on the country's growth rates has been modest.

Between 1980 and 1994, low growth was directly related to the foreign debt and fiscal crises, which translated into high inflation rates. The foreign debt crisis was a solvency issue for the entire nation, whereas the fiscal crisis was a failure of the state that tied in with the

Table 1.3 Average Annual GDP Growth (%)

	GDP	Per Capita GDP
1971–1980	8.67	6.10
1981–1990	1.67	−0.47
1991–2000	2.67	1.09
2001–2007	3.27	1.84

Source: Data are from the website of the Instituto de Pesquisa Econômica Aplicada (the Institute for Applied Economic Research): www.ipeadata.gov.br.
Note: Calculations are based on GDP and per capita GDP data in 2005 reals.

exhaustion of the import-substitution model. For better or worse, these problems were faced in the 1980s and early 1990s and were reasonably under control when the Real Plan finally succeeded in stabilizing inflation. The reform of the Brazilian economy began with the successful exchange devaluation of 1983; then, with the country reporting substantial trade surpluses, it proceeded with the financial reform of the Ministry of Finance that did away with multiple budgets (1983–1987); it continued with the debt renegotiation and trade liberalization policies begun in 1987 and completed in early 1990; it finally came to a conclusion with the neutralization of inflationary inertia under the Real Plan in 1994.[1]

What matters now is to understand the second period, when Brazil had every reason to resume development and still did not. Why did growth rates remain so low in a period in which prices were at last stable and huge capital inflows demonstrated confidence on the part of the North? Although this is the question of the book, a first response may be offered here. The central problem was the persistence of a low investment rate. As we can see from Table 1.4, investment as a share of GDP averaged 18.5 percent in the 1995–2007 period and was just 17.6 percent in the last year—an investment rate much smaller than those of the dynamic Asian countries and the Eastern and Central European countries. Why has Brazil been unable to increase its investment and savings rates? Many answers may be given to this question: the preferred explanations given by the conventional orthodoxy are that public expenditures and the tax burden are too high and also that Brazil's institutions are not business friendly. There is some truth in explanations of this kind, because there

Table 1.4 Investment Rates in Groups of Countries: 1995–2007 (percentage of GDP)

	1995–2007 Average	2007
Developed countries	21.2	21.1
Africa	21.4	24.4
Eastern and Central Europe	23.1	25.0
Dynamic Asian countries	33.7	37.9
Latin America	20.8	20.6
Brazil	18.5	17.6
World	22.2	23.3

Sources: Data from IMF, www.imf.org; World Bank, www.worldbank.org; and Instituto Brasileiro de Geografia e Estatística (Brazilian Institute of Geography and Statistics, IBGE), www.ibge.gov.br.

are many reasons for the decrease in the Brazilian savings rate during the 1980s and its failure to recover in the 1990s.[2] Yet the central thesis of this book is that the main cause—the one that depends directly on policymakers—is that after 1995, Brazil adopted the mistaken recommendations of the conventional orthodoxy: high interest rates, an uncompetitive exchange rate, and a loose fiscal policy. These policies not only lowered the savings capacity of the country but also diminished the export-oriented investment opportunities that, in Keynesian terms, would have increased investment and, in consequence, the savings rate.

The Real Plan had been a successful strategy to neutralize inflationary inertia. It was based on a theory—the theory of inertial inflation—developed fundamentally by Brazilian economists. This success was a clear indication that the country's macroeconomic problems should be tackled by Brazilian economists, based on a specific analysis of the constraints and opportunities the economy faces within the framework of the world economy. Nevertheless, neoliberals had been successful in attributing high inflation and stagnation in the 1980s to the national-developmentalist strategy. On the other hand, the triumph of capitalism over communism and of market economies over command economies contributed to the neoliberal hegemony's reaching its apogee in the 1990s. It is probably for these reasons—because the Brazilian nation was weakened by crisis and because the North's ideological hegemony, and in particular that of the United States, had become so strong—that in 1995 the Brazilian government decided to adopt the recommendations of the conventional orthodoxy.

At that time, after the foreign debt crisis, governmental and quasi-governmental agencies in Washington and the financial players of New York proposed a "new" development strategy for emerging countries: "to open up the capital account and grow with foreign savings." This strategy went against the grain of the historical experience of economic development, according to which a country always achieves development with its own resources; it also went against the stabilization policies proposed by the International Monetary Fund itself, which, as late as the 1980s, recommended exchange rate depreciation when a country faced a balance-of-payment crisis. Since the early 1990s, however, the agency ceased concerning itself with current account deficits (which are the obverse of foreign savings), based on the assumption that the inflow of foreign savings would lead to a consequent increase in a country's investment rate, and focused its attention exclusively on controlling inflation, which was to be achieved through fiscal adjustment, interest rate policy, and a foreign exchange anchor.[3] According to the new version of the conventional orthodoxy that set in,[4] foreign equilibrium would be automatically achieved by fiscal adjustment combined with the twin-deficits hypothesis. Countries that had barely overcome the great foreign debt crisis were now called upon to take on new debt in order to grow with foreign savings. First, they should dedicate themselves to confidence building, that is, to become "deserving" of these savings, in the form of credit or direct investments provided by advanced countries; second, after becoming indebted, they should become even more subservient to the dictum of the conventional orthodoxy to simply roll over the foreign debt already incurred.

The confidence-building policy so required meant that a country would stop thinking for itself and start following the policies the conventional orthodoxy recommended. What were these policies? Each country, in addition to (1) competing for the foreign savings of rich countries, should (2) broaden market-oriented reforms, especially financial openness (so that foreign finance faced no obstacles), and (3) fight inflation with three instruments: fiscal adjustment, a foreign exchange anchor, and, where needed, hikes of the central bank's short-term interest rate. When the foreign exchange anchor policy failed within a few years, it was promptly replaced with free-floating exchange rates (now the market would automatically solve foreign balance problems) and by a new anchor, or quasi anchor: the inflation targeting policy that would give an even sounder justification for high interest rates while keeping disguised the exchange rate anchor.[5]

Of the economic policies proposed by the conventional orthodoxy, only fiscal adjustment was appropriate, but even this stayed within the realm of intentions, as it failed to be realized in the form of exacting goals and strict fiscal policies. The fiscal goal set was not, as we will see, a reduced budget deficit, but an increased primary surplus, which could be achieved in combination with a large budget deficit as long as the total interest rates paid by the state remained high. As Cardim de Carvalho notes (2005, p. 336), the fiscal policy, "instead of reducing the public debt as it was expected deepened the fiscal unbalance because, among other things, debt service expenditures increased as a result of exceptionally high interest rates." At the foreign accounts level, opening up the capital account in order to grow with foreign savings, that is, with current account deficits, meant accepting increasing foreign indebtedness together with a higher exchange rate. To use the exchange rate as a foreign exchange anchor meant an even steeper appreciation. To use, instead, a free-floating rate policy meant losing control over the exchange rate in addition to letting it appreciate. Internally, keeping short-term interest rates at high levels based on the notion that the neutral, or equilibrium, rate (that which does not add momentum to inflation) was high involves substantial fiscal costs and prevents the credit operations needed to fund investments besides implying exchange rate appreciation.

When the balance-of-payment crisis of 1998 led to the foreign exchange anchor's being abandoned, the free-floating exchange rate policy that replaced it in 1999 continued to promote a chronic appreciation of the exchange rate, as two other appreciation factors (the free inflow of capital and high interest rates) remained in place, as they still do. As a result, the Brazilian economy remained vulnerable to balance-of-payment crises.

I will discuss the implications of all of these problems, as well as the substitution of a free-floating exchange rate for the foreign exchange anchor strategy that soon took place under pressure from the successive balance-of-payment crises that marked the 1990s. It is important to point out that the direct outcome was high interest rates, exchange rates with a constant tendency to appreciate, and recurring financial crises; as a consequence, the investment rate failed to grow and quasi stagnation remained. The primary objective of raising the investment rate was not achieved, and Brazil continued to report annual capital accumulation rates of less than 20 percent,[6] much lower than those achieved by dynamic countries that were catching up.

Macroeconomic Instability

These economic policy decisions and their subordination to the conventional orthodoxy conspired to keep the Brazilian economy semistagnant. I will return to them as the book progresses. In this first chapter, which provides an overview of the macroeconomics of stagnation, it is worthwhile to further note the intrinsic macroeconomic instability that has characterized the Brazilian economy. Although the conventional macroeconomic policy adopted in Brazil is done under the banner of stability, what we have is permanent instability. Given the tendency to the overappreciation of the exchange rate, the stop-and-go pattern of the Brazilian economy is characterized by growth periods where the exchange rate appreciates followed by balance-of-payment crisis and sharp currency depreciation. Yet, Brazilians, scalded by the high and inertial inflation of the 1980–1994 period and satisfied with the nearly stable price levels since 1995, fail to clearly realize that the Brazilian economy is also marked by macroeconomic instability, which is the more direct and immediate cause of low growth. For a very long time, based on a misinterpretation of Keynesian economics, it was believed that there was a trade-off between growth and stability. In fact, there is such a trade-off in the short run: an economy that grows fast may be subject to demand inflation and, in the absence of a competitive foreign exchange rate, to balance-of-payment crises. In the medium run, however, macroeconomic stability is essential for development, and a competitive exchange rate is more important in ensuring demand for investments than a domestic expansive policy. The state's financial health, expressed in low public indebtedness levels and positive public savings, is a condition for macroeconomic stability and full employment. John Maynard Keynes defended budget deficits only as an anticyclical economic policy tool based on the assumption that the state's finances were in equilibrium and, at the same time, demand and employment were insufficient. In this particular case, running a temporary deficit would be legitimate (Bresser-Pereira and Dall'Acqua 1991).

Macroeconomic stability is defined not only in terms of relatively stable prices and a fiscal adjustment expressed as primary surpluses but also in terms of full employment, inflation under control, moderate interest rates, a competitive foreign exchange rate, and intertemporally sound state and nation-state accounts. From the public accounts perspective, macroeconomic stability exists when the ratio of public debt to GDP and the ratio of the state's fiscal expenditure on interest payments to GDP are within acceptable boundaries; where these ratios are high, a large primary surplus will not be enough: the budget deficit–to–GDP ratio must be low enough for it to drop gradually, and the interest rate must be gradually reduced so that the ratio of the state's expenditure on interest payments to GDP will drop. From the perspective of the country as a whole, there will be macroeconomic stability where the foreign debt–to–exports ratio remains within acceptable limits and any eventual current account deficit is small enough not to raise this additional indebtedness index; otherwise, the current account deficit must become a surplus, or exports must increase to make for a comfortable debt-to-exports ratio. In either case, it is the size of the flows—public deficit or current account deficit—that matters because over time they determine whether the economy is in equilibrium or on its way to crisis. It is not enough, therefore, that inflation is under control and that primary surplus goals are being attained. As noted by José Antonio Ocampo (2003, p. 93), "fiscal equilibrium and price stability" replaced the Keynesian view that defined macroeconomic stability as "full employment and stable economic growth with low inflation and sustainable foreign accounts." Ocampo argued that removing real economic activity from center stage is not economically justified given the high cost of real crises and the procyclical character that uncontrolled markets take on as they exacerbate times of both euphoria and crisis. Balanced states' public accounts and nation-states' foreign accounts are not enough to ensure stability and growth: strategic macroeconomic prices must also be appropriate, that is, the interest rate must be "moderate," as required by the US Federal Reserve Bank Act, and the exchange rate must be stable, which allows exporters to plan ahead, and competitive, which ensures the competitiveness to tradable industries utilizing technology in the state of the art.

Finally, in addition to keeping inflation under control, macroeconomic stability requires reasonably full employment. I don't mean full employment alone—the level of activity that admits only frictional unemployment (workers in between jobs), because this rate is difficult to determine. And I reject the concept of a nonaccelerating inflation rate of unemployment (NAIRU) because this rate is even harder to measure and, mainly, because the concept has been used by conventional economists to hide unemployment because unemployment is inconsistent with neoclassical macroeconomics. For years, conventional economists used this concept to argue that there was no unemployment in the United States when the average rate was in excess of 6 percent of the active workforce; when this rate dropped two percentage points without any structural changes, the old full employment rate was quickly forgotten. I say "reasonably full employment" because I understand that there is a rate of unemployment a little above the frictional rate that acts as a compromise between, on the one hand, workers and members of the professional middle class, who would like unemployment to be lower, and, on the other, the rentiers who would like it to be higher in order to prevent any threat of inflation arising from lower unemployment eroding the value of their assets. James Galbraith (1997) showed how weak the evidence was that exceeding the hypothetical NAIRU leads to an unacceptable increase in inflation: the cost of attempting to restrict demand to this level is high and the benefits meager.

Since 1980 the Brazilian economy has failed to meet the criteria for macroeconomic stability. Unemployment remains very high, and not even the staunchest conventional economist and advocate of the NAIRU would dare speak of full employment in Brazil. The real short-term interest rate is the world's highest and is lower than 9 percent only by "accident," as was the case in 2003. Brazilian society may be "used to" such high rates since 1995, as it was used to high and inertial inflation between 1980 and 1994, but this does not neutralize the essentially sick nature of the phenomenon: if high inflation was the great source of disequilibrium in that period, since 1995 high interest rates have been the main ailment the Brazilian economy faces, an anomaly that cannot be explained by the mechanics of the market alone. This anomaly translates into low investment and growth rates and into a need for higher taxes. The exchange rate, finally, in addition to being highly unstable, tends to appreciate as a result of the inflow of capital attracted by the high interest rates, depreciating only in times of crisis or the threat thereof. Only the rate of inflation fits the bill for a stable economy, albeit still unsatisfactorily; the current rate of 4.5 percent is not safe because it has been attained largely by an exchange rate appreciation that is not sustainable in the medium run.

In fiscal terms, the Brazilian economy is far from equilibrium. Even though it has, since 1999, met the primary surplus goals that cater to the interests of creditors and the IMF, public savings are still negative and investment rates remain a cause for concern, in particular the state expenditure on interest-to-GDP index. There has been a drop in the public indebtedness rate to about 51 percent of GDP from a high of 57 percent. But this improvement is due not to a real decrease in debt but to the fact that the foreign public debt, now practically eliminated in net terms, was relatively high, so that the appreciation of the real led to a drop in the public debt–to–GDP ratio. The current level of 51 percent is apparently reasonable relative to other countries. This is, however, misleading. As any good economist and finance practitioner should know, flow metrics are always more relevant than stock metrics. The interest rate on this debt must be taken into consideration. From this perspective, Brazil's fiscal situation is precarious: the country is no longer in the "fiscal crisis of the state" that I identified in the 1980s;[7] since the early 1990s it can no longer be said that fiscal insolvency is a characteristic of the Brazilian economy, but, as we will see in Chapter 4, fiscal disequilibrium persists.[8]

Only the foreign indebtedness ratios and sovereign risk have improved substantially since 1999, thanks to the enormous increase in exports. As we will see in Chapter 7, the foreign debt–to–exports ratio dropped from a high of 5 in 1999 to a little more than 1.2 in 2007. Note, however, that the foreign debt–to–GDP ratio also improved, but not by as much. The former ratio is more significant, but the difference between the two shows that the improvement was due mostly to the increase in exports, which practically doubled after 1999. As discussed earlier, this improvement implied a significant foreign adjustment of about 6.4 percent of GDP during the period, as the current account deficit of 4.75 percent of GDP in 1999 became a surplus of 1.6 percent of GDP in

2005. Such improvement was due to the major increase in the price of the commodities exported to Brazil. Nevertheless, although the Brazilian government, in June 2008, announced that the net foreign debt, excluding the patrimonial (direct investment) debt, had turned negative, the real continued to appreciate. With the exchange rate around 1.60 reals per US dollar, exports fell, imports increased, and a current account deficit again materialized. In this way, the intertemporal equilibrium of foreign accounts was again lost.

Development cannot take place in the absence of macroeconomic stability. This is so not only because the instability indicators include open unemployment, which automatically reduces the growth rate but also because high interest rates reduce investment (and, in the case of Brazil, imply a heavier tax burden and fiscal deterioration) and because a higher exchange rate reduces exports, investment, and savings; increases imports and consumption; and leaves the country under the constant threat of balance-of-payment crises. Where macroeconomic instability prevents a country from growing, one finds oneself in the shoes of the captain who, when asked to explain to his commanding officer why he had failed to fire a 21-gun salute in honor of the visiting king of a friendly country, began by saying: "Sir, I have ten reasons for my failure; the first one being that there was no gunpowder." As of 2008, Brazil has not resumed sustained growth in 28 years (since the beginning of the chronic and lasting crisis it finds itself in) or 14 years (since the stabilization of prices), chiefly because there is no macroeconomic stability. Among instability indicators, the main culprits are the high short-term interest rate and the volatile and principally the chronically overappreciated exchange rate. These lie at the root of most other forms of disequilibrium. What is interesting about these high interest rates is that they are almost uniquely Brazilian. The conventional orthodoxy certainly encourages high interest rates, in the name of "financial deepening" or to bring about "bigger savings," and because they are compatible with a high exchange rate and growth with foreign savings—the bedrock of the "development strategy" that rich countries have to offer to their middle-income competitors—but nowhere is it as successful in bringing about high interest rates as in Brazil. In relation to the exchange rate, however, Brazil is not alone. Most developing countries are also unable to neutralize the tendency to its overappreciation. Now, since the exchange rate is an economy's most strategic macroeconomic price, we should remember a phrase that Mario Henrique Simonsen often repeated: "if inflation cripples, the exchange rate kills."

An improved foreign scenario, together with high primary surpluses, has led to a significant improvement of Brazil's sovereign risk in the past few years, as we will see in Chapter 7, and Brazil was "investment graded." We should, however, not be misled by this fact. Brazil's international credit improved, but the overappreciated exchange rate and the return to current account deficits show that such improvement is transitory.

A Perverse System

The long-lasting quasi stagnation or low growth rates and macroeconomic instability that characterize the Brazilian economy are the consequences of a perverse macroeconomic system whose main traits and interrelations I examine in this book. A system is a set of elements articulated in such a manner as to make up a whole. This articulation or coordination of elements follows a certain logic: in the case of a living organism, it is the logic of survival; in the case of a social system, the minimal objective is likewise survival or security, but, made up as it is of actors endowed with free will, there is an additional economic objective—that of well-being. Man does not work for survival alone, but to better his living standards. Finally, in the case of a modern social system, with the democratic state as instrument for collective action, and equipped with the market as the main coordination mechanism, well-being is promoted from an implicit to an explicit objective: the governments of nation-states, supported and legitimized by their people, or their nation, start developing strategies to pursue economic development—the system's logic becomes that of development.

In Brazil, however, the incumbent economic system does not abide by the logic of well-being or development. Its logic since the mid-1990s has been that of high interest rates and uncompetitive exchange rates. To use economists' jargon, its "objective function" is to secure revenues that meet the interests of rentiers and their commission-earning associates in the financial industry as well as to maintain a high exchange rate to neutralize the nation's ability to compete internationally and to allow multinationals to expatriate bigger hard-currency profits to their headquarters. The entire logic of macroeconomic policy, which is naturally part and parcel of this perverse system, points in that direction. Its consequences are macroeconomic instability and the quasi stagnation of income per capita. I am probably among those responsible for casting "rentiers" in a decisive role in Brazilian macroeconomic policy. But there is nothing theoretically novel about it. The best economists have always concerned themselves with abusive interest rates that benefited rentiers, knowing that this amounted to a terrible disease in any economic system.

Keynes spoke of the need for the "euthanasia of the rentier." Bhaduri and Steindl (1985) showed that the rise in interest rates after the Bretton Woods Accords met the interests of rentiers and bankers; Pasinetti (1997) called this rise the "revenge of the rentiers." These authors, however, never imagined interest rates as high as those rentiers get in Brazil—truly usurious ones.

Ultimately, the high interest rate is a consequence of this perverse logic. The interested parties and monetary authorities clearly differ. For them, the objective is to control inflation. Still, as common sense should show, keeping inflation under control does not necessitate maintaining the Central Bank's short-term interest rate at a level much higher than Brazil's long-term interest rate that can be inferred from Brazil's sovereign risk. On the other hand, if it were true that maintaining control over inflation is the main objective of economic policy, at times when aggregate demand dropped and inflation correspondingly declined, the Ministry of Finance and the Central Bank would have taken advantage of the opportunity to develop a strategy to lower the base rate toward international levels compatible with Brazil's risk rating. This has been unthinkable for the leaders of both institutions in past administrations, as it has been also to do away with indexed short-term interest rates and indexed government contracts—which are essential to reduce inflation and the interest rate. When the economy cools down, the Central Bank does lower the interest rate, but the floor of 9 percent in real terms is ever present.

Fiscal policy, too, is subordinated to an interest rate that satisfies rentiers. Once this rate has been set, public debt must be prevented from rising relative to GDP. In other words, the debtor must be kept from contracting so much debt that it becomes insolvent and thereby endangers the rentiers' investments. The 4.25 percent primary surplus has been calculated to achieve this end. If the objective had been to use fiscal policy to fight inflation, the fiscal goals would be a reduced budget deficit and increased public savings rather than a primary surplus, and these goals would vary according to the economic cycle; but this practice, too, is off the agenda. The problem that rentiers and the financial industry face is how to use the primary surplus to make "the debt fit into GDP." They are ever fearful that it will not, although, as we will see when we examine the state's two indebtedness indexes—the ratio of public debt to GDP and the ratio of the state's interest expenditure to GDP—it will become clear that it is the interest plus current expenditures that don't fit GDP. Finally, the exchange rate is also subordinated to the logic of the satisfactory interest rate. Because this rate is so high, it draws capital from abroad. Capital flows appreciate the domestic currency until it reaches the perverse equilibrium of high interest rate and uncompetitive exchange rate—an equilibrium that pushed Brazil over the edge and into crisis in 1998 and, partly, in 2002 as well.

In sum, although the logic of a macroeconomic system is ideally that of economic development or national interest, the logic of the prevalent system in Brazil is that of high interest rates and uncompetitive exchange rates, which serves not the nation but the rentiers, who live off interest revenues; the financial industry, which benefits from commissions; multinationals, which are able to expatriate more hard currency profits with the same profits in reals; and every country in trade competition with Brazil. It is a perverse, but well-constructed, logic whose economic foundation is that the equilibrium interest rate—the rate that exerts no pressure on inflation—is around 9 percent a year in real terms in Brazil and whose political foundation rests, on the one hand, on powerful domestic and foreign interests and, on the other, on the ideological dependency of Brazilians and their fear of the return of inflation. One cannot understand the macroeconomics of stagnation that prevails in Brazil without combining economics and politics because the macroeconomic system is itself made up of both purely economic variables, such as the marginal propensity to consume, and economic policy variables, such as the inflation targeting policy. Economic policy variables are institutions that, once set and reiterated, become intrinsic elements of the economic model. These policies, as their name implies, are the result of politics in the broader sense: the arguments and compromises the citizens of a nation make through politicians and high-ranking bureaucrats (as are the governors of central banks). An economic system may be, and usually is, a win-win system, as the majority therein benefits; this has been the secret of capitalism's success. But it may also be a zero-sum system where many lose. Political struggle and conflicts exist precisely to somehow address such problems. In certain cases, however, as in the Brazilian economy, the disequilibriums become so massive that they serve the interests only of a minority in league with foreign interests. In this case we have before us an extremely perverse situation that requires the nation to rebuild and reorganize itself and resume the defense of its interests.

Notes

1. My analysis of the 1980–1994 period can be found mainly in the essays collected in Bresser-Pereira (1992).

2. Surprisingly, Dani Rodrik (2007, pp. 79–81) endorses this explanation. To him, the reform to which the country should give priority is "lower taxation." Indeed, to reduce some entitlements and the corresponding taxation is desirable, but this is definitively not the main problem Brazil faces, nor the one that can be tackled more directly and effectively.

3. Textbooks continue to refer to "monetary policy" instead of "interest rate policy." But the fact is that central banks have relinquished the classic strategy of controlling the interest rate by managing currency supply and demand and, more specifically, the monetarist policy of achieving monetary goals, choosing instead to manage the interest rate directly. As a consequence, the LM curve in the IS-LM model has been replaced with the MP curve, which makes it the IS-MP model (Nakano, 2002).

4. Initially, I called the conventional orthodoxy, as it presented itself in the early 1990s, the Second Consensus of Washington, to set it apart from the previous consensus of the 1980s. The term *conventional orthodoxy* is more generic and, therefore, more convenient.

5. I refer to a "disguised" exchange rate anchor because, as we will see in Chapter 5, the high interest policy "controls" inflation not by checking aggregate demand but by appreciating the exchange that remains the real nominal anchor.

6. After all, in 2006, according to an analysis by IPEA, the investment rate rose to 20.8 from 20.4 percent of GDP.

7. I examined the state's fiscal crisis based on the paper I delivered in Cambridge in April 1987, a few days before being sworn in as minister of finance, "Mudanças no padrão de financiamento do investimento no Brasil." This and other works addressing the crisis are collected in *A Crise do Estado* (The Crisis of the State) (Bresser-Pereira 1992).

8. The state's fiscal crisis ends during the administration of Fernando Collor (1990–1992), which was also the one that showed the most determination to solve it. For an appraisal of Brazil's fiscal sustainability, see Bicalho (2005), who applied a test to the 1997–2004 period.

2

The Old
Developmentalism

This chapter is in the nature of a brief flashback—a summary historical analysis of why Brazil, during the 50 years between 1930 and 1980, set up a developmental state and adopted a successful national-developmentalist strategy, but then in the major foreign debt crisis of the 1980s surrendered to the conventional orthodoxy and is now experiencing only modest economic growth. From the 1930s to the 1970s Brazil and other Latin American countries grew at an extraordinary pace. They took advantage of the weakening of the center to formulate national development strategies that, in essence, implied the protection of national infant industries and the forced promotion of savings through the state. This strategy was called "developmentalism" or "national developmentalism." The purpose of such a name was, first, to emphasize that the policy's basic objective was to promote economic development and, second, to emphasize that in order for this to happen, the nation—that is, business leaders, the state bureaucracy, the middle classes, and the workers joined together to face international competition—used the state as its principal instrument of collective action. Latin American economists who, together with a group of international economists, took part in formulating "development economics" were affiliated to three complementary schools of thought: the classical economics of Adam Smith and Karl Marx, Keynesian macroeconomics, and Latin American structuralist theory.[1] Developmentalism was not an economic theory but a national development strategy. It employed economic theories to formulate, for each country on the capitalist periphery, a strategy capable of gradually leading to the development level attained by central countries. It used market-based theories, for there is no

45

economic theory that does not spring from markets, but also theories that cast the state and its institutions in a leading role as an auxiliary co-ordinator of the market economy. Developmentalism faced opposition from neoclassical economists who, when dealing with developing countries, practiced the conventional orthodoxy—that is, the set of diagnoses, economic policies, and institutional reforms that rich, or Northern, nations prescribed to developing, or Southern, countries. At the time of national developmentalism, their opponents were called "monetarists" owing to the emphasis placed on the money supply as a means of controlling inflation.

Since Brazil was a peripheral, or dependent, country, whose industrial revolution was taking place 150 years after that of Britain and more than 100 years after that of the United States, the remarkable development from the 1930s to 1970s was possible only insofar as Brazil as a nation was able to use its state proactively as an instrument to define and implement a national development strategy. This was not about replacing the market with the state but, rather, about strengthening the state in order to enable it to create the requisite conditions for business enterprises to invest and innovate. All countries, beginning with Britain itself, required a national development strategy to bring about their industrial revolutions and to continue to develop. The use of a national development strategy was particularly evident among latecomer central countries such as Germany and Japan, but these countries were not colonies nor did they suffer from dependency. Due to the different experience of peripheral countries such as Brazil and other Latin American countries that had lived through the colonial experience, they remained ideologically dependent on the center after becoming formally independent. Both late-development central countries and former colonies needed to formulate national development strategies, but the task was easier for the former. For peripheral countries, there was the additional hurdle of facing their own "dependency," that is, the submission of the local elites to those in central countries, who were interested in nothing other than their own development.

National developmentalism adopted a nationalist ideology that had nothing in common with ethnical nationalism; it was just the necessary ideology that nations use to form an autonomous national state; it was the affirmation that, in order to develop, countries needed to define their own policies and institutions, their own national development strategy.[2]

In the 1940s, 1950s, and 1960s, developmentalist and Keynesian policymakers prevailed in Latin America; they were the mainstream.

Governments used their theories first and foremost in economic policy-making. From the 1970s on, however, in the context of the great neoliberal and conservative wave that began to build up, Keynesian theory, development economics, and Latin American structuralism were successfully challenged by neoclassical economists, most of whom adopted a neoliberal ideology. Since the 1980s, in the context of the great foreign debt crisis that added to the rich nations' political power, these economists have managed to redefine in neoliberal terms their prescriptions for developing countries. The neoliberal ideology targeting these countries became hegemonic, expressing itself through the Washington Consensus and its macroeconomic conventional orthodoxy. Today, there is no longer a "consensus" insofar as the corresponding hegemony has weakened, and many speak of a post–Washington Consensus. Yet, a systematic economic critique of it is lacking. People see that the consensus did not produce the promised outcomes but fail to explain why. When they try to explain, they come back to old national-developmentalist ideas—principally citing the lack of industrial policy—which certainly is not the main reason why the Washington Consensus failed economically. In this book I am trying to develop this systematic critique that has been lacking, using Brazil as a reference.

Before discussing the causes of the failure of the Washington Consensus, however, we must consider why, during the 1980s, national developmentalism faced a major crisis and was replaced with a foreign strategy: the conventional orthodoxy. Several factors help explain this. First, during the 1960s the national alliance that served as the political foundation of developmentalism fell apart as a direct consequence of the military coup supported by Brazilian industrialists and the US government. The national-developmentalist approach assumed the existence of a nation and, thus, of a national agreement involving industrialists, workers, and the state bureaucracy—a reasonable assumption insofar as, after the lengthy period of dependency that followed the independence movements of the early nineteenth century, these countries since 1930 had taken advantage of the crisis in the North to begin their national revolutions and form autonomous national states. Accordingly, developmentalism proposed that each country's new industrial businesspeople should become a "national bourgeoisie," as had been the case in developed countries, and should, in association themselves with government officials and urban workers, bring about a national and industrial revolution. Therefore, in every country the sense of nation, of national society, was reinforced, and the possibility dawned that this society might implement a national development strategy. This strategy was at once a proposal and an assessment of the reality represented by the accelerated industrialization process that Latin America was then experiencing.

The Cuban Revolution of 1959, by radicalizing the left wing, and the economic crisis of the early 1960s led, however, to the dissolution of the national developmental alliance and set the stage for the establishment of military regimes in Brazil, Argentina, Uruguay, and Chile, with support from each country's businesspeople and from the United States. As a consequence, the national coalition that was so essential to the constitution of a nation broke up, and Latin America's moderate left embraced the mistaken theses of the "associated dependency," which rejected the possibility of a "national bourgeoisie" (Bresser-Pereira 2005b). In doing so, it rejected the very idea of nation and of national development strategy on which national developmentalism was based.

Second, because old or national developmentalism was based on import substitution, it contained the seeds of its own demise. Protection of national industry, the focus on the market, and the reduction of an economy's openness coefficient, even in a relatively large economy such as Brazil's, are greatly constrained by economies of scale. For certain industries, protection becomes absurd. As a result, the import-substitution model that was maintained through the 1970s led Latin American economies into deep distortions. On the other hand, as Furtado remarked (Furtado 1966), after the initial import-substitution phase of consumer-goods industries, continued industrialization implies a substantial increase in the capital-labor ratio, with two consequences: income concentration and reduced capital productivity or product-capital ratio. The response to income concentration was to be an expanded production of luxury consumer goods, characterizing what I have termed the *industrialized underdevelopment model,* which, besides being perverse, contains the seeds of the dissolution of the national prodevelopment alliance.

Third, the great debt crisis of the 1980s, which was not directly related to the import-substitution model but already an outcome of the growth-with-foreign-savings strategy, further weakened the national coalition supporting national developmentalism. The debt crisis paved the way for the rise of high and inertial inflation, which would be the scourge of the Brazilian economy for 14 years. The military government had indexed prices since 1964, but it was only in the early 1980s that inflation topped 100 percent a year as a result of exchange rate depreciations caused by the foreign debt crisis: from this moment up to 1994, inflation would be measured in monthly terms (5, 10, 20 percent a month), configuring high and inertial inflation. Thereafter developmentalism was supported by only a populist left wing that, while in office in the second half of the 1980s, proved unable to manage the Brazilian economy. This became apparent in the Cruzado Plan—the 1986 attempt to control inertial inflation—which ended in a disastrous populist episode (Sachs 1989).

The fourth reason for the replacement of developmentalism with the Washington Consensus lies in the strength of this ideological wave that was coming from the North. In the early 1980s, in response to the foreign debt crisis, a new and stronger conventional orthodoxy established itself bit by bit. The Baker Plan (1985), named after US Secretary of the Treasury James Baker, completed the definition of the new ideas by adding market-oriented institutional reforms to orthodox macroeconomic adjustment. Developmentalism then became the target of systematic attack. Taking advantage of the economic crisis that derived, in part, from the discredited development model and from the distortions it had suffered at the hands of populist politicians and the middle classes, the Washington Consensus imparted to developmentalism negative connotations, identifying it with populism or irresponsible economic policies. In its stead, the Washington Consensus proposed the panacea of orthodox and neoliberal institutional reforms. It further proposed that developing countries abandon the antiquated concept of "nation" that national developmentalism had adopted and accept the globalist thesis according to which, in the age of globalization, nation-states had lost autonomy and relevance: worldwide free markets (including financial ones) would be charged with promoting the economic development of all.

Twenty years later, the failure of the conventional orthodoxy to promote Latin America's economic development was evident. While developmentalism prevailed, between 1950 and 1980, per capita income in Brazil grew almost 4 percent a year; since then, it has grown around 1.2 percent a year, that is, three times less. The performance of other Latin American countries has been no different, with the exception of Chile. In the same period, however, dynamic Asian countries, including China since the 1980s and India since the 1990s, maintained or achieved extraordinary growth rates.

Why such different growth rates? In this book I argue that, at the more immediate level of economic policies, the fundamental problem relates to loss of control over the most strategic macroeconomic price in an open economy: the exchange rate. Latin American countries lost control over their exchange rates via financial liberalization or the opening of financial accounts. As a consequence, Brazil stopped neutralizing the tendency to the overappreciation of the exchange rate. Now, the Dutch disease and the growth-with-foreign-savings policy were free to appreciate the real and, so, limit on the demand side the export-oriented investment opportunities. At the same time, Asian countries mostly ran current account surpluses and retained control over their exchange rates. At the reform level, Latin American countries indiscriminately accepted all liberalizing reforms, irresponsibly privatizing monopoly utilities and opening their capital accounts, whereas Asian countries were more prudent. It gradually became clear to me, however, that the main difference was to be found in a new, fundamental fact: Latin American countries interrupted their national revolutions and watched as their nations became disorganized and lost cohesiveness and autonomy.

Summing up, between 1930 and 1980, Brazil adopted national developmentalism as a national development strategy. In this period, and mainly from 1930 to 1960, Brazil and many other Latin American countries were firmly nationalist, finally providing their formally independent states with a basic solidarity when it came to competing internationally. Yet the weakening brought about internally by the great economic crisis of the 1980s and by dependency theory, combined externally with the hegemonic force of the ideological neoliberal wave coming from the United States since the 1970s, interrupted the process of national-state formation in Latin America. Local elites stopped thinking for themselves and accepted advice and pressure from the North, while the countries, devoid of a national development strategy, saw their development stall.

Economic Inequality and Populism

At the beginning of this chapter, I briefly listed both the false and the true economic causes of the poor performance of the Brazilian economy since 1994. Before coming back to them in Chapter 3, however, I must briefly discuss a structural problem that haunts the Brazilian economy and society. I refer to economic inequality. The radical inequality in the country widened under the military regime; since redemocratization it has been tackled by increased public spending on social welfare. Yet such a major problem does not involve social injustice alone. Of course, this moral element can and should be regarded independently of any other consideration, but I want to emphasize the economic aspect here: economic inequality is a severe obstacle to Brazil's economic development. The internal structural cause of the Brazilian economy's insufficient growth over more than a quarter of a century is the vast gulf between the masses and the elites, expressed in high income concentration.

Deep inequality is not simply unfair. On the one hand, it keeps the elites and even the middle class insensitive to national problems and, therefore, submissive to the ideological hegemony of wealthy competitors from the North; on the other hand, it causes politicians to adopt populist policies to win votes.

Before the military takeover, Brazilian inequality, whose roots lie in the plantation system and in slavery, was already great. This inequality, however, found an appropriate political response in the political populism of President Getúlio Vargas and in the labor protection policies that granted a cluster of social rights to urban workers. National developmentalism came under the critique of neoliberal representatives because it would be a populist strategy. This criticism confused political populism—a classic concept of political sociology—and economic populism, a more recent concept used by economists since the late 1980s. Political populism is defined as direct contact between a political leader and the people, or the masses, without the mediation of political parties. This populism is generally the first means by which the poor become party to the political process—massive participation, subject to mistakes of all kinds, which liberals reject because they oppose popular participation, and socialists equally reject because they expect the people to engage in an ideological, revolutionary participation, which never happens. Nevertheless, political populism is a step forward from the authoritarian past because it is an early form of popular participation, a manifestation of the emerging democracy of the elites.[3]

In a developing country such as Brazil, when industrialization began in the 1930s, political populism was inevitable. The political backwardness of the country as well as the prevailing economic inequality left no alternative. Even today there is room for political populism in Brazil. Brazil is an industrialized middle-income country that remains underdeveloped because it is still a dual economy where a significant portion of the workforce is not incorporated into the capitalist labor market. Although the country is fully capitalist, its stock of capital is not sufficient to employ all of the existing labor, so that a significant part of the workforce continues to live at a subsistence level on the fringes of the system—and excluded from its benefits. A "traditional" sector no longer exists in Brazil, but the semiemployed or unemployed population is large enough to provide what Arthur Lewis (1958 [1954]) called "unlimited labor supply"—the essential trait of an underdeveloped country. Brazil is an underdeveloped, inequitable country, but not a poor one. Brazil's is an industrialized underdevelopment. It has a large capitalist sector made up of the three social classes typical of modern capitalism:

the capitalist class, the professional middle class, and the working class that originally was just urban but today is also rural. This class system is completed by an urban and rural underclass of poor or socially excluded, which cannot be seen as precapitalist, but as the source of existing unlimited supply of labor. Medium-development countries share several structural characteristics, such as low average per capita incomes and wages, moderate scientific and technological development levels, and the presence of a large informal sector. But one structural aspect of the Brazilian economy and society deviates from the average in a negative way: high income concentration. Every indicator available is clear in this respect. Time and time again statistics are published listing Brazil as one of the world's most unequal countries. Table 2.1 presents the same picture and leaves no room for doubt: it shows the ratio of the income earned by the 10 richest percent and the 10 poorest percent of the population in Brazil and other selected countries, both developed and developing.

Economic populism is a different matter. It too has a political content, but also a clear and direct economic aspect: it happens where the government spends more than the revenues it collects, in an effort to please the voters. The government may cause the state apparatus or organization to spend more than it earns, and in this event fiscal populism arises. Or the nation-state may import more than it exports, leading to what I have termed *exchange rate populism*. In the case of fiscal populism, the end result is a budget deficit and increased public debt; with foreign exchange populism, a current account deficit and increased foreign debt. The two forms of populism are independent: political populism can exist in the absence of economic populism. Although economic

Table 2.1 Inequality Index, Selected Countries (income of the richest 10% against the poorest 10% in different countries, ca. 2000)

	Index of Income Concentration
India	9.6
Turkey	14.0
Peru	22.1
Russia	22.8
Mexico	32.1
Brazil	68.6

Source: World Bank, www.worldbank.org.

populism is always negative, political populism has both positive and negative aspects. It all depends on how it is used. Getúlio Vargas was a political leader who, over two administrations (1930–1945 and 1950–1954), used political populism to acquire political legitimacy in a country where the gap between the elites and the people was massive and, thanks to this legitimacy, to be able to promote industrialization or the Brazilian national industrial revolution. He did not resort to fiscal populism—he maintained strict fiscal discipline at virtually all times—or to foreign exchange populism, but he did maintain direct contact with urban workers and gave them a sequence of real benefits that materialized in the form of the Consolidated Labor Law. On the other hand, through the national development strategy that national developmentalism was, he struck a reasonable compromise among workers, industrial businesspeople, and government technicians, inasmuch as all stood to gain from the accelerated economic development between 1930 and 1960. His successor, Juscelino Kubitschek (1956–1960), consolidated Brazil's industrialization over the five years of his term, but, owing mostly to the decision to build Brasília, erred on the side of fiscal and foreign exchange populism, leaving the country's fiscal and foreign accounts unbalanced. The economic and financial crisis that began in 1961 was largely the result of this policy. During the military period, national developmentalism was not populist, except during the 1979–1980 period; the error here was failure to adjust the economy after the first Organization of Petroleum Exporting Countries (OPEC) oil shock (1973) and, above all, after the second one (1979) and to delay any adjustments until 1981, when the foreign debt had already become too large.

Economic populism is a distortion that haunts the developmentalist and the conventional orthodox alike. The conventional orthodoxy—despite its constant accusations of its adversaries as populists—with its policy of growth with foreign savings, causes a foreign exchange appreciation that implies foreign exchange populism. Thanks to the appreciated rate, wages and salaries rise in real terms and, for a period, the country experiences euphoria, until a balance-of-payment crisis puts an end to the party. This happened in Brazil from 1995 to 1998, after the Real Plan, and has been repeating itself since 2005, always to the applause of Washington and New York.

Behind these populist experiences—both the fiscal and the foreign exchange varieties—lies Brazil's radical economic inequality. When this inequality coincides with quasi stagnation, the sole alternative politicians perceive for gaining votes and legitimizing their power is to resort to economic populism. Of course, this is a short-lived policy, but it may last long enough to ensure election or reelection. If a better distributive balance prevailed in Brazil, the poor would be less vulnerable to being deceived by politicians. But it is not just politicians who change their behavior in light of income concentration. The wealthy, too, the greatest beneficiaries, take advantage of it to perpetrate abuses that would be unthinkable in more equitable—and, therefore, more democratic—societies. Their relationships with the state remain perverted, marked by capture—by violence against citizens' republican rights. Tax evasion remains high, notwithstanding a system based on indirect taxes that are highly regressive but easier to oversee.[4] No one dares speak of criminal prosecution for tax evasion involving fraud. Significant efforts have been made to pass laws defining and punishing corruption in other areas, but the results have been modest. This is illustrated in the area of governmental purchases, where a strict law reduced, but did not prevent, corruption. In the case of payments to owners of land that the state expropriated for public purposes, for example, gangs of lawyers and businesspeople continue to exist and misappropriate public funds. Other sectors remain devoid of specific institutional protection. With the privatization of a series of monopolistic firms, the regulatory agencies then created have often been captured by the very firms they regulate. Finally, the excessive interest rate in force in Brazil is tantamount to confiscation of the public wealth. Corruption among politicians, in turn, may on occasion pose a threat to democracy, as in the "Mensalão" scandal of 2005 and the "Sanguessugas" scandal of 2006. Although the amounts involved are much lower than those found in the private sector, this type of political corruption receives large coverage in the media. Brazilian society is beginning to show indignation, but not enough to prevent the reelection of obviously corrupt politicians and the punishment of embezzling civil servants and businesspeople. After all, the elites tacitly accept and expect impunity, rejecting the notion that its members should be subjected to the same criminal treatment as the poor, which can be explained only by the radical inequality found in Brazil. The poor, in turn, seem numb before such corruption. The middle classes are traditionally more demanding in this respect. At a more abstract level, it appears clear that this is the fundamental obstacle to an active civil society and a cohesive nation.

Democratic Transition and Distribution

Since the transition to democracy, Brazilian society has been making a great fiscal effort to fund education, health, and welfare, and, thanks to it, social indicators have improved. Brazil's social policy is the greatest achievement of the democratic regime. Social spending has increased and its quality has improved in Brazil as a consequence of the pressure exerted by voters for more and better education and health services and for the introduction of several minimum-income programs, combined in 2004 into Bolsa Família, that have produced an indisputable social protection effect.[5] Although the incompetent and unfair economic policy, run by alienated elites, keeps the Brazilian economy semistagnant, a consolidated democracy has been meeting with success in the social area, especially at the municipal and state levels. The data provided in Table 2.2, concerning three basic social indicators, show that social spending has borne fruit. Average life expectancy for Brazilians has risen from 62.5 years to 72.4 years in the period; the infant mortality rate has dropped to less than half its earlier level; and illiteracy rates have dropped by about half. Although the quality of basic education in Brazil is still wanting, basic education coverage now extends to 97 percent of children.

Conservative critics argue that social spending in Brazil has concentrated purely on welfare activities. True, there has been a significant increase in welfare expenditures in Brazil, particularly since the implementation of the minimum-income mechanisms now concentrated in Bolsa Família. As can be seen from Table 2.3, between 1987 and 2004 a 3.1 percent increase occurred in the extension of welfare benefits to recipients who had made no prior contributions or only partial contributions. As such, about 3 percent of GDP—out of the 10 percent increase in social spending by the Brazilian state since the 1980s—can be attributed to the welfare policy; the other 7 percent went to education and health.

But this welfare policy, through minimum-income programs that the incumbent administration consolidated and expanded under Bolsa Família,

Table 2.2 Improved Social Indicators: 1980, 2000, and 2006

	1980	2000	2006
Life expectancy at birth (years)	62.5	70.5	72.4
Infant mortality rate (thousands)	69.1	30.1	25.1
Illiteracy rate (%)	31.9	16.7	13.9

Sources: Instituto Brasileiro de Geografia e Estatística (IBGE, Brazilian Institute of Geography and Statistic), www.ibge.gov.br.

Table 2.3 Brazil—Welfare and Subsidized Benefits: 1987–2004

	1987	2004
Benefits as percentage of GDP	0.5	3.6
Beneficiaries (millions)	5.2	21.8

Source: Instituto Brasileiro de Geografia e Estatistíca (IBGE, Brazilian institute of Geography and Statistics), www.ibge.gov.br.

Notes: Benefits to recipients who had made no prior contributions or only partial contributions; payments of the value of the minimum wage or less, except for unemployment insurance, which on average is valued at one and a half times the minimum wage. The number of beneficiaries is an estimate.

effectively eliminated or substantially reduced absolute poverty.[6] A study by Fundação Getúlio Vargas (FGV) shows a significant drop in poverty levels in Brazil between 2003 and 2005.[7] In 2003 poverty affected 28.2 percent of the Brazilian population; by 2005 it had dropped to 22.7 percent. A study by the Instituto de Pesquisa Econômica Aplicada (Institute for Applied Economic Research; IPEA), in turn, shows that from 2001 to 2005 average income rose by 8 percent a year among the poorest 10 percent, 6 percent a year among the poorest 20 percent, and 5 percent a year among the poorest 30 percent.[8] On the other hand, recent studies prove that income distribution in Brazil has been improving since 1989 and at a brisker pace since 1996.[9] In that year, the income of the richest 20 percent of households was 29.3 times larger than that of the poorest 20 percent; the ratio had dropped to 21.9 by 2004.[10] But these data are not entirely reliable because 76 percent of the total income surveyed by Pesquisa Nacional por Amostra de Domicílios (National Household Survey; PNAD) in 2004 (the latest official information available) pertained to labor income. According to the national accounts of the Instituto Brasileiro de Geografia e Estatística (Brazilian Institute of Geography and Statistic; IBGE), labor income (of wage earners and the self-employed) accounted for 40.1 percent of the country's total national income.[11] On the other hand, it is known that in that period the amount rentiers received as interest rose remarkably. In the early 1990s, it was close to 2 percent of GDP; by 2005, it had risen to 8.3 percent of GDP.[12] With this in mind, IPEA researchers and Marcio Pochman carried out studies in 2006 that indicate that inequality rose in recent years instead of falling.[13] I hypothesize that this increase in inequality took the form of income increases for the richest 2 percent, and not for the richest 10 percent, which includes the middle class; but this hypothesis is yet to be verified. It is the members of this richest group that benefit from high interest rates. When middle-class income falls relative to that of the poor, the usual income distribution indexes show gains, even if the income of the wealthy shows great growth. And what happened after 1999 was a marked drop in middle-class income. If we define the middle class as those who earn more than three times the minimum wage (more than R$1,050), nearly two million formal middle-class jobs have disappeared since 2002. The income of those who managed to enter the market at wages in excess of R$1,050 dropped 46 percent in real terms (adjusted to inflation) from the level paid to those who were dismissed.[14] Perhaps the simplest illustration of income distribution in the relevant period for this book is that as the income of the (business and professional) middle class fell in relative terms, the wealthy, who largely consist of the rentiers and of some high professional executives and financial operators who are no more than 2 percent of the population, benefited from interest rate hikes, and the very poor benefited from Bolsa Família. As a result, given the much larger drop in middle-class incomes, the indexes normally used to show income distribution appear favorable, whereas in fact they were favorable to the poor and the very rich and harmful to the middle class.

This is not the place to discuss how to implement a redistribution policy oriented toward mass consumption, as has been proposed by Bielschowsky (2006). This will certainly be needed, but it must involve the middle class instead of excluding it, as has been the case so far. Solving the fundamental macroeconomic problem of interest rates will be a significant step. The funds so saved must then be used in part to fund public investment and in part to reduce public debt. Soon, however, with resumed economic development, there will be many more funds to continue basic education and health policies, welfare and minimum-income policies, and small manufacturing and land reform policies and also to implement policies to foster job creation and to incorporate the poorest into production. On the other hand, continuing and deepening the 1995 Public Management Reform is essential to improve the quality, and reduce the cost, of the state's social services.

Crisis and Surrender to the North

Civil society and nation are two political forms through which a national society organizes and manifests itself. Society as civil society is more concerned with civil rights, democracy, and social justice; society as nation focuses on national security and economic development. A democratic nation-state, where institutions effectively guarantee citizens' rights, needs an active civil society strong enough to prevent abuse; an autonomous nation-state, capable of ensuring its own autonomy and development, requires a strong and cohesive nation capable of standing up for national interests in the framework of global competition. Brazil's weaknesses in connection with these two forms of political social organization are considerable and should remind us that a cohesive nation is essential for national autonomy and economic development, as a vibrant civil society is a precondition for the protection of civil, political, and social rights. Social inequality, which makes Brazilian society heterogeneous, also makes it authoritarian as a nation and as a civil society. Before being a characteristic of the state, authoritarianism is a trait of the society the state represents—of the two political forms modern societies take: nation and civil society. Only by reducing inequality can this social authoritarianism be countered and democracy promoted at the level of the state. Inequality has always been great in Brazil, but we have seen that the democratic transition allowed some democratization of society itself through the distribution system. On the other hand, the loss of the concept of nation and the weakening of the Brazilian nation that took place in two stages—at the social level after the 1964 military coup and then at the state level with the surrender to the Washington Consensus that began in 1990—have not yet been rectified, even though the conventional orthodoxy's failure in recent years to promote the country's economic development has led a growing number of individuals to review the national problem. The weakness of the Brazilian nation is partly due to inequality, but other reasons exist for this lack of what Aldo Ferrer (2004) calls "national density," reasons that have to do with the rootless nature of local elites and their tendency to mimic rich countries' ideas, institutions, and consumption patterns.

Brazil has been politically independent since 1822, but its independence has always been more formal than real, insofar as the country's elites have always been marked by a strong cultural dependency on the outside world. By cultural dependency we do not mean acknowledgment of the cultural superiority of wealthier countries, which are in fact better educated and have longer cultural histories, but the way Brazilians regard this superiority: as a legitimate source of tutelage. An autonomous means for an economically lagging country to relate to the outside world involves, first, recognizing the superior knowledge of wealthier countries and making efforts to learn from it; second, imitating their technologies; third, importing their institutions and adapting them. The dependent view uncritically emulates institutions and cultural practices, assumes that the relationships between wealthy and poor countries are essentially cooperative, and believes that the advice of and pressures from the North are intended to help developing countries. The autonomous or nationalist view, in turn, in addition to adapting ideas and institutions in a critical manner, does not deny cooperation, but emphasizes competition and mistrusts advice that can just as easily turn into pressure. The dependent, or globalist, view naturally accepts pressures from rich countries and their public policy prescriptions, above all their macroeconomic policies, even if, in their dealings with Brazil, these countries arduously defend their own interests. When it comes to what monetary policy Brazil should adopt, the dependent assumption is that the IMF and the World Bank are guided by the country's interests, rather than by those of their main stockholders.

Cultural dependency is a phenomenon that Brazilians have long pointed out. In 1836, poet Domingos José Gonçalves de Magalhães, in his *Discurso sobre a história da literatura brasileira* (Speech on the History of Brazilian Literature), already criticized Brazilians' "star-struck mimicry" (Lucas 2002, p. 123). Oliveira Vianna wrote passionately on the subject. Sérgio Buarque de Holanda said of Brazil's transplanted institutions: "We are expatriates in our own land." The aforementioned ISEB intellectuals and Álvaro Vieira Pinto spoke eloquently of the cultural mimicry or inauthentic nature of Brazil's culture. Roberto Schwarz (1973), at a time when the concept of nation had again lost momentum and was almost forgotten, was independent enough to coin the term *misplaced ideas.*

In the period in Brazilian history beginning with the Great Depression and the Revolution of 1930, society as a whole reacted vigorously against the national alienation. It reacted materially to bring about the Brazilian industrial revolution; it reacted politically and culturally to carry forward its national revolution. The country finally discovered itself as a nation. The ability to formulate and implement a national development strategy—national developmentalism—is a clear indication that the Brazilian nation was fully under construction; as Celso Furtado used to point out, Brazil after the 1930s was bringing the decisionmaking center within its borders. The setting up of a military regime in 1964, with the support of businesspeople and the United States, was the first blow against the National-Developmentalist Pact, by assigning a prevalent role to multinationals and excluding workers and the left wing from the political pact. In the 1970s the theory of dependency, by denying the possibility of a national bourgeoisie in Brazil—that is, of businesspeople committed to national economic development—further widened the chasm between businesspeople and workers that the Cuban Revolution of 1959, the pre-1964 coup, political radicalization, and the military coups in the Southern Cone had already opened.

The emergence of the theory of dependency in Latin America was, at the time, a reaction from the left wing that only further weakened the nation. The crisis of the 1980s was not simply the crisis of national developmentalism, of its "intrinsically mistaken" nature as affirmed by the Washington Consensus: it was also and principally the crisis of the growth with foreign savings policy, a foreign debt crisis. The fact that this national development strategy had fostered 50 years of extraordinary growth was overlooked. In 1990, after 10 years of crises, Brazil surrendered to the North, or to the neoliberal, globalist wave that had taken over the United States after the early 1980s. In the 1940s, 1950s, and 1960s, developmentalist and Keynesian economists were prevalent in Latin America; they were the mainstream. Governmental economic policy adopted their ideas above all. From the 1970s on, however, within the context of the great neoliberal and conservative ideological wave that prevailed in the United States and Britain from the early 1980s on, Keynesian economics, development economics, and Latin American structuralism were successfully challenged by the neoclassical economists, most of whom embraced a neoliberal ideology. Since the 1980s, within the context of the great foreign debt crisis that added to the political strength of rich countries, these economists were able to redefine their prescriptions for developing countries according to the neoliberal precepts of the Consensus of Washington and its conventional orthodoxy: a national development strategy was replaced with an outside strategy.

The previous section suggests many factors that may explain this national demise. First, we have to consider that old developmentalism was based on import substitution—a strategy that contained the causes of its own obsolescence. Protection of national industry, attention to the domestic market, and a reduced economic openness coefficient, even in the case of a relatively large economy such as Brazil's, are strongly constrained by economies of scale. For certain industries, protection becomes absurd. As a result, when the import-substitution model was maintained during the 1970s, it led Latin American economies into deep distortions. On the other hand, after the initial stage of import substitution for consumer goods industries, continued industrialization implied a significant increase in the capital-to-labor ratio, with two consequences: income concentration and reduced productivity of capital, or of the product-to-capital ratio. The response to income concentration was expanded production of luxury consumer goods, an industrialized underdevelopment model, which, in addition to being perverse, carried within itself the seed of the demise of the national prodevelopment alliance.

The second reason concerns the dissolution in the 1960s of the national alliance that was the political foundation of national developmentalism. The national-developmentalist approach assumed nation building in each Latin American country. It was a reasonable assumption, since, after a long period of deep dependency that followed the formal independence movements of the nineteenth century, starting in 1930 these countries took advantage of the crisis in the North to begin their national revolutions. Based on this, developmentalism proposed that each country's new industrial businesspeople should stand as a national bourgeoisie, as had been the case in developed countries, and associate themselves with government technicians and urban workers to bring about the national and industrial revolution. The nation, or national society in each country, thus established or reinforced itself and made possible the definition and implementation of a national development strategy (developmentalism), using the state as its instrument for collective action. This was at once a proposal and an analysis of the reality that was represented by the accelerated industrialization process then underway in Latin America. But the Cuban Revolution of 1959, by leading to the radicalization of the left and to the economic crisis of the early 1960s, brought about the end of the national alliance and created the conditions for the establishment of military regimes in Brazil, Argentina, Uruguay, and Chile, with the support of the businesspeople in each country and of the United States. As a consequence, that alliance, essential as it was to the constitution of the nation, broke up, and the Latin American moderate left embraced the theses of the "associated dependency theory," which rejected the possibility of a national bourgeoisie. In doing so, it rejected the very idea of nation and the national development strategy that was the basis of national developmentalism. The great crisis of the 1980s—the definitive crisis of the import-substitution model that developmentalism had supported since the 1940s—further weakened it. Since then, developmentalism, still supported by the bureaucratic-populist left that formed under the protection of the state based on the distortions this development strategy suffered but without the support of businesspeople, of the modern left, or even of a large portion of the state bureaucracy itself, gradually lost the ability to face down the neoliberal ideological wave from the North.[15]

The third reason for the substitution of the Washington Consensus for developmentalism lies in the strength of this ideological wave. The conventional orthodoxy slowly established itself in the early 1980s, as a response to the foreign debt crisis. The Baker Plan completed the definition of the new ideology by adding market-oriented institutional reforms to orthodox macroeconomic adjustment. Developmentalism then came under systematic attack. Taking advantage of the economic crisis that was partly due to the exhaustion of the old developmentalist strategy and to the distortions it had endured in the hands of populist politicians, the conventional orthodoxy gave the term *developmentalism* a negative connotation: it came to be identified with populism or with irresponsible economic policies. In its stead orthodox economic policies and neoliberal institutional reforms to solve all problems were proposed. The conventional orthodoxy also proposed that developing countries should give up the old-fashioned concept of "nation" that national developmentalism had adopted and accept the globalist thesis according to which, in the age of globalization, nation-states had lost autonomy and relevance: worldwide free markets (financial ones included) would be responsible for promoting the economic development of all.

In essence, the surrender to the North's ideological hegemony meant ignoring elements that had been crucial to the lives of modern nations since they emerged but had become even more strategic in the current stage of capitalism. It meant forgetting that generalized competition among firms supported by their respective national states is the guiding principle of the entire world system. Nation-states have become more interdependent in the age of globalization and have stopped threatening one another with wars, but, on the other hand, economic rivalry among them has become much fiercer. They also need to cooperate with one another, as competition requires regulatory institutions for the global system, but cooperation is limited to clarifying the rules of competition and is, where possible, biased in favor of advanced countries, as seen in the Uruguay Round of trade negotiations or every day in the advice and pressures originating from the IMF or the World Bank. It also means accepting as true something rich countries keep telling us, but do not themselves observe—that no difference any longer exists between domestic and foreign work, capital, and knowledge. National developmentalism was a nationalist strategy. The term *nationalism* has been systematically demonized by the world's hegemonic ideology. Some forms of nationalism are, in fact, perverse. Ethnic and religious nationalism can be extremely violent, even if used in national liberation struggles. The nationalism of rich countries that reject immigrants, which can easily take on a racist trait, is equally unacceptable. The nationalism I refer to—and the one that is relevant for Brazil—is the nationalism of nation-state building, the affirmation of the national interest in international competitive arenas. It is, therefore, a liberal and democratic nationalism, as is the nationalism of rich countries. It is the nationalism of those who have no doubt that it is their government's duty to defend national labor, knowledge, and capital. In advanced countries, no one, or practically no one, harbors any doubt about this—they are all, therefore, nationalists in the sense in which I am using the term. As a result, they do not need to call themselves nationalistic because nationalism is not a characteristic that distinguishes some citizens from others, and, so, many of them can use the term in a pejorative sense; domestically and in relation to other rich countries they associated nationalism with right extremism; in relation to developing countries, with economic populism. If Brazilian society were not so divided between the rich and the poor and not as subject to cultural dependency (which means that it is divided between nationalists and globalists), the reaction to the crisis would not have been the deconstruction of the Brazilian nation, and Brazilians would not so easily accept the economic policy recommendations and pressures from the North. A country that stops differentiating domestic capital and labor from foreign capital and labor, a country that stops thinking with its own head, is a country that has ceased to be a nation. And in the absence of a nation there is no development strategy. Only by chance, haphazardly and unstably, can economic development then take place.

In sum, the collapse of old developmentalism, the rejection of nationalism by the right and the left for different reasons but in both cases under the banner of dependency, the foreign debt crisis, and high inflation all interrupted the Brazilian national revolution. As nations build and grow strong, so, too, they can lose cohesiveness, become frayed, and weaken. If the nation is an everyday construction, as Ernest Renan wrote (1993 [1882]), it also faces the ever-present threat of deconstruction in the absence of the common effort to preserve it and strengthen the necessary solidarity ties. The dependency of Brazilian society, with its radical inequality, was always an obstacle to the formation of a true nation, but this didn't prevent, for a certain period, a national industrialization project from somehow uniting Brazilians under Getúlio Vargas and, later, Juscelino Kubitschek. The military excluded workers and the left-wing intellectuals from the power pact, but the national development strategy remained. In the 1970s the theory of dependency distanced workers from national businesspeople, eliminating the political relevance of the distinction between rentiers and active businesspeople. The 1980s were marked by a deep crisis that was mainly a foreign debt crisis but interpreted as the crisis of national developmentalism. It is not surprising, therefore, that after 10 years of crises Latin American elites, Brazilian ones

included, should have surrendered to the neoliberal and globalist ideological wave that had been sweeping down from the North since the late
1970s. Nor is it surprising that this depletion of the concept of nation,
this weakening of the democratic, social, and liberal nationalism that
every country requires, should be a root cause of interrupted economic
development.

Notes

1. In Brazil, the two leading economists who contributed to development
economics were Celso Furtado and Ignácio Rangel. The former's international
profile made him a member of the founding group of development economists,
which included Paul Rosenstein-Rodan, Arthur Lewis, Ragnar Nurkse, Gunnar
Myrdal, Raúl Prebisch, Hans Singer, and Albert Hirschman.
2. Nationalism can also be defined, following Gellner, as the ideology that
attempts to endow every nation with a state. Although this is a good definition,
it is applicable to Central Europe rather than to Latin America. In Latin America, nations were not yet fully formed, and yet they were endowed with states.
The nations, however, were incomplete, and their regime was semicolonial; following independence, the main change was that the dominant power shifted
from Spain or Portugal to Britain and other major Central European countries.
3. Based on the popular participation criterion, I adopt a threefold historical classification of democracy: elitist democracy, public opinion democracy,
and participatory democracy (Bresser-Pereira 2004a).
4. On the highly regressive nature of the Brazilian tax system, see the recent study coordinated by Maria Helena Zochun (2006).
5. These mechanisms are due mainly to the tireless efforts of Senator Eduardo Suplicy. On this topic, see, among others, Marques (1997); Suplicy (2003);
Barros, de Carvalho, Franco, and Mendonça (2006); and Soares (2006). The
two latter papers, in providing an in-depth examination of the problem of the
recent evolution of inequality in Brazil, evaluate the Bolsa Família program and
outline its limitations but emphasize its positive effect on distribution.
6. In 2006 Bolsa Família provided benefits to 11.1 million families (three
times more than all preceding programs put together), and its cost was estimated at R$8.3 billion, a mere 0.04 percent of GDP.
7. Fundação Getúlio Vargas (Getulio Vargas Foundation), available at
www.fgv.br.
8. IPEA is a think tank of the Brazilian government.
9. These data originate from research coordinated by Marcelo Neri, director of FGV's Social Studies Center, and by IPEA's Ricardo Paes de Barros,
based on the 2005 Pesquisa Nacional por Amostra de Domicílios (PNAD). According to Kakwani, Neri, and Son (2006), in the 1995–2004 period, although
per capita income dropped at an annual rate of 0.63 percent, the per capita incomes of the poor rose by 0.73 percent annually.

10. Results based on the National Household Survey (PNAD) of the Instituto Brasileiro de Geografia e Estatística (IBGE). All other inequity indexes, such as Gini and Theil, show the same trend.

11. PNAD is the biannual census survey held by IBGE, the Brazilian census bureau.

12. Barros, Cury, and Ulyssea (2007) made a careful analysis of the problem of the underestimation of the income of population deciles by income level and found that this underestimation also occurs at the level of the poor. Once adjustments are made to all deciles, however, the numbers offset one another so that the general underestimation of the inequality level is slight.

13. The IPEA study by Marcelo Medeiros and Sergei Soares has not yet been published. Marcio Pochman, using National Accounts in addition to PNADs, calculated the functional distribution of income and found that, between 1995 and 2005, although national income as a whole rose by 24.4 percent, labor income rose by 7.62 percent and other income rose by 37.6 percent. Therefore, the period was marked by a substantial functional concentration of income, which is incompatible with the improved personal distribution of income as calculated on the basis of PNADs.

14. These figures are from the Ministry of Labor, Cadastro Geral de Empregados e Desempregados (General Roll of the Employed and Unemployed; CAGED). Data compiled by Mendonça de Barros Associados.

15. I analyze this crisis, which was, in broader terms, a crisis of the state, in Bresser-Pereira (1992).

3
Reforms and Institutions

A
mong the false causes of the poor performance of the
Brazilian economy since 1994, the argument attributing it to
"lack of reform" or "insufficiency of reform" is paramount.
Since the Baker Plan of 1985 (which defined reforms in developing countries as a US policy to be followed by IMF and World Bank), the conventional orthodoxy has used the argument to explain countries' high
interest rates and low economic growth rates, failing to distinguish the
medium-term problem of institutional reform from short-term macroeconomic imbalances and ignoring the fact that reform is more often a
consequence than a cause of economic development. Market-oriented
reforms are an integral part of the economic development process but
must follow a sequence over time to gain legitimacy and effectiveness.
In the early stages, the state tends to play a strategic role, raising the investment rate by means of several forced savings mechanisms; the state
itself makes investments in the infrastructure of transports and energy
and deploys active industrial policies. As growth takes place, however,
the division of labor increases and the production system becomes more
complex, the number and frequency of transactions increase, markets
tend to be strengthened and better regulated, and market-oriented reforms impose themselves as a necessity, even though the state's regulatory role remains decisive. I have no doubt, therefore, that market-
oriented reforms are needed. At the times when I was a member of the
government, I was deeply involved in reforms, such as the public budget
reform and the beginning of trade liberalization in 1987 and the privatization and public management reform between 1995 and 1998. But there
is no sense in using long-term arguments to explain a short-term problem

such as macroeconomic instability and the resulting economic quasi stagnation.

Until the mid-1980s, the IMF, which took it upon itself to guide developing countries' balance-of-payment adjustment policies, was quite aware of this. Its remedies might have been too harsh, but they were limited to fiscal adjustment and foreign exchange depreciation. Since the Baker Plan, however, and since the passion for institutions that then arose in the universities of rich countries (which could then deprioritize or simply dismiss structural and cultural variables), the conventional orthodoxy has ceased to make the distinction between long-term and short-term problems: all would be solved by miraculous reforms. In this chapter my objective is to criticize this view. As Dani Rodrik (2007, p. 190) correctly points out, "large scale institutional transformation is hardly ever a prerequisite for getting growth going." On the other hand, although many correlation exercises trying to link reforms to growth show that there is a high *final* correlation (the richer the country, the stronger the institutions), they fail to show correlation between reforms being done and rates of economic growth. This fact shows clearly that reforms go hand and hand with economic growth but do not explain growth. They do not do so principally because in developing countries formal institutions tend to be ahead of effective institutions, the reason being that although it is relatively easy to approve new laws and regulations, it is very difficult to enforce them when society is not prepared. In the case of Brazil, this is certainly true. Reforms are necessary, but they take time to mature and to be competently defined so as to respond to the actual needs of society—to be legitimate—and still more time to be put into operation; reforms are an everyday and gradual process in which all societies are permanently involved; when a country is growing insufficiently, what we have to look for are the policies that really make a difference—the strategic policies that are lacking. And in order to arrive at them, I first discuss the criteria for establishing priorities among them.

The Criteria for Choosing Strategic Policy Variables

The development process is an integral process where economic structures, institutions, and culture or ideology maintain a relatively strong correspondence relationship. There is no economic and social development without cultural and political development. Economic development takes place when income per inhabitant increases with productivity and the population's well-being improves; social development occurs when income distribution among classes and races becomes more equitable; cultural development occurs when the education level rises and the nation frees itself from ideological dependency on wealthier and more powerful nations; political development occurs when the citizens' freedom increases (i.e., when democracy affirms itself) and when the nation's freedom increases (i.e., the nation gains autonomy in relation to rich countries). Long-term institutions (the constitutional system) are more correlated to economic and cultural factors, and more difficult to change, than short-term macroeconomic policies. But these policies, too, are conditioned: behind macroeconomic economic policies and practices that cause quasi stagnation are institutions and, behind these, lie culture and economic structures.

To attribute the low growth rates of Brazil after 1994 to poor long-term institutions is unreasonable because Brazil has in the past achieved higher growth rates within the framework of an institutional system far more adverse to economic development than the one today existing. The three societal "instances" or societal levels—the structural or economic, the institutional, and the cultural or ideological—are mutually correlated; considering different moments in time, one or another may become retarded; yet rarely is it the general institutions that are backward. In the case of Brazil, they do not represent a fundamental obstacle to economic growth unless we include among institutional reforms short-term and strategic macroeconomic policies. If we are able to detect which are the strategic institutional variables—preferably short-term policies having a major effect on overall economic conditions—we will be able to overcome the real bottlenecks or traps to which the Brazilian economy is subject.

On examining the causes or determinants of economic and social phenomena, we have to consider a hierarchy of causes behind slow growth. Some causes are directly related to the problem, others are relevant at an earlier stage, and still others precede the latter, and so forth. Thus, in order to understand the modest growth rates that prevail in Brazil and in many other developing countries, we must build such a causal chain. This is a difficult task because, in economic and social relations, causes are frequently also consequences; cause and effect are mutually reinforcing. Nevertheless, in an attempt to outline the hierarchy of the reasons for the Brazilian economy's slow growth, I understand that its immediate or first-level causes are the low investment and domestic savings rates and the low productivity of invested capital.[1] Brazil invests between 19 percent and 20 percent of GDP, when it should invest at least 25 percent or 26 percent. We must then understand the main cause of such low investment, which brings us to the core of this book. The root cause of the semistagnation of the Brazilian economy is not insufficient savings, but, in Keynesian terms, the lack of opportunity for profitable investment—particularly export-oriented investment.

So far, I have presented two criteria for determining the key policy or short-term institutional variables required for growth: we should not look for long-term institutions because they are strongly correlated with the level of economic and cultural development, and we should look for the causal chain leading to the variable that directly affects growth: the investment rate. From this analysis, I concluded in Chapter 2 that the problem was in the macroeconomic policy area, because the lack of investment opportunities existing in the country is directly related to the high interest rate and the uncompetitive exchange rate. While rich and developed countries adopt moderate interest rates and competitive exchange rates and grow with domestic savings, they advise Brazil to grow with foreign savings, high interest rates, and an uncompetitive exchange rate.

A third criterion for arriving at the priorities that a country should set in order to grow—and at the same conclusion in relation to Brazil—is to select the policy variable that may be changed relatively more easily and more rapidly. Problems that depend on short-term macroeconomic policies can be addressed with relative effectiveness, and its outcomes may be sizable in the short term. Although long-term policies—usually legal if not constitutional—are difficult to formulate and take time to bring about results, the correction of macroeconomic policies can have rapid and major outcomes in terms of growth rates.

In light of these three criteria, which are the factors behind the lack of investment opportunities? Throughout this book I will argue that it is a macroeconomic problem: on the demand side, high interest rates and an uncompetitive exchange rate reduce the opportunity for profitable investments and leave vast human and material resources underutilized. High interest rates discourage enterprise and productive investment, and the appreciated exchange rate reduces expected profits on export-oriented investments. On the other hand, the domestic market suffers from an unlimited supply of labor that keeps wages growing more slowly than productivity. Together, these two out-of-balance macroeconomic prices and this distortion in the labor market lower the country's investment and savings capacity, besides causing greater inequality.[2] For the investment rate to grow, effective demand would need to be increased, and, for that, the exchange rate should not be chronically overvalued and wages should not grow less than productivity. As we will see below, there is a tendency for the exchange rate in developing countries to be overvalued, and, thus, only an economic policy that neutralizes this tendency will ensure the competitive exchange rate that is required for sustained economic growth. Between 1930 and 1980 Brazil was able to neutralize this tendency by managing the exchange rate and imposing a disguised tax, the *confisco cambial* (exchange confiscation), on exported commodities, principally coffee. Yet, since the early 1990s, when trade and financial liberalization were radically implemented, Brazil was unable to counter the tendency for the exchange rate to be overvalued as a result of the Dutch disease and the excessive capital inflows attracted by high interest rates. The success of old developmentalism was principally based in the neutralization of this tendency. Since the early 1990s, however, Brazil has lost its two defenses against the Dutch disease: trade liberalization eliminated the system of import tariffs and subsidized exports, which implied a tax on the export of Dutch disease–causing goods, and financial openness made capital inflows impossible to control. As if that were not enough, at this moment Brazil actively adopted a policy of growth with foreign savings that further appreciated the exchange rate and promoted a high rate of substitution of foreign for domestic savings.

To sum up, the problem behind Brazil's low growth rates is not a lack of major institutional changes—the quality of institutions is reasonably consistent with the level of economic development of the country and it is extremely difficult to make them substantially better—but the lack of competent macroeconomic policies: fiscal austerity, a moderate basic or short-term interest rate policy, and a competitive exchange rate. To come to this conclusion I used three criteria: first, the fact that, in outcome terms, the economic, institutional, and cultural instances are highly correlated; second, a causal chain where it is clear that the low investment rate is principally related to the lack of investment opportunities on the demand side (here the assumption is that, although the supply side of growth, principally education, should not be disregarded, there are idle resources such that a competitive exchange rate on the export side combined with a moderate policy of income distribution on the domestic side would ensure the required demand for investments and cause the rate of savings to increase substantially); and finally, the difficulty-outcome criterion: if the problem is macroeconomic, it is not so difficult to change macroeconomic policy (this does not mean that it is easy), and the results may be rapid and strongly positive.

Yet this summary analysis of the causes of, and of the criteria to choose the remedies for, Brazil's quasi stagnation is far from uncontroversial. Even though we are in a post–Washington Consensus era, the conventional orthodoxy is still alive insofar as it represents the hegemonic thinking with its claim to be the only way to ensure macroeconomic stability. This book criticizes the conventional orthodoxy because it urges developing countries to adopt two macroeconomic policies—high basic interest rates and uncompetitive exchange rates—that developed countries don't themselves adopt—because the conventional orthodoxy is not a growth strategy but a counterstrategy recommended and pushed by competitors. The conventional orthodoxy's representatives recently became aware of Brazil's low growth rates, but the recent (since 2004) higher GDP growth rates reassured them. In any circumstance, they do not accept that the immediate cause of quasi stagnation lies in macroeconomic policy. In fact, they deem this policy highly successful, principally because the inflation rate remains low—which should prove that the "macroeconomic tripod" (fiscal adjustment, floating exchange rate, and inflation targeting) is successful. Wherein, then, lies the problem? Why does India invest 28 percent of GDP and China 40 percent? Conventional orthodoxy's answer is simple: "a tax burden at 35 percent of GDP" and institutions—i.e., a state—that create "a very bad climate for investment." Not a word on the real macroeconomic tripod: on poor fiscal adjustment, on the high interest rate (that unduly increases the tax burden), and on the overvalued exchange rate that reduces export-oriented investment opportunities and constrains domestic savings.

The mistaken view on the causes of Brazil's slow growth is not the prerogative of conventional economists. Dani Rodrik (2007, p. 80), who has displayed independent thinking in relation to the conventional orthodoxy, offers a poor explanation for this slow growth. He correctly sees that the central problem in Brazil is the insufficient investment rate, but instead of explaining the corresponding low savings rate by reference to investment, he adopts the neoclassical approach of explaining the low investment rate in terms of insufficient savings. Why is the savings rate low? High taxation and negative public savings reflecting very high levels of bureaucratic entitlements, waste of resources by the state, and a high level of inherited debt are the explanation. Although, as we will see, the high tax burden is a problem, and although perverse entitlements favoring the public bureaucracy explain it partially, the major causes of the high tax burden are the necessary social expenditures (which compensate low wages) and the unnecessarily high interest rate favoring rentiers and the financial system. Rodrik mentions only the high interest rate and makes no reference to the exchange rate in his account. Besides, he ignores how these recommended policies neutralize the international competitive capacity of developing countries.

Institutional reforms are long-term policies: they can be designed and implemented only gradually, and their effects are a long time coming. Reforms are everyday chores for any nation; every democratic country has a parliament or congress precisely for this purpose; the legislative process is essentially a process of introducing institutional reforms that gradually adjust the rules of the game to economic and social reality. In addition to senators and representatives, the process involves thousands of government technicians and thousands or millions of citizens interested in this or that reform. Market-oriented reforms are needed in Latin America, where countries have been implementing them: public budget reform, trade reform, privatization, social security reform, and administrative reform. To say that reforms were not implemented is untrue; to say that they are incomplete is truthful, but the chronic incompleteness of reform does not explain the country's macroeconomic instability. Macroeconomic instability is, in theory, a short-term problem to be solved with short-term policies, whereas most institutional reforms show results only in the medium term. Even economic reforms that involve short-term results, such as trade liberalization, do not automatically lead to stability and growth. The same Dani Rodrik (1999), after an in-depth regression analysis based on many countries, found that trade reform was not significantly related to growth in the 1980s and 1990s: the significant variables were capital accumulation and macroeconomic stability.[3] The only reform directly related to macroeconomic stability is the "fiscal reform," but even its effects occur in the medium run; short-term expenditure-cutting policies are more important.

The Role of Institutions

Chapter 2 showed that economic development depends directly on capital accumulation and the incorporation of technical progress into capital and labor; at an intermediate causal level, it depends on a competitive exchange rate, a moderate interest rate, and balanced fiscal accounts; at a third level, on the relevant economic policies; at the next level, on education and macroeconomic stability; and, finally, it depends on the nation's ability to share beliefs and values and to define institutions comprising a national development strategy. If an economist says that economic growth depends on accumulation of capital and technical progress, this is the fundamental response of the classical school of Adam Smith and Karl Marx—the school of economic thinking that best and most broadly addresses the issue of development. If the same economist adds that this development will further depend on a social structure and institutions compatible with capitalist development, he will be thinking in terms of Marx. If he should assign importance to culture or religion, then Max Weber is present. If he states that economic development depends basically on business innovation, a competent Schumpeterian dimension is being added. If he mentions the crucial role of education or human capital, this will be an acceptance of the most important contribution neoclassical economists have made to the theory of growth. If he highlights problems that hamper the operation of markets, such as social duality, infant industries, the role of externalities, and the tendency of the exchange rate to overvaluation that I stress in this book, the approach will be typical of development economics and Latin American structuralist theory. If the economist should further add that the fundamental institution is a national development strategy that combines macroeconomic and microeconomic policies, his strategy of choice will be new developmentalist. But, if based on neoclassical growth models, he should say that development depends not on capital accumulation but on technical progress, or if he should reduce development-promoting institutions to those that ensure property and contracts, he will be falling back on ideological reductionism and impoverishing the analysis. Institutions are often obstacles to development, but in a nation that is able to turn its state into an instrument for collective action, a set of institutions and policies that I call national development strategy will play a decisive role in fostering economic development. It is not enough to carry out market-oriented reforms and ensure the activities of businesspeople; they must be given real conditions in which to innovate, profit, and innovate again and to encourage workers and the middle class, bringing them in to share in the fruits of development.

Since the 1980s, conservative and neoliberal thinking that coalesced as the conventional orthodoxy has understood that the lack of institutional reforms is the core problem of Brazil and every other developing country. Institutions, that is, the country's constitutional and legal system, as well as other informal standards that organize social life, are crucial to encourage work and productive investment as well as to protect public wealth and "republican rights" (Bresser-Pereira 2002b). Often, the Brazilian legal system fails to encourage economic activity and is powerless to control the interests of, and abuse and corruption by, the powerful. Therefore, reforms are certainly needed, but two things about them must be kept in mind: first, how far they can be seen as short-term solutions; second, whether they are truly necessary for national development or, on the contrary, represent the interests of foreign countries or interest groups that have little, if anything, to do with economic development.

Discussing reform is inevitably difficult, as it means different things to different people. For the conventional orthodoxy, it means a minimum state and reduced public spending, with the elimination of bureaucratic privileges. For businesspeople, it means, perhaps, reduced taxes, flexible labor laws, judicial reform, reduced red tape, and so on. For new developmentalism, the required reforms aim to strengthen the state and democracy, preventing the state's capture by certain groups and turning it into an effective instrument of the nation, so that the country can resume development and, at the same time, reduce inequality, adding legitimacy to the legal order itself.

A capitalist economic and social structure already prevails in Brazil and, therefore, early capital accumulation and the industrial revolution are already completed, so that the country has the businesspeople, wage earners, and technicians that development requires. As for education, although the country has been irresponsibly slow in promoting it, since the democratic transition no one doubts its importance, and a significant effort is under way. Concerning economic stability and development, however, an important debate is taking place between new developmentalism and the conventional orthodoxy. Both agree on the importance of institutions; but whereas the conventional orthodoxy emphasizes assurance of property and the enforcement of contracts, assuming that the market will take care of the rest, new developmentalism understands that the central institution should be a national development strategy, that is, a set of economic policies, legal and governmental steps to encourage investment by businesspeople and to offer profitable investment opportunities to those capable of innovation. As for macroeconomic stability, the conventional orthodoxy believes it has been attained in Brazil, whereas new developmentalism shows that its absence is the main cause of the country's quasi stagnation. Since price stability was achieved in 1994, the representatives of the prevailing conventional orthodoxy assure us that resumed development is "just around the corner." But resumed development never seems to take place—which prompts a twofold excuse: lack of fiscal adjustment and lack of reform. I agree with the first excuse, but not the second. My thesis in this book is that what is really missing, the thing that can make Brazil resume economic development, is competent macroeconomic policy aimed at national interests and capable of effectively attaining macroeconomic stability, not just price stability. To this end, we must change not only fiscal policy but also interest rate policy and foreign exchange rate policy. Institutional changes are also needed, but we must still determine which reforms to implement, how, and when to expect them to bear fruit. In the short run, it is far more important to change the three macroeconomic policies: fiscal, interest rate, and foreign exchange rate. These changes should, naturally, be part of the broader institutional framework of a national development strategy.

Classical economists always assigned great importance to institutions. Because they understood that the main institution was the state itself, they called themselves political economists: markets, contracts, institutions, and state are intrinsically overlapping concepts and realities. In Marx's model, historical lags and the necessary correspondence between the economic and social structure on the one hand, and institutions, on the other, are dialectic movements essential for capitalist development. The German historical school and the US institutionalists assigned a leading role to institutions. The same is true of development economics and Latin American structuralism, for which economic planning was fundamental—and planning is nothing if not an institution. Neoclassical economics, in turn, with its hypothetical-deductive method and its radically abstract models, has left institutions in the background since its foundation in 1870. From the early 1980s, however, faced with the great foreign debt crisis, the conventional orthodoxy (which uses neoclassical theory) started assigning to institutional reforms a central role in overcoming that crisis. Realizing that the adjustment policies employed by the IMF were insufficient to solve the issue of foreign debt and unwilling to admit that the crisis embodied a national solvency problem (rather than just a liquidity problem), Washington's conventional economists outlined the Baker Plan soon after the emergence of the great foreign debt crisis of the 1980s. According to that document, in addition to promoting fiscal adjustment and devaluing their currencies, countries should commit to market-oriented institutional reforms in order to overcome the foreign debt crisis and resume growth. It was not a coincidence that, five years later, economic historian Douglass North (1990), who had Marxist roots but has long been integrated into the neoclassical school that revolves around the University of Chicago, published his book on institutions and development, where he attempted to apply neoclassical economics and the neoclassical institutionalism of Ronald Coase (1937, 1988) and Oliver Williamson (1985) to the problem of economic development.[4] North won the Nobel Prize for his efforts, and reforms gained academic respectability among conventional economists.

Economists such as myself, trained in development economics and Latin American structuralism, watched this change with a blend of sympathy and criticism. Sympathy, because the conventional orthodoxy thus finally became a little more realistic; criticism, because its view of institutions remained incurably abstract and hypothetical-deductive and also because the proposed reforms were reductionist and ideological. According to this view, the state, the greatest institution and the matrix of all other institutions, was still "the market's adversary," as if a strong market could exist in the absence of a strong state; on the other hand, the only really important institutions were those that ensured property and contracts, when, for economic development to take place, more must be drawn from institutions: they must encourage growth. Furthermore, this new institutionalism does not understand that institutions are not just a cause but also a consequence of development and that a strong correlation exists between the standards that organize a society or set the rules of social and economic gain and its ever-changing economic and social structure. The Washington Consensus took a reductionist stance in assuming that it would be enough to reform institutions, ensuring property and contracts, for development to be guaranteed. It failed to see that institutions can play a truly positive role in economic development only when they stand as a national development strategy: when they form a set of policies, of economic practices and legal instruments that, in addition to ensuring property and enforcing contracts, positively encourage investment and work, which free markets cannot alone foster (Bresser-Pereira 2006a). Businesspeople are defined as such because they are willing to take risks: respect for property and contracts is important to them, but even more so are opportunities for profit and firm growth, which a national development strategy ensures.

What Reforms?

For the Washington Consensus, *reform* became a magic word, an endlessly repeated mantra, capable of solving any problem. A government is good or bad if it is for or against reform—if it is or is not carrying out the market-oriented institutional reforms that will automatically promote development. Institutions, instead of being at once a cause and a consequence of development, become causes only: reforms are a requirement for growth, and there is a clear institutional model to follow—the one in force in rich countries, and in the United States in particular. This is the straitjacket, the one path possible for countries that want to develop, as put without hesitation by Thomas Friedman (2000), one of the many ideologues of this hegemonic thinking. No matter that one of the most important exponents of development economics, economic historian

Alexander Gerschenkron (1962), had already proved this false in the early 1960s; that different paths exist to economic development; and that a significant literature already exists on this topic discussing the varieties or models of capitalism.[5] Washington, with the World Bank as its main instrument, has the standard model of institutional reforms to be undertaken by developing countries. Its technicians certainly know that institutions should adapt to reality, but the reasoning behind the entire US hegemonic system, which is exported not only to developing countries but to Europe as well, is that the US, or Anglo-American, model is the efficient model for the economy, society, and institutions; it is the model to copy.

When the Washington Consensus states that developing countries must reform their institutions, it is largely repeating something that is self-evident. When, after the 1980s, it announced that these reforms should be market-oriented, even though it was acting ideologically, it was also indicating that the previous national-developmentalist strategy had been excessively based on the state and that it was now time to give the market more room. This was certainly needed. Countries that had not yet become open to trade needed to change, as they no longer had infant industries, and, mainly, those such as Brazil that insisted on the import-substitution model needed to switch to an export-driven model. Competitive industries, such as base manufacturing (steel, petrochemicals, etc.), and semicompetitive ones (mobile telephony) had to be privatized. But the market must not be opened up haphazardly; it was important to reject the World Trade Organization's (WTO) Uruguay Round prescriptions of limiting developing countries' ability to make industrial policy while allowing rich countries to continue subsidizing agriculture; it was important to reject abusive protection of property rights within the scope of the WTO itself; it was important not to quickly privatize even monopolistic industries, where regulatory agencies tend to be captured by the firms they regulate. It was important to reform public management, and Brazil was the first developing country to start down that path, but this reform should not be used as an excuse to tear down the state.

But there was one reform in the list the Washington Consensus provided that was not microeconomic, but macroeconomic, and that should definitely not have been done: opening the capital account or the country's financial opening. The reforms mentioned earlier were all needed, in a way. The problem was how to implement them gradually and competently. The opened capital account, on the other hand, coupled with the policy of growth with foreign savings, was disastrous for developing countries, as we will see in Chapters 6 and 7. Even developed countries opened their own capital accounts only recently. Countries with very strong currencies and very stable economies, such as the United States, Japan, the United Kingdom, and the European Union member states, can afford to open their capital accounts and let the exchange rate float somewhat freely, but even they must be careful. The exchange rate is an economy's most strategic macroeconomic price. An appreciated exchange rate, such as one that results from the policy of growth with foreign savings, has negative effects on a national economy. Developing countries could and should gradually liberalize their foreign accounts, but this must be done with the greatest care, preserving at all times control over the exchange rate.

The neoclassical notion that "the long term real exchange rate cannot be managed" is false both empirically and theoretically. It is empirically false because countless cases of control or administration exist in the past and the present; it is theoretically false because countries can control their exchange rates whether by buying reserves and sterilizing the resources they use to fund themselves domestically or by imposing capital controls. Economic policy, however, is not made up of such discrete and exclusive choices, and intermediate situations exist where the exchange rate is managed or follows a crawling peg—two circumstances dealt with separately in the literature but equivalent in terms of exchange rate management. Exchange rate management does not mean a pegged rate, nor does it imply rejecting a floating one. What it does mean is that the "fix or float" polar choice is false. Robert Mundell's triangle of impossibility is a brilliant model but faulty, owing to the lack of gray areas where economic policies effectively operate. The presence of some exchange fluctuation does not prevent the rate from being managed, nor does it prevent application of an interest rate policy, because fluctuation cannot ever be complete.[6] The exchange rate is an economy's most strategic price and cannot be kept fixed indefinitely, nor can it float freely in markets that are still far from perfect. To manage the exchange rate, the Central Bank must have an interest rate that enables it to purchase reserves and sterilize them, and the government must be able to control capital flows when necessary. Brazil renounced control of its capital account in 1992, and the high interest rate prevents it from managing the exchange rate through the purchase of reserves as intensively as needed. The most mistaken of all of the conventional orthodoxy's theses in the form this orthodoxy took in the 1990s was, perhaps, the failure to distinguish trade globalization from financial globalization and, therefore, the equating of financial liberalization with financial

openness. Although strong arguments exist in favor of trade liberalization, the same is not true in relation to financial liberalization. That
countries should move in this direction, giving up control over the capital account, and so over the exchange rate, is debatable even for advanced countries—what, then, for developing ones? Even though trade
liberalization should lead to a more efficient allocation of resources at
the global level, the same cannot be expected of financial liberalization:
"Market forces will not appropriately allocate financial resources to
maximize growth rates in developing countries" (Kregel 2006, p. xiii);
on the contrary, by making the foreign exchange rate unstable and increasing its tendency to appreciate, a completely open capital account
will form an obstacle to the development of these countries.

Even though capital controls were included in the list of forbidden
practices by neoclassical economics and conventional orthodoxy, these
controls have a long tradition in sound economics. John Maynard Keynes
was a strong advocate. Capital controls were created in the 1930s to
protect national economies from high international economic volatility,
and the main European countries retained them until the 1980s. Keynes's
main concern, expressed in his 1924 *Tract on Monetary Reform,* was
protecting the economy from external shocks. According to Carvalho
and Sicsú (2006, p. 4), the logic of capital controls involved arguments
similar to the discussion of regulatory intervention in domestic financial
markets. Today, arguments such as the incompleteness of markets, externalities, and information asymmetry are used to continue defending
limits for capital account openness. Concerning developing countries,
and Brazil in particular, much literature already exists on this topic.[7]
Rodrik (1998) showed that there is no correlation between growth and
an open capital account; he did not, however, go as far as proving a negative correlation. Damasceno (2008), studying 16 countries, came to the
same conclusion for Latin America. Still, if instead of emphasizing the
problem of the shocks and allocation failures involved we were to consider that unrestricted capital flows, in addition to causing instability, are
one of the causes of appreciating exchange rates in developing countries—a trend that is broken only by balance-of-payment crises or near-
crises—we would then have sound reasons to use such controls, especially those over incoming capital, whenever needed. By doing so, we
would reduce the likelihood of crises, so that there would be no need for
controls over outgoing flows.

In Brazil, as in all of Latin America, the notion that institutional reform would solve all problems was followed to the letter. After the early
1990s, reforms picked up speed in an attempt to make institutions more

market-oriented. The public budget was regulated, trade and financial liberalizations were executed, extensive privatizations took place, several partial tax reforms were implemented, social security was partly adjusted, the public management reform was formulated and advanced in large steps, the bankruptcy law was amended, and so on. Therefore, a great effort was made. But development failed to materialize. Why? In certain cases, because reform was simply not needed; on the contrary, it went against the national interest, as was the case with opening the capital account. In other cases, development failed to materialize because the reforms were not competently implemented and benefited only certain groups, as with several privatizations of monopolistic companies, such as power utilities, or of firms whose profits derive from economic rent, such as mining companies. In almost every case, development failed to materialize because the effects of reform are of necessity slow and gradual. The "reformists," however, have a different explanation. The Washington Consensus inevitably explains away its failure to promote development with the claim that the reforms were insufficient—they should have been deeper and more comprehensive. The reasoning is similar to the one adopted by monetarist economists who planned to end runaway inflation by controlling the currency supply. When the strategy failed, as it had to, the explanation was always that monetary and fiscal controls were insufficient. Even at the height of the Collor Plan, when the fiscal and monetary adjustment had been massive, this was the argument the conventional orthodoxy had to offer.[8] To maintain the credibility of their new credo that all will be solved with appropriate liberal institutions, the conventionally orthodox insist that reforms have been insufficient instead of looking for the actual causes of the problems. It counts for little that many countries vigorously have implemented fiscal adjustments at various times, that trade liberalization and privatization are faits accomplis in Latin America, that the public management reforms in Brazil and Chile have gone further than in many developed countries, that the labor markets have become more flexible in relative terms, that competition protection has improved, that several social security reforms have been implemented. All of this is dismissed, and the conclusion is that the reforms have been insufficient, or that new reforms are needed.

At certain times, the attitude verges on the comic. According to the view of the Washington Consensus adopted by the organization Economic Freedom of the World, everything can be solved with the institution of "economic freedom," which can be measured and converted into an index. According to this curious index, China has more freedom than

Brazil, and Peru holds a higher rank than Denmark.[9] Nevertheless, the index is used by the chief herald of the conventional orthodoxy, namely, *The Economist.* Bill Emmott (1999, p. 28), while editor of *The Economist,* in a special feature asked himself why poorer countries failed to recover in the course of the twentieth century. He dismissed answers such as the lack of skilled labor or of capital, or of enterprise, to conclude with an obvious statement: what was missing was economic freedom, the due protection of property rights, because "the freer an economy, the greater the development and the richer the country." Reforms would lead to this freedom, reduce the state, and deregulate the economy, allowing the market to do its job. If growth didn't happen, it was because reforms were not done or were incomplete.

But the problem is not limited to international agencies or media organizations. University economists also join in the game of institutions in a most embarrassing manner. Xavier Sala-i-Martin and Arvind Subramanian (2003) asked themselves the causes of the total lack of development in a country such as Nigeria, despite the fact that it became a major oil producer. It was the curse of natural resources, they replied—correctly—and then offered their view of this curse as based on an econometrics effort that professed to be scientific: the problem was not the Dutch disease, that is, a foreign exchange rate overvalued by the presence of a product whose production cost has nothing to do with the selling price, but the fact that Nigerian institutions were not appropriate for economic development. The issue of the appreciated exchange rate, which is clearly fundamental in oil-exporting developing countries—a problem that the conventional orthodoxy views with no theoretical sympathy whatsoever—is later dismissed after its inappropriate inclusion in the econometric equation.

Explaining the paralysis of Brazilian development in terms of a lack of reform is nonsensical. The country achieved remarkable growth, without reform, in the past. New historical facts of tectonic proportions might have emerged that required completely new institutions. This was the case, for example, in Eastern Europe, whose countries moved from a state-based to a capitalist economic system. In Brazil, however, no sufficiently significant new facts emerged to make the lack of institutional reform an impediment to economic development. True, many institutions are still obstacles, but this is part of the development process, not an impediment to it. They did not prevent development in the past, and there is no reason why they should do so now, as long as the country maintains macroeconomic stability and has available a national development strategy. What did occur, as we will see in Chapter 10, was the capture of the state by several groups or, mainly, by a political coalition: on the one hand, the dominant coalition made up of rentiers, the financial industry, and multinational companies, interested in high interest rates and an uncompetitive exchange rate; on the other hand, and taking advantage of loopholes, groups of bureaucrats and politicians interested in all manner of benefits and transfers from the state. Reforms are important to prevent captures such as this, to prevent such violence against the republican rights of Brazilian citizens,[10] but far more important are the formation of a national coalition with its sights on economic development and the constitution of a democratic state that is an effective instrument for collective social action. If a strong correlation exists between a country's development level and its institutions, of course an economically late country will also have late institutions. It is not by chance that countries such as Switzerland or Sweden, better examples of economic, social, and political development than the United States or the United Kingdom, should also have strong states and efficient markets—that is, institutions compatible with their development level. Therefore, to blame Brazil's failure to resume growth on the lack of reform would make sense only if Brazil had not, since the early 1990s, committed to a major reform program—and, in broader terms, if the development level of its institutions was clearly mismatched with the country's economic and technological development level. This is not the case. Brazil was always characterized more by "far too advanced" institutions—unsuited to the country's nature—than by outdated ones. Of course, there are institutions that protect unacceptable interests, but this is the case in any country, and solving these problems is a long-term effort that will require the commitment not only of lawmakers but of the entire society.

The 1995 Public Management Reform

Brazil has long been implementing institutional reforms. In the 1980s, the fiscal reform that eliminated the *conta movimento* (movement account) with Banco do Brasil and unified the budgets was fundamental;[11] in that decade, trade liberalization began at the end of 1987 with the policy of eliminating administrative controls over imports and with privatization. In the 1990s, trade liberalization and privatization were completed, and a longer-lasting reform began—the 1995 Public Management Reform, or the state's managerial reform, whose greatest concern was and still is to make the Brazilian state apparatus more efficient. This reform is crucial for economic development because it makes public spending, which became massive after the welfare state was implemented in many countries, much more efficient than it can be under a classic bureaucratic administration framework.

The state is, on the one hand, a legal order or political system and, on the other, an apparatus or organization. As a political system, in more advanced countries the state is initially absolute, transitions to liberal in the nineteenth century, and becomes democratic in the twentieth century. At the same time, as an organization, it is initially patrimonial, becoming bureaucratic in the nineteenth century and managerial by the late twentieth century. "Public administration" was the means to manage the bureaucratic state; "public management" is the means to manage a state on its way to becoming managerial. Having so defined our categories, it is understood that the history of the modern state includes only two fundamental administrative reforms: the bureaucratic reform that promoted the transition to the Weberian bureaucratic state in the second half of the nineteenth century and the public management reform, which now outlines the transition to the managerial state. These two reforms did not take place, or are not taking place, arbitrarily. They are the needed changes in the manner of organizing and managing the state as a political system. Although administration could be patrimonial under the absolute state, as the monarch's need to set apart his and the aristocracy's wealth from public wealth was limited given his power over subjects, after the great liberal revolutions (Glorious, American, and French) this became an imperative, as it became a requirement under the liberal state to clearly distinguish between the wealth of rulers and that of taxpaying bourgeois citizens who demand ensured freedoms. The reform of public services and the resulting bureaucratic state became a necessity for effective state organization. When, in the twentieth century, the state became democratic and the citizenry included not only the bourgeoisie but all the people, its social functions expanded enormously, and public management reform, intended to turn the merely bureaucratic state into a managerial, and therefore an efficient, body, became inevitable.

Brazil was the first developing country, in 1995, to begin its public management reform; this was after Britain and the United States had implemented similar ones, but prior to countries that pioneered the bureaucratic reform, such as Germany or France. In the late 1960s, Decree-Law No. 200 had pointed in this direction, but it was only after the 1995 *Plano Diretor da Reforma do Aparelho do Estado* (White Paper on the Reform of the State Apparatus) that the reform process gained consistency and scope. Since then, the 1995 Public Management Reform has been making advances in Brazil, particularly at the state and municipality levels. There is nothing surprising about this, if we keep in mind that this reform is inevitable for a country whose state has attained the dimensions of the Brazilian state. As the public management reform is historically the second relevant administrative reform of the modern state, it will sooner or later take place in every country. And, once begun, there is no turning back. The paths are many, because the reform is very broad in its institutions and practices. It will gather speed at certain times and, at others, the groups that feel harmed by it will force it to stall, but the course toward greater efficiency and, therefore, greater legitimacy for public spending in the social (including security) and scientific areas that every democratic society demands will have to be run.

The bureaucratic public administration was appropriate to lend effectiveness to a small state, such as the liberal state was; public management is essential to make the democratic state managerial and thereby efficient. Bureaucratic public administration could be centralized and based on strict regulations; public management, or managerial public administration, must of necessity be decentralized and driven by results-based controls. Under bureaucratic public administration the state can directly provide all of the few services it is obliged to offer (particularly justice and police); under public management, the state must outsource ancillary services to firms and social and scientific services to nonstate public entities (social organizations); in addition, its own exclusive activities must be delegated to executive and regulatory agencies.

Upon examination of the events at the federal level between 1995 and 2008, and what has taken place in states and large municipalities, the progress of the 1995 Public Management Reform is evident.[12] True, at the federal level, from 2003 to 2005, the reform all but stopped for ideological reasons. In the second Luís Inácio Lula da Silva administration, however, the quasi consensus today existing on the public management reform prevailed. A careful examination of Bolsa Família, the government's most ambitious social program, leads one to realize that its success is largely due to the adoption of a strictly managerial strategy of decentralization in the direction of municipalities.

At the level of states, in turn, progress is impressive. Although the strategic core of the state continues to strengthen with the creation of management careers, there is a simultaneous attempt to decentralize activities, create social organizations with greater operational and decisionmaking autonomy, and control them based on results while advancing with e-government (the use of information technology by government in dealing with citizens). Each study shows this trend differently, but they all point in the same direction. These gains in the states are due not only to the fact that the public management reform is inevitable. Two other, more specific, reasons exist. First, from 1995 to 1998 the states' administration secretaries were intensely involved in the formulation of the reform and in the efforts to pass Constitutional Amendment No. 19—the public management amendment. Second, states (and municipalities) dedicate a much larger share of their activities to directly serving citizen-customers than does the federal government, whose unmediated contacts are limited mainly to issues related to welfare, health, and minimum income. Therefore, state and municipal governments desperately need the efficiency that modern public management ensures. The federal government needs this efficiency as well, but many of its activities are still closer to policymaking than to the provision of services and, for this very reason, efficiency is not a requirement for them. At the federal government level, significant changes have occurred in the three areas mentioned above and especially in the latter two. In health care, gains began in 1996 with the reform of the universal health care system; in social assistance and in the administration of basic income systems, progress has been seen more recently; only in the area of social security and federal universities and technical schools have advances failed to be realized or remained very small.

The goal of the 1995 Public Management Reform is to contribute to the creation of a strong state. In the twenty-first century, this expression may sound odd because it diverges from the liberal hegemony that formed in the 1980s and from the Washington Consensus, which acts as the hegemony's instrument in developing countries. But in the competitive world of globalization, nothing is more important than a state that is strong in terms of fiscal policy, administration, and political legitimacy. The strong and democratic state is the state of law, based on a legitimate and effective constitutional and legal system where institutions correspond to existing social and economic structures. Its institutions are democratic; they allow the election of politically legitimate governments. All of these topics refer us to the necessary political reform. Financially, a strong state is a fiscally and monetarily strong state, one whose finances are firmly based on fiscal balance and that is equipped with a stable currency. Organizationally, the notion of a strong state relates to an efficient administrative structure and a professional and managerial public service.

The proposed reforms to increase the state's capacity, as described earlier, were introduced in Brazil in 1995, with the State Apparatus

Reform Master Plan of the Ministry of Federal Administration and State Reform. They covered three dimensions: (1) an institutional and legal dimension intended to reform the public sector's legal and normative framework and to create new organizational formats, in particular social organizations; (2) the introduction of new management instruments (management contracts, managerial and cost accounting, strategic planning and control, process analysis and improvement, quality management procedures, and more) to enable the "autonomy vs. accountability" attributes pair by means of granting administrative flexibility to public managers, combined with new forms of control (social control, results-based control, managed competition) and accountability channels;[13] (3) a cultural dimension that involves a mindset shift, with the goal of moving from the general mistrust that characterizes bureaucratic administration to the increased, albeit limited, reliance typical of managerial administration.

One of the guiding principles of the 1995 Public Management Reform was that the state should directly perform only tasks that are exclusive to it or that use the state's resources. Among the state's exclusive tasks, however, we must distinguish centralized public policy and legal formulation and control activities, to be carried out by state bureaus or departments, from executive tasks that must be decentralized and assigned to autonomous executive and regulatory agencies. Not all of the other services that society decides to provide with funds from tax revenues should be performed by public servants within the scope of the state's organization; some could be outsourced to third parties. Social and scientific services, whose respective markets are particularly fraught with imperfection owing to information asymmetry, must be hired from nonstate public service organizations, the "social organizations," whereas others may be hired from private firms. The three managerial forms of control—social control, results-based control, and managed competition—must apply to both agencies and social organizations. The 1995 Public Management Reform did not underestimate the patrimonial and clientelist elements that still exist in a state such as Brazil, but instead of continuing to concern itself exclusively with them, as did the bureaucratic reform begun in the 1930s, it moved in the direction of a more autonomous administration, with greater accountability to society. The assumption is that the best way to deal with clienteles and other forms of state capture is to take a step forward and make the state more efficient and modern. A struggle against corruption and waste is required, but this struggle cannot be successful if limited to constraining public administration with the piling up of controls. Instead, there must be a combination of trust and control, giving public managers additional autonomy and additional responsibility for their actions.

The 1995 Public Management Reform began in a severely adverse climate. The proposed reform, which included a constitutional amendment, was initially understood to be neoliberal and contrary to the interests of public servants. Gradually, however, as a result of public debate, the logic of the managerial reform gained support, even as the constitutional amendment that made job security for public servants more flexible was improved and gained political legitimacy through debate. Three years later, the amendment was passed almost in full, with the support of public opinion. At the end of four years, deep cultural change had been effected in Brasília as a result of the 1995 Public Management Reform: the language of results-based management was disseminated as part of a new public management ethos that replaced its bureaucratic forerunner. The institutional change was also significant, thanks in particular to the ratification of Constitutional Amendment No. 19 and the Social Organizations Act. At the implementation level, however, the reform's impact can be felt mainly in the states and municipalities, where the social services provided directly to citizens are more substantial. At the federal level, during the first Lula administration, the reform stalled because the new administration identified with the interests of unionized mid- and low-level bureaucrats, who do not derive any particular benefit from the reform as it envisions a transfer to social organizations of the social and scientific services that employ this class in great numbers. Even so, at the Instituto Nacional do Seguro Social (Social Security National Institute, INSS), a typically managerial reform was under way in 2006. In the structural aspect of the reform, however, despite the practical adoption of the social organizations' model by sending to Congress a law creating the "state foundations," we are seeing a number of organizations being created based on traditional formats, as it is the case of the creation of seven new universities with the same inflexible institutional format as the existing public federal universities, or attempts to impose strict standards on entities with some level of administrative autonomy. The backward steps are clear in terms of public service organization—admission contests, wages policy, extended benefits for retirees, politicization of positions by appointment.

Institutions can and should be "imported" by the interested developing countries, not "exported" by rich countries that would "know better" what the former need. When imported by a country's nationals, the odds are good that they will select institutions compatible with the country's reality and will make the necessary adaptations; when exported by international organizations, the likelihood of their being mere artifacts, devoid of legitimacy and harmful to the country, increases. The 1995 Public Management Reform is an example of an imported reform and therefore is adapted to the Brazilian reality rather than imposed contingently by international organizations. In this particular case, in fact, the opposite happened. The World Bank, in its guise as the body behind the neoliberal reforms that became official policy after the Baker Plan, in 1985, not only withheld support from the managerial state reform but actually opposed it. In the early 1990s the Bank decided that the time had come for "second generation" reforms, which included state apparatus reforms. But its proposals were fundamentally different from the public management reforms I have discussed here. For the World Bank, state reform in developing countries meant, and still means, first off, downsizing.[14] It also involved the classic public service reform—the bureaucratic reform rich countries carried out in the nineteenth century and Brazil in the 1930s—and anticorruption measures. When, in the late 1990s, World Bank economists finally studied the public management reform (the alternative developed countries adopted after the 1980s) and considered adopting it, they finally rejected the notion based on their "sequencing argument": the developing countries, including those at intermediate development levels, were not ready for it. They would first have to downsize the state apparatus; second, fight corruption; and third, "complete" the public service reform. Only then would they recommend public management reform.

In sum, the three problems discussed here—radical inequality, the loss of the concept of nation, and the lack of reforms or institution inadequacy—are important causes of the difficulties the Brazilian economy faces. Yet, they are not the root cause of Brazil's interrupted growth, because they are not new problems and because no relatively simple steps can be taken to address them in the short run. One exception might be radical fiscal reform, of the sort that Ireland implemented, which could have short-term effects (Godoi 2007), but a decisive fiscal reform or adjustment is essentially a macroeconomic measure that is central to the new developmentalist alternative I offer in the final chapter of this book. The public management reform, for example, will of necessity take about 30 years to complete.

Notes

1. The low productivity of invested capital, although related to other microeconomic factors such as inadequate institutions, deficient economic infrastructure, and low expenditures on education and technology, is mostly a function of the investment rate itself.

2. Ferreira, Baptista, and Pessoa (2006) did a significant econometric study to determine why Brazil's investment rate did not rise after 1994, finding two main culprits: the high interest rate and the high tax burden. Their test did not include the exchange rate: had it done so, they would probably have found that this rate, too, was significant. Miguel Bruno (2006, p. 103), in turn, also used econometric studies to show that the average gross profit rate and the rate of accumulation dropped systematically in Brazil between the mid-1970s and the early 1990s. Since then, however, the two rates became uncoupled, with the rate of accumulation dropping as the profit rate rose. The increase in the profit rate, which partially offset the interest rate hike, is related to the reduction of the wages share as a portion of income.

3. According to Rodrik (1999, p. 1): "The claims of enthusiastic advocates of international economic integration are often exaggerated or completely false. . . . The evidence based on the past two decades' experience is clear: the countries that grew fastest since the mid-1970s are those that invested a large share of GDP and preserved macroeconomic stability."

4. The dates of the works by Coase and Oliver Williamson are also significant. Although Coase has an article dating back to 1937, his 1988 book *The Firm, the Market, and the Law,* like those by Williamson and North, coincides with the neoliberal wave that gained momentum in the United States in the early 1980s and with the Baker Plan in 1985.

5. See, in particular, Esping-Andersen (1990); Albert (1991); Goodin, Headey, Muffels, and Dirven (1999); Hall and Soskice (2001); and Stephens (2002).

6. According to this triangle and assuming a floating exchange rate, the country will only keep autonomy in defining its monetary policy if capital flows are left free.

7. On Brazil, see Paula (2003); Oreiro, Paula, and Silva (2004); Carvalho and Sicsú (2006); and the papers in the collection edited by Sicsú and Ferrari Filho (2006).

8. In April and May 1990, Yoshiaki Nakano and I wrote a paper that we presented, in June, at the Second International Post Keynesian Workshop. We then went to Washington and visited the World Bank and IMF economists involved with Brazil. In our paper, we wrote that the Collor Plan had already failed by ignoring runaway inflation. Our interlocutors, however, assured us that the plan would succeed because of its monetary and fiscal strictness. Some months later, when failure was evident, they said that the adjustment had been insufficient (Bresser-Pereira and Nakano 1991).

9. See Gwartney and Lawnson (1999) and Economic Freedom of the World's website: www.freetheworld.com. The organization uses data from 53 institutions around the world to produce its Economic Freedom Network Index. In Brazil, where the practically unknown institution operates, the freedom index in 1997 was 5.5 (on a 0–10 scale), out of a total of 119 surveyed countries.

10. By "republican rights" I mean the rights each citizen has that the public wealth be used for public purposes rather than captured by interest groups (Bresser-Pereira 2002b).

11. Banco do Brasil's *conta movimento* was an institution that allowed the state to print money without limits.

12. For an appraisal of these gains, see Consad (2006).

13. See Bresser-Pereira (2004a).

14. Martin Rama (1999, p. 1), who organized a Symposium on Efficient Public Sector Downsizing (Simpósio sobre o Enxugamento Eficiente do Setor Público), says: "Downsizing is not an end-objective of economic policy, but economic reforms may require mass dismissals. . . . The World Bank has indirectly supported more than forty attempts to downsize the public sector in developing countries between early 1991 and late 1993." On the World Bank's support for public service reform instead of public management reform, see Nunberg and Nellis (1995).

4
The Fiscal Debate

I demonstrated in Chapter 3 that the "lack of reforms" explanation of low growth in Brazil makes no sense. Reforms are necessary, but they are being implemented. Roughly the same applies to the conventional orthodoxy's second argument—the "lack of fiscal adjustment"—but with an important addition: its demand for fiscal discipline is rhetorical rather than real. Since 1999 Brazil has regularly achieved the primary surplus target, but the financial health of the public sector remains fragile. What the conventional orthodoxy is really interested in is maintaining the public debt–to–GDP ratio under control in order to keep the state solvent for treasury bond investors, not to reduce the ratio, because this would depress the interest rate—something that is definitely beyond its objectives.

Fiscal balance—budget deficits under control and low indebtedness indexes—is essential to the stability of any macroeconomic system. The fiscal problem is crucial to any country. It is not by chance that the main struggle of any ministry of finance is to limit public spending. The pressures that other state ministers and the head of government exert on the ministry of finance are always great, but a successful finance minister is, in principle, one who can resist these demands. Public resources are inevitably scarce because, being free to those who receive them, they are in infinite demand. But a state that incurs constant deficits and goes into debt is a weak state, incapable of performing the tasks with which national society charges it. Society pays taxes but wants a series of services in return, beginning with price stability, which is seriously jeopardized by public indebtedness in the medium run. Public deficits are not only inflationary but also result in a financially fragile state, incapable of playing its role. It is reasonably normal that, even in the best democracies, politicians follow the rules of the political cycle, which leads them to organize public finances in the first two years of their terms and to spend a little more near the end of their terms, as long as it is done in a limited way. When chronic deficits occur, instead, either they are letting themselves be corrupted by the powerful and becoming rent-seekers associated with groups of local or foreign capitalists or they are indulging in fiscal populism to please voters. Factors other than these two are unlikely to be encountered. Citizens of more advanced countries are well aware of this fact and, besides punishing rent-seeking and fiscal populism by their votes, they prevent corruption and clientelism through appropriate institutions.

Brazil has not been so successful. The privateers of the state have always been powerful, but one group in particular—the rentiers who live off interest income—has had, since 1994, an extraordinary opportunity to benefit from the fear of inflation. Fiscal populism, in turn, although still present, has been kept under better control, because it was the subject of many denunciations and because institutions such as the 1999 Fiscal Responsibility Act have met with some success. It has, however, been replaced with foreign exchange populism, which is far from being kept in check.

In this chapter, I show that, despite all of its efforts, Brazil remains in fiscal imbalance, expressed above all in the high ratio of state interest expenditure to GDP, in negative public savings, and in the high tax burden. I then emphasize that there is no disagreement, but coincidence, between new developmentalism and the conventional orthodoxy as to the severity of this crisis and the importance of a strict fiscal adjustment policy. But I argue, first, that the behavior of the conventional orthodoxy fails to confirm its willingness to solve the issue of fiscal imbalance: on the one hand, it adopts a fiscal performance index, namely, the primary surplus, that is inappropriate for signaling the overcoming of the fiscal imbalance; on the other hand, since 2000 the primary surplus goal the orthodoxy sets for its fiscal policy has been met, but fiscal balance remains unattained. Obviously, therefore, the goal is insufficient; it is not a goal truly meant to solve the problem. Second, in the final part of the chapter I show that there is a basic disagreement as to both the causes of fiscal imbalance and the means of tackling it. While the conventional orthodoxy balks at admitting that a central cause of the imbalance is the interest rate itself and wants first to overcome fiscal imbalance, then to reduce the interest rate, I argue that this policy, in addition to expressing linear thinking that is incapable of dealing with complex economic realities, clearly reveals the undeclared objective of delaying as long as possible a reduction of the interest rate to normal levels.

High Tax Burden and Negative Public Savings

Given Brazil's difficult fiscal situation, one of the primary objectives of any macroeconomic policy must be to combat fiscal imbalance. A populist left wing exists that invokes John Maynard Keynes and the principle of effective demand to justify chronic budget deficits, as well as a shortsighted orthodoxy that is unable to realize when an expansionist fiscal policy is legitimate. Efforts must be dedicated to reducing spending because Brazil, according to the new developmentalist view, is still submerged in fiscal imbalance. This imbalance, which I identified in the 1980s as a "fiscal crisis of the state," was partly overcome in the massive adjustment made during the administration of Fernando Collor (1990–1992) but renews itself with every mandate. It is defined by a tax burden that is incompatible with the country's economic development level yet still does not stop public savings from being negative and the state's indebtedness indexes, in particular the ratio of state interest expenditure to GDP, from being too high. The obligation to make gargantuan interest payments leaves the state's creditors ill at ease; they are attracted by the high interest rates but at the same time remain uncertain of how sustainable the public debt of a nation that accepts such rates can be. Although the economists who are responsible for this crisis, and who have managed the country's public finances since 1993, avoid speaking of a fiscal crisis—while they paradoxically insist on pointing out that the country's main trouble is fiscal in nature—the fact is that, despite the improved foreign exchange situation since 2002 and the fact that the country got "investment grade" in 2007, the Brazilian economy remains vulnerable. Why is that, despite the great improvement in Brazil's sovereign risk levels? The more generic answer is that the Brazilian fiscal situation remains negative because, as this chapter will show, the state's fiscal crisis is perpetuated as a result of the interest rate that weighs on Brazil's public debt and, principally, as we see throughout the book, the tendency to the overappreciation of the exchange rate was not neutralized. Contrary to the conventional orthodoxy, this rate is not a consequence but a cause of the disquieting fiscal situation of the Brazilian economy. The Brazilian public indebtedness index is high compared with that of other countries, but it is much higher in light of the interest rate of the indebtedness index that takes it into consideration: the ratio of state interest expenditure to GDP.

Let us begin our analysis of the fiscal crisis with the tax burden. As Table 4.1 shows, the tax burden in Brazil is high compared with those in similar countries. True, but this high tax burden finances high social expenditures that partly offset the radical economic inequality present in the country. Social expenditures—particularly expenditures on health care that increased strongly after the 1988 constitution made it a universal right—must be viewed in Brazil as indirect wages, despite the regressive nature of the Brazilian tax system. Yet, even if we take this into consideration, the tax burden is inconsistent with Brazil's development stage. The data provided in the table show that the tax burden in countries with per capita income levels a little higher than Brazil's—such as Mexico, Chile, and Argentina—is about half that found in Brazil as a percentage of GDP. On the other hand, countries with similar tax burdens, such as Spain, Germany, the United Kingdom, and Canada, have per capita income three or four times higher than Brazil's. The only country in the table with both per capita income and a tax burden similar to Brazil is Turkey.

A second basic indicator of fiscal imbalance is negative public savings. Since 1999 Brazil has been meeting the primary surplus objectives agreed upon with the IMF, as seen in Table 4.2. But the same table also shows that the country continues to run a budget deficit and that public savings are still negative. The primary surplus is an index that matters

Table 4.1 Tax Burden and Per Capita GDP (selected countries)

	Per Capita GDP (US$ PPP)[a]	Tax Burden (% of GDP)[b]
Brazil	9,695	32.8
Mexico	12,774	19.0
Chile	13,936	16.2
Argentina	13,307	16.6
Turkey	12,888	31.3
Spain	30,120	34.8
Germany	34,181	34.7
United Kingdom	35,134	36.0
Canada	38,435	33.5

Sources: IMF, www.imf.org; OECD, www.oecd.org; and ECLAC, www.eclac.org.
Notes: a. Data are for 2007 (PPP = purchasing power parity).
b. Data are for 2004.

Table 4.2 Fiscal Results: 1994–2005 (all as percentage of GDP)

	Public Savings	Budget Deficit[a]	Primary Surplus[a]
1994	4.4	−1.57	5.64
1996	−3.0	3.40	−0.10
1998	−4.2	7.40	0.02
2000	−2.5	1.17	3.47
2002	−2.3	−0.01	3.55
2004	−2.8	−1.83	4.17
2005	−1.0	2.23	4.35
2006	0.5	1.38	3.86
2007	2.3	−1.41	3.97

Sources: Instituto de Pesquisa Econômica Aplicada (the Institute for Applied Economic Research), www.ipeadata.gov.br.
Note: a. Data with exchange devaluation.

to creditors, who are soothed when the country achieves a primary surplus that stabilizes its public debt–to–GDP ratio and satisfied because this hides the effects of the interest rate on the country's fiscal status. But the fact that an economy has a high primary surplus does not mean that it is fiscally sound. If the interest rate is very high and applies to a high level of debt, the weight of interest on GDP will be great, as is the case in Brazil. Under these circumstances, a high primary surplus is needed to prevent the public debt–to–GDP ratio from growing, and the country may nevertheless continue to have a budget deficit and negative public savings. Given that the interest on public debt has been amounting to about 8 percent of GDP, a primary surplus close to 5 percent has not prevented the budget deficit from hovering around 2.5 percent and, since public investment must be a little under 1 percent of GDP, has not prevented public savings from being minus 1.5 percent of GDP. As Câmara Netto and Vernengo (2004, p. 338) note, a high primary surplus combined with a budget deficit is no indication of a healthy economy for creditors "but represents a transfer of resources from society in general to the rich." The consequence, however, is not limited to unfair distribution: in economies led by wages rather than profits, such as Brazil's, "redistribution to the rich with low propensity to consume should lead to stagnant production."[1]

For the country's development and macroeconomic stability, no index is more important than positive public savings to finance a substantial portion of the required public investments. I have been emphasizing this fact, which I deem a fundamental indicator of the Brazilian crisis, since the 1980s. The objective of fiscal policy cannot be to simply increase primary surplus–to–GDP ratio, as the conventional orthodoxy wants. The primary surplus—the budget deficit minus interest expenditure—is a perverse concept that can be relevant to the state's creditors and the IMF but is no indicator of fiscal health. On the contrary, as it must increase as interest payments grow, its high levels are a sure indication of public finance crisis. Public deficit and the public savings–to–GDP ratio are far more significant. Public deficit is a sign that the state's indebtedness is on the rise; very small or negative public savings is a sign that there are no funds for public investments. Given the oblivion into which the concept of public savings appears to have fallen, it is worthwhile to bring up some identities. Public savings, S_G, equals current revenue, T, minus current spending, C_G, which includes interest payments:[2]

$$S_G = T - C_G$$

Public savings is thereby distinguished from the budget deficit, D_G, which equals the government's current revenues minus all of its spending, including investment spending, I_G:

$$(-) D_G = T - C_G - I_G$$

As such, the state's investments are funded with either public savings or budget deficit:

$$I_G = S_G + D_G$$

Public savings is a simple concept of extreme importance to fiscal balance and economic development, because it is needed to finance public investments and, more specifically, infrastructure investments that the private sector has no interest in providing (low-traffic roads, streets, water, sewage, communications, transportation, power), social investments (schools, hospitals, cultural equipment), and security investments (police stations, prisons, military and police equipment). If public savings approaches zero, the only alternative left to the state to maintain such investments is to finance them through budget deficit. If public savings is close to zero and the budget deficit must be reduced (or the primary surplus must increase to prevent growth of the public debt–to–GDP ratio), the perverse solution that ends up being used is to reduce, or even eliminate, public investment. This is what took place in Brazil, especially after 1995. Since then, public investment dropped by half—from 2.92 percent of GDP to 1.5 percent in 2003—and dropped to around 1 percent of GDP in 2005 and 2006. The public investments that dropped the most were those in the areas of health, education, culture, security, and transportation, which amounted to 47.2 percent of public investments in 1995 and by 2006 were down to 26.5 percent.[3]

Assigning importance to public savings in fiscal policy therefore has a clear meaning; still, few economists use it. It is not part of the conventional orthodoxy's lexicon, and although part of the national accounts system, in the fiscal and financial statistics of every country that the IMF compiles and publishes annually, in *Financial Statistics,* the concept and the corresponding figures are absent. Until the 1970s the Fund required debtor countries to reduce budget deficits and current account deficits. Since the 1990s, however, dedicated as it is to the policy of growth with foreign savings, the IMF has "forgotten" current account deficits; on the other hand, showing that it had been captured by the financial interests of rentiers and large international banks, it started to cast the public deficit itself in a secondary role in the explanation of fiscal imbalance, as public deficit includes the cost of interest, and focused its undivided attention on the primary surplus. The concept of public savings no longer matters to the IMF and the conventional orthodoxy, because it is the source of funds for public investments. Because from a conventionally orthodox view public investments are not necessary in practice, there would be no need to discuss public savings. Keynes drew a clear distinction between the current budget and the capital budget in his discussion of fiscal issues. Kregel (1994/95) analyzed this distinction, emphasizing public investment. Recently, after the publication of a paper by Blanchard and Giavazzi (2004), who use the concept of "government current account savings," the topic has gained renewed relevance.

Given the extremely low levels of public investment, Brazilian economists have started discussing the problem of public savings (Afonso, Amorim, and Biasoto 2005; Silva and Pires 2006, p. 20; Pires 2006, p. 75). Pires has developed a model where he shows that public savings "can contribute to decelerating the ratio of public debt to GDP, given the positive effect it has on economic development." Silva and Pires show that "replacing the concept of primary surplus with public savings does not lead to any substantial change to the intertemporal path of the public debt–to–GDP ratio." In other words, there is a change in the fundamental fiscal objective—public savings occupies the central role it must and cutting public investment is no longer a means—but fiscal sustainability is not affected.

A truly independent country that makes decisions based on its own interests rather than the suggestions of international agencies will not set merely the primary surplus as an economic policy objective: in addition to attempting to reduce the budget deficit, its objectives will include increasing public savings in order to finance the necessary public investments. As a result, fiscal objectives will not be attained by simply reducing public investments, as has been the case in Brazil. Public investments did once play a decisive role in Brazil's development. But given, on the one hand, the neoliberal view that places no emphasis on public investment and, on the other, the fiscal crisis that translates into negative public savings, it is no wonder that these investments have dropped so drastically in Brazil: in the 1970s they were at around 5 percent of GDP; by 2005 they had dropped to a mere 0.9 percent. Some reduction was to be expected as a result of the country's different development stage, but not a drop as large as this.

A third way of assessing the Brazilian fiscal crisis is through indebtedness indexes. The generally preferred index relates public debt to GDP. The papers constantly write that the public debt–to–GDP ratio "is very high" or "is dropping." We have seen that the primary surplus is an instrument to control this index and thereby assuage the state's creditors. If the Selic base rate increases,[4] one simply has to increase the primary surplus for the public debt–to–GDP ratio to remain stable, and therefore the state's creditors, who are practically the only rentiers in Brazil, as only the state is truly in debt, will be reasonably satisfied if this index is kept at around 50 percent. But the index, among other limitations, varies not only with the interest rate and the primary surplus but also with the exchange rate in the presence of public foreign debt. While there was US dollar–denominated public debt, the index rose when the local currency depreciated and dropped when it gained in value.[5] In recent years, the government has bragged about the drop in this index, which was once close to 60 percent of GDP and is now around 50 percent; but when the drop occurred, it was related to the increased value of the Brazilian real.

On the other hand, as can be seen from Table 4.3, which lists countries whose average income is not very different from Brazil's, the Brazilian debt-to-GDP ratio is relatively very high, although three countries in the table have worse indexes than Brazil.[6] Examination of the ratio of state interest expenditure to GDP, however, shows that Brazil is in a worse situation than Turkey, and incomparably worse than other countries. The ratio of state interest expenditure to GDP is not commonly referred to in academic and journalistic discussions of public indebtedness,

Table 4.3 Public Indebtedness Indexes and Interest (selected countries)

	Public Debt/GDP (%)	Real Interest Rate (%)[a]	Interest Payments/GDP (%)[b]
Brazil	54.6	13.31	7.88
Turkey	74.4	5.60	4.42
Mexico	24.4	3.82	0.93
Philippines	71.5	1.03	0.73
Russia	34.8	2.00	0.70
India	62.2	0.68	0.42
China	29.6	1.30	0.38
Chile	14.8	1.22	0.18

Source: The Economist, www.economist.com.
Notes: a. The 2006 data are computed by removing the high consumer price index of April 2006 from the short-term interest rate.
b. The assumption is that the entire debt is subject to the rate in the previous column, which is not necessarily true.

but this is not to say that rating agencies and creditors in general do not take it into consideration or that it is not an important factor, in addition to low growth rates,[7] in Brazil's inability to attain investment grade. It is a known fact that in economics, as in finances, flow measures are always more important than stock measures: in the corporate world, profit and loss statements are more significant to managers, shareholders, and creditors than are balance sheets. Stock statements are static by definition, reflecting a snapshot, whereas flow statements show a process and its trend. In economies as dynamic as modern capitalist economies, the very concept of capital has changed from a stock concept—equity—to a flow concept, namely, the present value of the firm's cash flow (Bresser-Pereira 2005a).

Interest and Social Spending

What are the causes of the fiscal imbalance and the excessive tax burden whose indexes we have just discussed? The causes that the conventional orthodoxy usually suggests to explain the precarious state of Brazilian public finances are, on the one hand, fiscal populism (that is, expenditures with which politicians choose to please voters and meet their electoral interests) and a wasteful state bureaucracy, and, on the other, corrupt politicians and bureaucrats. The first pair of causes is important, but as we will see, legitimate social spending is hard to distinguish from populism; the causes related to the capture of the state by politicians and public servants, in turn, are quite real but are of less weight than capture by rentiers. The costs of congressional amendments—through which members of congress serve their clienteles—pale in comparison with the capture of the Brazilian state by various forms of corruption or rent-seeking. The same can be said of forms of corruption that are manifested as political scandals.[8] Most significant is the capture by the state bureaucracy in the form of a privileged retirement system and the excessive salaries certain public servants still receive, benefiting from the distortions caused by high inflation and from public servants' ability to incorporate several benefits into their wages as a result of court proceedings. These forms of capture taken together, however, including the public social security deficit of about R$46 billion in 2006, should add up to no more than 3 percent of GDP.[9] As we are discussing rent-seeking or the capture of public wealth, there is another form to consider along with its beneficiaries: the rentiers who benefit from excessive interest rates, just as some public servants benefit from excessive wages and, mainly, excessive pensions.

Then there is corruption, pure and simple, to consider. Let us also do a quick calculation of rentier capture. With an average real interest rate of 10 percent, state interest expenditures of 8 percent of GDP, of which one-third (or a real interest rate of 3.33 percent) is reasonable or legitimate from the public perspective, the capture would amount to 5 percent of GDP. Add to this the offset that must be offered to manufacturers and farmers as investment subsidies in light of the high market interest rates, and there is an additional 1 percent of GDP in the form of the rate gap of the *taxa de juros de longo prazo* (the long-term interest rate; TJLP) of the Banco Nacional de Desenvolvimento Econômico e Social (National Economic and Social Development Bank; BNDES)[10] and of the farming credit, leading to a total of 6 percent tied directly to the exorbitant interest rate or the rentier political coalition. Finally, and going into the realm of the illicit or corrupt, we must add the pillage of public wealth implied in the frauds or collusions that affect public bidding processes, and the mafia that overvalues expropriations carried out by the state. The excessive prices achieved in fraudulent public bids were, for a long time, the shape of this form of corruption par excellence. They still are, but the number of cases has dropped significantly since Law No. 4666—the Public Bids Act—was passed and since the governments of some states, such as São Paulo, started purchases via electronic auctions.[11] It seems reasonable to estimate that more than 3 percent of GDP is thus stolen from the state. The sum total is 12 percent of GDP—a high level of capture, of which 6 percent of GDP is due to the currently dominant political coalition (Chapter 10), 3 percent to the bureaucracy, and 3 percent to corruption.

Another cause of the Brazilian fiscal imbalance is allegedly the excessive number of public servants. Although there is some truth in this claim, blaming a significant portion of fiscal problems on personnel expenditures is a mistake consistent with the strategy of the neoliberal hegemony of demoralizing the public service by blaming it for the budget deficit and of dividing the nation by pitting businesspeople against the government's personnel; the claim has no basis in reality. Inefficiency and privilege certainly exist in the public sector, as they do in the private, but progress has been made in many areas. The state bureaucracy's cost increased substantially after the constitution of 1988 was enacted, expressed specially in a public social security system marked by privileges and the Unified Legal Regime Act. These privileges, however, were substantially reduced with successive social security reforms and a general revision of the Unified Legal Regime Act during the first phase of the 1995 Public Management Reform. There is still much left to do before the state becomes an effective element for development, thanks to its own efficiency, but a lot has been accomplished, not only at the federal level but at the state and local levels as well. As noted by Almeida, Giambiagi, and Pessôa (2006, p. 89), "the perception of a bloating of payroll expenditures over the past ten years, in particular, is mistaken . . . after the increase in personnel expenditures in the first half of the 1990s, this item stopped growing and remained relatively stable, considering the averages by period."

Since 1995, when the Public Management Reform I discussed in Chapter 3 began, there was a drop in public expenditures on public servants, followed by stabilization. The studies found in the collection *Gasto Público Eficiente* (Mendes 2006) point in the same direction, noting, however, that even though the executive branch's expenditures were kept in check, those of the legislative branch and above all of the judiciary branch skyrocketed.[12] The reform, although interrupted at the federal level since 2003, made it possible to achieve these results without reducing—in fact, while expanding and improving—the services provided by the Brazilian state. Under the current administration, however, with the admission of a large number of noncareer civil servants going against the principles of the 1995 Public Management Reform, which assumes that activities that are not exclusive to the state should be hired from third parties, personnel expenditures resumed growth. Associated with the criticism of public servants for appropriating the state is the charge that "bureaucrats are wasteful" and always act to maximize the budget for which they are responsible—exerting pressure for increased public spending regardless of results achieved. This charge, in addition to explaining little, lacks empirical evidence and disregards important advances made in public services delivery. For example, large efficiency and coverage gains occurred in the Sistema Único de Saúde (Unified Health System; SUS). Today, this instrument ensures universal access to health care in Brazil, at reasonable quality and at very low cost by international standards (an annual cost of approximately US$0.80 per capita). The system's reasonable quality, which has improved remarkably since 1998, is proven by the results of surveys, such as the National Public Services Users Satisfaction Survey held in 2000, that show an average 75 percent satisfaction rate among the effective users of public services, whereas better-off groups, who do not use such services, are more critical or less satisfied.

Populism, although not the main cause, is certainly an important cause of Brazil's fiscal imbalance. Through it, politicians and Brazilian elites in general attempt to reduce the lack of legitimacy that Brazilian institutions suffer from because of the structural heterogeneity of the society. But two other, and more important, causes exist: the interest rate itself and the policy of increased social spending that was decided during the country's redemocratization process. The previous section clearly showed the highly negative nature of the state interest expenditure–to–GDP ratio in Brazil when compared with other medium-income countries. In addition to being an indicator of the fiscal crisis, this indebtedness index shows that the interest rate the Brazilian state pays is more of a cause than a consequence of the fiscal crisis. It shows this in a straightforward and instantaneous manner. The index can only be so high compared with the public debt–to–GDP index because the interest rate that determines it is very high. Given, in addition, that the interest rate Brazilian public bonds pay has been very high for many years, it becomes clear that this rate, too, has been a central cause of the brutal increase in public indebtedness that took place after 1994. Table 4.4 shows how terribly interest payments weigh on the Brazilian economy. They have been around 8 percent of GDP; they have generally surpassed 20 percent of public spending or the tax burden. Imagine how much weight this means for the public budget: how much the tax burden could fall and how much expenditures on education, health, and needed public investments could increase.

As this gradually became clear to Brazilian society in recent years, the issue of the interest rate was finally included in the national agenda, and the ideological hegemony of the Washington Consensus started to

Table 4.4 Interest Expenditures

	Real Interest Rate[a] (%)	Interest Payments[b] (R$ billions)	Interest Payments/ GDP (%)	Interest/ Tax Burden (%)
1995	25.30	48.75	6.91	24.30
1997	19.53	44.97	5.20	18.19
1999	16.70	127.26	11.95	38.46
2001	9.65	105.63	8,111	25.45
2003	13.99	122.49	7.21	22.60
2004	8.61	124.92	6.43	19.59
2005	13.31	152.59	7.11	21.02
2006	11.94	157.80	6.76	19.75
2007	7.42	157.10	6.14	17.02

Sources: Instituto de Pesquisa Econômica Aplicada (Institute for Applied Economic Research), www.ipeadata.gov.br; Central Bank, www.bcb.gov.br.
Notes: a. Annual average of the overnight/Selic rate net of Índice de Preços ao Consumidor Amplo (Extended Consumer Price Index; IPCA).
b. Nominal interest with foreign exchange devaluation.

face challenges. It became clear that this is a central and perverse cause of fiscal imbalance. In the early 1980s, the state's interest payments were around 2 percent of GDP; they now hover around 7 percent. As such, about 5 percentage points in the growth of the tax burden that has occurred since the early 1980s can be explained by interest rates.

Another fundamental cause of the great increase in the state's spending since the late 1980s lies in the growth in social expenditures since the democratic transition. As can be seen from Table 4.5, transfers to welfare and social security rose by almost 8 percent of GDP. In addition, "other primary expenditures" increased by 5.43 percent of GDP. Given that about half of these other expenditures was also dedicated to social spending, particularly in the areas of education and health, the total increase in social spending between 1985 and 2003 was 10 percentage points of GDP. Add to this about 6 percentage points of GDP in increased interest, and we will have explained practically all of the increase in the tax burden over the period.

Another way of looking at the increased social spending in Brazil is depicted in Table 4.6, which compares GDP growth and social spending increases between 1980 and 2000. The two figures can be compared directly. Although income per inhabitant increased by a mere 8.5 percent—something that used to be achieved in Brazil in two or three years between 1930 and 1980—per capita social spending grew 43.4 percent,

Table 4.5 Public Spending Between 1985 and 2003 (percentage of GDP)

	1985 (1)	2003 (2)	Spread (2 – 1)
Investments (capital formation)	2.60	1.68	–0.92
Welfare and social security	7.69	15.62	7.93
Other primary expenditures	12.16	17.59	5.43
Total primary expenditures	22.45	34.89	12.44

Sources: Instituto Brasileiro de Geografia e Estatística (Brazilian Institute of Geography and Statistics; IBGE), www.ibge.gov.br; and the Instituto de Pesquisa Econômica Aplicada (Institute for Applied Economic Research; IPEA), www.ipeadata.gov.br.

Table 4.6 Per Capita GDP and Social Spending Growth, 1980–2000 (in percentage)

	Growth
Per capita GDP in 2002 prices	8.5
Per capita social spending	43.4

Sources: Instituto Brasileiro de Geografia e Estatística (Brazilian Institute of Geography and Statistics; IBGE), www.ibge.gov.br; Instituto de Pesquisa Econômica Aplicada (the Institute for Applied Economic Research; IPEA), www.ipeadata.gov.br; Instituto Nacional de Estudos e Pesquisas (National Institute for Studies and Educational Research; INEA), www.inep.gov.br.

or five times more. The conventional orthodoxy has insisted on attempts to reduce these expenditures. True, it is necessary to reduce the growth of social security and welfare spending to less than the growth of nominal GDP. But to reduce real social expenditures, as many propose, is neither politically feasible nor socially reasonable, given the commitments made during the Brazilian democratic transition. The significant rise in social spending in Brazil was a consequence of the great accord struck in the country after 1977 that eventually led to the democratic transition of 1985 and the 1998 constitution. This accord, which I have called the 1977 Popular-Democratic Pact, started as society's reaction to the "April package," a set of authoritarian measures implemented by then-President Ernesto Geisel. Indignation with the military regime also involved rejection of the high income concentration that the authoritarian system only made more severe and led every party—in particular PMDB, PT, and PSDB,[13] which would later and successively occupy the presidency—to commit to income redistribution programs through increased social spending. Increased social expenditures were, therefore, a strategy that the political forces that spearheaded the Brazilian democratic transition selected to tackle the radical inequality present in the country. Brazilians understood that the way to reduce income concentration was to increase social spending considerably, particularly in the areas of education and health. And so it was done.

The right wing usually argues that this spending is inefficient, doesn't reach end-users, and is all kept within the bureaucracy itself, but the marked improvement in social indicators (as was shown in Table 2.2) proves how mistaken this view is: inefficiencies exist, naturally, but public spending does reach the poor. Therefore, although social spending is a cause, along with interest, of Brazil's increased public spending, there is no political room or moral justification, or even an economic (efficiency-related) reason, for reducing social expenditures. It can and must be reduced relative to GDP so that public investment can rise and the tax burden can be alleviated. And its efficiency can be improved through public management reform. The space in the federal budget now available for expenditure cutting, however, is not in social spending but in the high interest rates that imply a cost of about 7 percent of GDP, or 20 percent of the state's revenues.

Fiscal Adjustment First?

Finally, one of the root causes of fiscal imbalance is the conventional orthodoxy's lack of interest in addressing it, notwithstanding its endlessly blaming such an imbalance for high interest rates and low growth. "The entire problem lies in public spending," its adherents tell us, but stop short of showing any real dedication to facing the problem and, naturally, never admit that public spending includes interest, which "lies below the line"—using technical jargon to gloss over it. Evidence of this lack of interest can be found in the use of the primary surplus as an adjustment criterion, in the goals set, and in their attainment.

In 1999 the conventional orthodoxy set a primary surplus of 3.5 percent of GDP as its major fiscal goal; in 2003 the goal was raised to 4.25 percent. Since 1999 these goals have been met with room to spare, but the conventional orthodoxy continued to use fiscal arguments to explain away every problem in the Brazilian economy. The contradiction is self-evident. If the objective were truly to address the fiscal problem, the goal would be zero nominal budget deficits, at least. In this case, the corresponding primary surplus goal would be exactly the same as the share of state interest expenditure in GDP. That is, instead of 4.25 percent of GDP, it would have to be around 7 percent! Any reasonable soul, of course, would deem that excessive. The obvious alternative would be to lower the share of interest expenditure in GDP by at least half in order to attain the same zero deficit. But this alternative holds no attractions for the advocates of conventional orthodoxy. In fact, they are more interested in maintaining a stable fiscal imbalance with the interest rate at the same average levels as in recent years.

The Brazilian fiscal issue involves a false controversy and a real controversy. The false controversy concerns the criticism that new developmentalism, being Keynesian, would be fiscally lax. The real controversy has to do with the sequence of the steps to be taken for the country to escape the interest rate trap: either to first perform and adjust, and then lower interest, or to embrace a strategy that combines adjustment with a series of financial reforms leading to a lower interest rate.

The conventional orthodoxy criticizes its adversaries as if they were all still stuck in the "populist Keynesianism" that flourished in Latin America, particularly in the midst of the crisis of the 1980s, when the old national developmentalism was already exhausted. The notion that any economic agent must control its expenditures—be "economical"— is probably the oldest and most basic principle in economics. A famous discussion exists between neoclassical, or orthodox, economists and Keynesian economists about the effectiveness or lack thereof of countercyclical fiscal policy, but this is a false controversy in the case of Brazil's post-1994 economy, as Keynesian analysis assumes intertemporally balanced public accounts as a starting point—something absent in Brazil since the early 1980s. The notion that, whatever the circumstances, the budget must be balanced in the short term is, after all, just a manifestation of market fundamentalism, a means to achieve the reduction in the size of the state that neoliberals dream about. In practice, the governments and good economists of rich countries do not hesitate to adopt an expansionist fiscal policy in times of recession. Such a policy may imply increasing spending and the budget deficit, as Japan did to try to escape from the depression that engulfed its economy in the 1990s, or it may take the form of tax cuts—an alternative that brings two benefits from the conservative point of view: it pleases the rich and reduces the tax burden, that is, the size of the state.

Keynes was the great economist of the twentieth century not because he eliminated the principle of the balanced budget, but because he showed there may be exceptions to it. An agent may go into debt in certain cases in order to invest, as Joseph Schumpeter emphasized in other cases in order to rekindle aggregate demand. Keynes always distinguished between the current budget and the investment budget. Charging him or Keynesian economists with lack of fiscal policy rigor makes no sense.[14] Keynes showed in an innovative way that a policy such as this was justified because capitalist economies are under the constant threat of insufficient demand—of the mismatch between aggregate demand and supply that the classical and neoclassical schools deemed was ensured. But by justifying an expansionist fiscal policy in such periods, Keynes assumed that the public sector was starting from fiscal balance, departing from it for a brief period, only to return as soon as the economy picked up and tax revenues resumed growth (Carvalho 1992). Keynes did not, as good macroeconomists (who are always Keynesians at some level) do not, consider supporting chronic public deficits that led to fiscal crisis, such as those that were often seen in Brazil and Latin America generally When public deficit and indebtedness reach high levels, not only do creditors require higher interest rates but investors retrench instead of being encouraged by increased public spending.

In light of the Keynesian caveat, each country or nation-state should be guided by the principle of economy. Otherwise, when the state shows chronic deficits and debt increases, creditors will become concerned, start stipulating unacceptable conditions for their continuing to provide funds, and, ultimately, lead to bankruptcy. At the limit, when the state starts losing credit, interest rates go up and the problem of "fiscal dominance," that is, spiraling interest payments and debt, arises, as was the case in Brazil with the crisis of 2002. Before this happened, however, stimulating demand, which is the theoretically intended result of an expansionist fiscal policy, would cease to work because investors would lose trust in the government and the future and lower their expectations of profit, and aggregate demand would fall instead of rising as a consequence of increased spending. The problem lies not in the phantom fact that economic agents rationally neutralize the fiscal policy, or that public indebtedness always implies increased interest and the crowding out of private investments, but in the security and expected profits of investing businesspeople. No neutralization exists because economic agents are not as rational and capable of acting intertemporally as the rational expectations hypothesis assumes; crowding out does not necessarily stem from the public deficit because, for this to happen, increased public spending would have to be the cause of increased interest rates, rather than interest rates being the main cause of excessive state spending, as is the case in Brazil. It must be clear, however, that any expansionist fiscal policy in a framework of chronic fiscal crisis such as Brazil's is ineffective, because businesspeople, doubting the sustainability of public indebtedness, stop investing.

On the other hand, in the presence of a floating exchange rate regime, an inflation targeting policy, and ample capital account convertibility, as is the case in Brazil, the need for balanced fiscal accounts becomes especially strategic, almost as much as balanced foreign accounts. When capital flight occurs, the Central Bank is forced to raise interest rates until creditors calm down. At this point, in addition to having ample international reserves, it is important that the country's fiscal situation be comfortable if the crisis is to be tackled.

But beyond the false controversy—as there is consensus about the need for and importance of fiscal adjustment—lies the true controversy, the real disagreement. This disagreement can be most simply summarized in the following proposition: for the conventional orthodoxy, even if its representatives regard fiscal imbalance as the cause of high interest rates, they all agree that, *first,* the imbalance must be faced with a much greater fiscal effort in order *later,* or *as a consequence,* to achieve a lowering of the short-term interest rate on public debt; whereas, for new developmentalism, fiscal adjustment and reducing the interest rate must be done concomitantly.

In fact, with this rhetorical strategy of "first" and "later," the conventional orthodoxy's aim is to delay—or altogether prevent—a drop in interest rates. Instead of clearly stating opposition to a certain event, a common strategy is to condition such an event on certain future facts. In firms, for example, those that are against decentralization but lack the courage to directly oppose it resort to the argument that "first" the managers must be trained, or the rules better defined, in order "later" to decentralize. In the case of the interest rate, "first" the fiscal problem must be solved so that, "later," interest rates can drop automatically or naturally. According to conventional orthodoxy's representatives, every sensible economist is fully aware that a drop in real interest rates and a rise in the real exchange rate will lack consistency without a prior structural solution to Brazil's unresolved fiscal problem. The required "structural solution" thus becomes an excuse for doing nothing in connection with the interest and exchange rates. The reasoning is similar to that of the conventional orthodoxy between 1980 and 1994. Unwilling or unable to diagnose inflation as runaway inflation, it said that the fiscal adjustment had to be done "first" because then, and "automatically," inflation would subside. In the meantime, the critics of the conventional orthodoxy said that the adjustment had to be done simultaneously with neutralizing runaway inflation. When, in 1990 and 1991, the real budget deficit dropped to zero and inflation failed to follow suit, the conventional orthodoxy's monetarists fell silent, and there was finally room for the Real Plan to neutralize runaway inflation and bring the high inflation rates to an end.

A stiff fiscal adjustment is fundamental, not to reduce the state's size but to make the state financially and fiscally healthy and, as a result, to enable it to play its role as the instrument par excellence for the nation's collective action and to make businesspeople self-reliant and ready to invest. Although Asian countries are always exemplary in terms of fiscal discipline, Brazil's governments have often been lacking in this respect. I harbor no doubt that this is one of the reasons why Asian countries have been much more successful than Latin American ones. With their actions, they strengthened their states and were able to turn them into effective instruments for national collective action, whereas Latin American countries fell victim to inflation. In addition to rejecting fiscal populism, which implies state expenditures in excess of revenues, the Asian countries were wary of foreign exchange populism, that is, a nation-state's imports exceeding its exports. South Korea in the 1970s, and Thailand, Malaysia, and Indonesia in the 1980s, developed for a long time with current account deficits (Gala 2006). They did not, however, act in an "orthodox" manner, that is, avoiding budget deficits or current account deficits under all circumstances. At times, and for limited periods, one or the other deficit might be justified. Good economists and good economic policymakers are precisely those who can examine each case, each peculiar situation, and make the right decision.

Lowering the interest rate without causing a rise in inflation requires reducing public spending: not because a reduction of the short-term interest rate causes increased demand to the point where it significantly pushes up inflation rates, as the conventional orthodoxy maintains, but because such a reduction would cause the exchange rate to depreciate with the temporary result of higher inflation rates. Although this inflation acceleration process should be light and temporary, it must be offset with fiscal adjustment. Reducing public spending will send the market a signal that the strategy of reducing the interest rate is serious. Let us suppose that this reduction, done over a period of six months, amounted to 1 percent of GDP. Add to this value the great fiscal savings due to the lower interest rate—savings that may easily reach 5 percent of GDP over a period of about two years (see Chapter 11). The savings of 6 percent of GDP so achieved and maintained through strict fiscal oversight can then be divided into two parts: one devoted to achieving positive public savings to fund the public investments needed to resume growth and the other devoted to lowering the tax burden. I assume a relatively small spending reduction because I must not overestimate the government's ability to reduce nonfinancial current public expenditures. Useless expenditures must be cut: this is an everyday task for any good government. But expenditure cuts must in the short term not embrace mandatory social expense items. These are not arbitrary: they reflect the country's inequality and Brazilian society's decision to provide them through social spending.

To conclude, there is a fundamental difference between new developmentalist and conventionally orthodox economists. The latter are mired in insoluble contradictions. They have been in power since 1993 and, for this very reason, are in effect criticizing themselves when they blame the country's ills on poor fiscal management. They would probably be satisfied with meeting the primary surplus agreed upon with the IMF, as in fact they are, as exemplified by Afonso Bevilaqua (2006), economic policy director at the Central Bank since 1999: "We have been mentioning in our minutes that our hypothesis with regard to the path of public accounts is that the government will continue to meet the 4.25 percent primary surplus targets. Such a target assures a sustainable path of the public debt–to–GDP ratio over time, which is a fundamental working hypothesis." And so they begin saying that, thanks to the "macroeconomic tripod" they chose, based on a floating exchange rate, primary surplus, and inflation targeting policies, everything is fine with the country and resumed growth is just around the corner. Then, when criticized for the high interest rates, they return to the fiscal problem they had just claimed was resolved and say that everything—reduced interest rates, resumed development—hinges on an adjustment that "populists" prevent. In fact, they themselves prevent the country from attaining fiscal balance, by setting and meeting fiscal targets that fail to address the problem.

For new developmentalism there is no doubt that the country has serious fiscal problems, that its fiscal management in the hands of the conventional orthodoxy has been generally loose, especially in terms of the interest rate. This sick rate that has for years prevailed in Brazil is a cause rather than a consequence of fiscal imbalance. The fiscal populism of governments is also a cause, but a secondary one: since 1990, governments, except on the eve of elections, have not been irresponsible spenders and, since 1999, the primary surplus target agreed upon with the IMF has been attained. The main cause of fiscal imbalance is none other than the short-term interest rate that the Central Bank sets based on the argument that it is needed to fight inflation. In addition to the astronomical interest rates, the severity of the ratio of state interest expenditure to GDP and negative public savings, despite the high primary surplus, leaves no doubt. A country whose state is financially healthy, paying, instead of 9 percent of GDP in interest, one quarter of that, can afford a much lower primary surplus. But unless Brazil's central economic distortion, the short-term interest rate—the main cause of the country's fiscal imbalance itself—is addressed, lowering the primary surplus will remain impossible.

Notes

1. See Taylor (2004) for the distinction between "wage-led" and "profit-led" economies.

2. We might understand that current expenditures and revenues do not include state-owned companies. In this case, the simplest means to take account of these companies' savings (positive or negative) is to add their profits (state-owned companies' savings) to or deduct their losses (state-owned companies' negative savings) from the public savings formula.

3. Unafisco/Delegacia Sindical de São Paulo (2006).

4. The Selic rate is the interbanking interest rate to one-day transactions. Its name comes from its origin in the Sistema Especial de Liquidação e de Custódia (Special System of Liquidation and Custody). Actually, it is Brazil's short-term interest rate.

5. Today, should the exchange rate depreciate, the public debt would fall because the government is long on US dollars; this is yet another reason to force a reduction of the interest rate, which would diminish public debt in two ways: less interest expenditure and active indexation to the US dollar.

6. Note that some developed countries, such as Japan, Italy, and Belgium, are in the same situation.

7. Brazil's per capita income grew, on average, a mere 0.9 percent annually from 2001 to 2005, against 3.3 percent in countries at the lowest investment grade.

8. My reference is to the scandals that became known as "Anões do orçamento," "Mensalão," and "Sanguessugas."

9. This deficit is not to be confused with the private social security deficit, which has been rising dangerously and will require the average retirement age to increase.

10. The TJLP is a subsidized interest rate created by the Brazilian government to make viable real investments that otherwise would not be possible given the high short-term interest rate (Selic) managed by the Central Bank.

11. The first electronic auction was held in the Mário Covas administration at the initiative of Yoshiaki Nakano, as São Paulo state secretary of finance. The e-government implemented since then is an international landmark for modern public management.

12. Between 1995 and 2005, while the executive branch's personnel expenditures rose by just 9.7 percent, the legislative branch's increased by 163 percent and the judiciary branch's by 233 percent, thanks mainly to excessive wage increases.

13. The PMDB was the party that united the democratic political opposition during the military regime (1964–1984); initially its name was just Movimento Democrático Brasileiro. PT, created in 1981, was the first split from PMDB, putting together union leaders and the Catholic left; PSDB is the center-left party born from a second split from PMDB in 1988. President José Sarney (1985–1989) was a member of PMDB; President Fernando Henrique Cardoso (1995–2002), of PSDB; and Luís Inácio Lula da Silva, elected president in 2003 and reelected in 2006, of PT.

14. For recent analyses of Keynesian fiscal policy, see Arestis and Sawyer (2004) and Berglund and Vernengo (2006).

5
Is Inflation
a Real Threat?

The next culprit of Brazil's low growth after lack of reforms and lack of fiscal adjustment is said to be inflation: not actual high inflation but the "threat of inflation." This is a mistake. Reasonable price stability is required for economic growth and is an objective of any responsible economic policy, but the more important objective is economic growth. Although inflation is a problem in Brazil as in other countries, Brazil no longer experiences high rates of inflation, and it makes no sense to believe that they may come back. In this book, I assume that the high and inertial inflation that prevailed in Brazil between 1980 and 1994 has been neutralized by a competent device—the adoption of an intermediary "real unit of value" attached to the dollar—and that there is no threat of its return. This is not to say that inflation is no longer a problem. Inflation is a permanent danger and must be kept under constant attack, but fighting it does not justify adopting treatment with side effects—the high interest rate and the uncompetitive exchange rate—that are more serious, in the end, than the inflation that now exists in Brazil. Irrational treatments such as the one adopted in Brazil after the Real Plan attack the patient's health and yet fail to result in acceptable inflation levels. There is no reason why Brazil should not have an inflation rate in line with international rates. With the economic policy recommended by the conventional orthodoxy, inflation may drop, as it has since 2002, but this has been mostly owing to the appreciation of the exchange rate. Since the exchange rate will rise (appreciate) again with the next balance-of-payment crisis, the low inflation rate (which was 4.5 percent in 2007) will sooner or later rebound. It will not reach the levels of the past runaway inflation—because inflationary inertia has been controlled, the risk no longer exists—but it will be enough to show that the stabilization policy adopted by the conventional orthodoxy has not in fact provided even price stabilization.

Since the beginning of 1999, when the floating exchange rate implied giving up the exchange rate as a nominal anchor, the new nominal anchor monetary policy adopted has been inflation targeting. It was as if Brazil could not do without an anchor—a kind of acknowledgment of our inability to manage our economy without relying on anchors. Generally regarded as successful insofar as the inflation rate has been kept under control, the inflation targeting policy has been showing problems, which can be divided into two main categories. First, the Taylor rule, which relates inflation to the interest rate and the potential product gap, can be accepted only in combination with other important variables, such as the exchange rate or the unemployment rate. The argument that the Central Bank should have only one target, because the monetary authorities have only one instrument—the interest rate—is neither reasonable nor realistic. In practice central banks often also consider employment and the exchange rate as informal objectives, and the interest rate is not the *only*—it is just the more important instrument they use. Second, an inflation targeting policy is intended to "manage" monetary policy, not to "change" the monetary policy regime: it determines the basic interest rate within a certain range (the range of the equilibrium interest rate) and is inadequate for tackling the interest rate and exchange rate trap in which Brazil has been caught for years.

An inflation targeting policy could be considered a monetary regime in itself, but I reserve the use of the term *monetary regime* for a broader purpose: a monetary regime comprises the average inflation rate, the interest rate, and the exchange rates together with the maturity of the public debt, the existing institutions, and the selected policies including inflation targeting. In the case of Brazil, the monetary regime includes the inflation targeting policy, the high interest and appreciated exchange rate, and institutions such as Selic, providing returns on bank reserves and public bonds. Monetary policy regimes persist for some time but must eventually change, whether because they conceal internal flaws or because new structural facts require change.

The inflation targeting policy was adopted in Brazil in 1999 without a prior change of the monetary policy regime being deemed necessary. The required change involved institutional reforms such as ending public bond indexation to the Selic and a series of additional steps intended to bring the interest rate back down to normal levels; it also involved the indexation of prices administered by the public utilities. By doing no more than managing an inflation targeting policy since 1999, the government shows that it lacks a clear strategy to reduce the interest rate and neutralize the tendency to the overappreciation of the exchange rate—the two main monetary problems that the Brazilian economy faces.

Because inflation was lower than many had predicted after the exchange rate was allowed to float in January 1999, the general conclusion of several authors analyzing the Brazilian inflation targeting policy was that the experience had been a success.[1] But in their haste they gave the inflation targeting policy adopted in July 1999 undue credit for the results. Conventionally orthodox economists have repeatedly overestimated the positive effects of the inflation targeting policy; they celebrate the low inflation indexes achieved by the Brazilian economy without realizing that they are largely due to the overvalued exchange rate. In fact, as many studies show, the results achieved by countries that use inflation targets are neither better nor worse than those of countries that do not use this tool (Ball and Sheridan 2003; Arestis, Paula, and Ferrari Filho 2006).

The purpose of this chapter is to provide a brief overview of the conduct of monetary policy in Brazil under the inflation targeting policy, from its implementation through to late 2006, and to criticize this policy for the timing of its adoption and the negative aspects of its practical and theoretical structure or framework. These negative characteristics are both theoretical and empirical, which means that Brazil's monetary authorities have used the inflation targeting policy inappropriately. I don't propose to hold a theoretical discussion of the inflation targeting policy. Suffice it to say that the inflation targeting regime is acceptable so long as the equilibrium interest rate is taken to be a mere "variable convention," that is, so long as the theory surrounding it is treated as an empirical generalization of how central banks operate and, in practical terms, the inflation target is combined with an undeclared but effective exchange rate target. In other words, within the framework of a pragmatic inflation targeting policy, the Central Bank should have a double mandate.[2] Strictly speaking, we should consider four objectives. The Federal Reserve Bank has a triple mandate: besides controlling inflation, it must attempt to maintain the employment level and a moderate interest rate. Brazil, like any country with stable growth, must also pursue these two additional goals—employment and a moderate interest rate—although they do not need to be directly assigned to the central bank.

As for the timing of the inflation targeting policy, although it was able to keep inflation low, this entailed extremely high fiscal and growth opportunity costs.[3] Inflation would have been lower and growth rates higher if the government had not rushed to import a monetary policy institution before appropriate conditions were present. Therefore, I will not go into the usual topics concerned with inflation targeting policy: how ambitious the target should be, what inflation index to use, what period to consider, what price indexes to use, and so on. These are administrative issues. Instead, I will discuss structural aspects and issues related to the timing of its adoption.

The Inflation Targeting Policy

After a decade of frustrated attempts to adopt a monetary rule to control inflation, central banks in advanced countries realized that a more pragmatic policy would be to control the inflation rate itself. Although this adoption resulted from the failure of the monetary targets policy and was a pragmatic call made by central bankers, neoclassical and monetarist economists soon found a theoretical explanation for it: the "credibility theory" associated with what has been termed the "new classical macroeconomics" (Kydland and Prescott 1977; Barro and Gordon 1983; Rogoff 1985). According to this theory, if monetary authorities fail to uphold their own rules, their decisions will lack credibility and higher inflation rates will ensue. As a consequence, a reliable central bank is needed to eliminate the "inflationary bias" present in the conduct of monetary policy.

This theory fails, however, to correspond with the practice of central banks. Adopting a historical rather than hypothetical approach, Edwin Le Heron (2003) sees in the case of the Central Bank of Canada the creation of a new monetary policy consensus—a Keynesian consensus. According to Le Heron, the inflation targeting policy clashes with the credibility literature because it is based on "confidence," not "credibility." The credibility approach requires complete central bank independence, whereas inflation targets require operational independency only, with inflation targets being defined by elected officials. Instead of emphasizing "rules versus discretion," the confidence approach emphasizes the expectations of economic agents, the behavior of financial markets, and the prices of assets. In a second paper, Le Heron and Carré (2006) note that central bankers do not simply follow the rules, assuming that they and economic agents are aware of the true model. Instead, central bankers gain economic agents' confidence as they act reasonably, now simply following the rules, now modifying them according to reasons economic agents themselves can understand—under the constant assumption that structural shocks may necessitate such changes. In every process, communication and understanding are the key variables to gaining confidence. As the authors note, "inflation targets involve an ambiguity: the target is almost invariably the goal of the credibility strategy—the target replaces the rule—but, sometimes, it is the beginning of the confidence strategy: the goal is a focal point, *that is,* as part of a communication strategy" (emphasis in original). Alan Greenspan exemplifies a central banker who thinks in terms of "confidence" rather than "credibility" (Blinder and Reis 2005; Aglietta and Borgy 2005).

Some of the institutional arrangements at the base of the inflation targeting policy are (1) a quantitative and explicit inflation target, as well as tolerance intervals established on a generally known price index selected by the National Monetary Council, based on a proposal from the minister of finance; (2) clear operational procedures implemented by the Central Bank of Brazil; (3) a high level of transparency and accountability, through inflation reports, conferences, and minutes (Svensson 1998); and (4) an institutional commitment to price stability, in line with the primary goals of a long-term monetary policy objective.

For Brazil in particular, in the event of failure to hit a target, the Central Bank must publish an open letter explaining the reasons for the failure and setting out the steps to be taken to ensure that inflation will return to tolerated levels and the time frame needed for such steps to produce effects. As for the ideal inflation and the ideal interest rates, it has become common practice to analyze the behavior of central banks according to Taylor's (1993) original formulation—the pragmatic equation known as the Taylor rule whose general form we saw in Chapter 3 but which is worth repeating for its simplicity and practicality:

$$i = i^* + \varphi\,(Y - Y^*) + \gamma\,(\pi - \pi^*) + \delta$$

where i is the nominal interest rate, i^* the equilibrium interest rate, $Y - Y^*$ the product gap, $\pi - \pi^*$ the spread between expected inflation and the inflation target, φ and γ are constants, and δ an exogenous shock factor. This interest rate rule says that the central bank must raise the interest rate above its long-term equilibrium level when inflation surpasses the goal and when production exceeds the total growth permitted by potential GDP.

According to the even more pragmatic original Taylor rule, with the United States as reference, i^* is estimated at 2 percent; the two coefficients, that is, the product gap and the difference between expected rate and inflation target, are 0.5; and the exogenous factor is 2. Thus defined, the Taylor rule and the inflation targeting policy were not, at first, the result of a concern with credibility, or of neoclassical hypothetical-deductive reasoning on inflation, but the generalization of historic experience: of how central banks started to behave to control inflation after abandoning monetary targets. Good macroeconomics adopts a prevalent historical method, making generalizations based on observations of how an economic system truly operates (Bresser-Pereira 2005d). The Taylor rule clearly is based on such a historical, pragmatic approach. The behavior of central banks, in turn, is also pragmatically based on a combination of many theories and findings about inflation, of which the Philips curve is an obvious confidence or credibility requirement.[4] Neoclassical credibility theories were added to the intuition of central bankers and of Taylor to make the inflation targeting policy consistent with the neoclassical view, but nothing prevents further considerations from being added to make it consistent with Keynesian macroeconomics.

The Inflation Targeting Regime

The Brazilian economy changed abruptly in 1994, when the Real Plan neutralized the inflationary inertia mechanism and, as a result, controlled the high inflation that had been affecting the country's development since the early 1980s. But although neutralization of the inertia through the URV mechanism was the true cause of the stabilization of the high inflation, a decision was made to adopt an exchange rate anchor too. At this point the economic team, which had been adopting a national strategy based on a theory of inflationary inertia developed by Brazilian economists, was already giving indications of a turn toward the conventional orthodoxy, which knew nothing of runaway inflation and, since the Argentine Convertibility Plan (1991), defended exchange rate anchors. Maintenance of an almost fixed exchange rate from mid-1994 to early 1999, legitimized by the "fight against inflation" and the policy of "growth with foreign savings," made the country accept high current account deficits and, therefore, become increasingly dependent on international capital inflows and vulnerable to external shocks. This weakness was confirmed in mid-1998, when international creditors decided to suspend the refinancing of the foreign debt, quickly resulting in capital flight. As a result of the endless loss of reserves, in January 1999 the Brazilian government was forced to freely float, and accept a devaluation of, its exchange rate and to enter into an additional agreement with the IMF.

The freely floating real led policymakers, used to regarding the exchange rate as a monetary anchor of the Brazilian economy since 1994, to fear the return of high inflation. Thus, they achieved a marked rise of the interest rate, even though the basic interest rate was already very high.[5] Their fear of inflation was not borne out by the facts; the increase in the inflation rate after the exchange rate was allowed to float was much smaller than conventional economists expected. Even so, Brazilian monetary authorities started working to achieve two main objectives: (1) severe control over inflation to calm the financial market and build credibility and (2) implementation of an inflation targeting policy as a new nominal anchor for economic policy.

Six months after the crisis and the adoption of a flexible exchange rate, the Central Bank put into effect a formal inflation targets policy and established its first rules. The Índice de Preços ao Consumidor Amplo (Extended Consumer Price Index; IPCA)[6] was selected as a benchmark for the targets because it registered seasonal factors as well as temporary shocks. The Selic overnight interest rate was chosen as the policy's instrument, and the inflation target became the responsibility of the Conselho de Política Monetária (Monetary Policy Council; COPOM). Tolerance intervals of up to two percentage points[7] were allowed to take into account the significance of uncertainty in Brazil's inflationary process as well as unexpected temporary shocks and/or seasonal effects (Figure 5.1 shows the targets for 1999–2005). Therefore, the monetary authorities continued to treat inflation control as their main task and failed to recognize that an extremely high basic interest rate was then the greatest impediment to true macroeconomic stabilization. In other words, it was a misguided political agenda, given that the main problem the Brazilian economy faced had shifted from inflation to the perverse combination of a high interest rate and an uncompetitive exchange rate. But the policy remained in place and was mistakenly given credit for the low growth of inflation in 1999, even though it had only just come into force.

After Luís Inácio Lula da Silva was elected president in October 2002, the monetary authorities decided to maintain and reinforce the previous monetary and fiscal policies as well as continue with microeconomic institutional reforms. The new administration's plans included a clear primary surplus objective and a newly announced reform of the social security system. Because the market took this as an indication that no significant policy changes would occur, there was a drop in the likelihood of default, an appreciation of the real, and a reduction in inflation (Blanchard 2005). In 2003, with the new administration in power and the orthodox behavior of the monetary authorities, Brazil's creditors

Figure 5.1 Real Inflation Rates, Targets, Tolerance Intervals, and GDP (1999–2005)

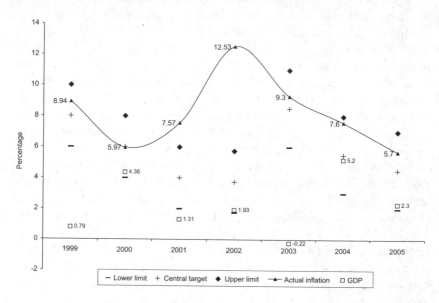

Source: Instituto de Pesquisa Econômica Aplicada (Institute for Applied Economic Research), www.igov.br.

started to calm down. At that time, in mid-2003, the clear improvement in Brazil's foreign accounts and the recovery of confidence in the government created an opportunity to begin an interest rate reduction policy. But the government made the opposite decision: interest rates rose. Its sole concern was to send a signal to the financial market that fighting inflation remained a priority for the new administration. According to Favero and Giavazzi (2005), Lula's announcement of a restrictive fiscal policy after his 2003 inauguration was enough to bring Brazil back to "normal conditions," with a quick drop in sovereign risk, exchange rate stabilization, and, as a consequence, stabilization of expected inflation, of inflation itself, and of the dynamics of public debt. The interest rate, however, remained at its absurdly high level, and the economy stagnated despite extremely favorable international circumstances.

Monetary authorities began 2005 with a monetary policy similar to the one of the previous year, and the inflation target was hit. The inflation targets as far ahead as 2008 had already been set by the National Monetary Council—4.5 percent each year. In 2006 and 2007 the target was met, but in 2008 it would not be fully met as a consequence of an unexpected event: the sharp depreciation of the real and of many other national currencies as a consequence of the global financial crisis. Inflation rates in Brazil are a little higher than the average of other emergent countries, but the difference is small and can be explained by the indexation of utility prices and of wages set by collective agreements, by the minimum-wage increase policy, and by the still relatively shut-off nature of the Brazilian economy (Werlang 2006). Managed prices, in particular, could be responsible for inflation rates in excess of international standards. In 2005 and 2006, inflation dropped and the target was hit. In late 2006 the conventional orthodoxy celebrated an inflation rate of around 3 percent as a "victory" against inflation: in fact, it was the result of foreign exchange populism, as the rate was attained thanks to a strong appreciation of the real. In 2007 the target was again reached, although the rate of inflation increased to the targeted 4.5 percent.

Monetary Policy Regime

While the inflation rate remains low, even though higher than international levels, the Brazilian economy's growth rate is still much lower than the average of developing countries, even though Central Bank officers and conventional economists go on and on about their successful policy. I cannot agree. If, instead of adopting an inflation targeting policy the monetary authorities had concentrated their efforts on changing the monetary policy regime and thus getting out of the trap they were in, if they had committed to controlling the factors that truly destabilize the Brazilian economy—the high interest rate and the uncompetitive exchange rate—then we might have not only added growth but also an inflation rate at international levels—lower, that is. By their devoting all their efforts to lowering inflation instead of attacking the Brazilian economy's real macroeconomic problem, the very goal of lowering inflation is threatened. This was clear, for instance, in 2008, when inflation rose all over the world, including in Brazil. Given the fact that the exchange rate was already highly overappreciated and the real interest rate remained at a very high level, the Central Bank's decision to resume the increase of the short-term interest rate to fight the surge of inflation will probably have little positive effect. If, while aggregate demand was not pressing, the Central Bank had lowered the short-term interest rate much more rapidly and firmly, on one hand, it might have avoided part of the appreciation of the real, and, on the other, the increase in the interest rate would have a greater impact on the economy.

The most straightforward reason for my claim lies in the exchange rate. The economic policy that the conventional orthodoxy proposes to developing countries and that the Central Bank of Brazil faithfully adopts implies an appreciated exchange rate. One of the reasons that make this policy appealing, besides foreign exchange populism, is that it causes an immediate reduction of the inflation rate. On the other hand, sooner or later, as the mismatch must be corrected as a result of either a crisis or a near-crisis, this correction implies a sudden depreciation and, therefore, a higher inflation rate. It is impressive how closely inflation rates in Brazil have matched exchange rate movements (Figure 5.2). If the monetary authorities and the government as a whole concentrated on avoiding the tendency of the exchange rate to become relatively overvalued, owing to either the Dutch disease or the massive supply of capital to developing countries, they would achieve not only greater general economic stability, particularly in the domestic accounts, but also a more stable and lower inflation rate in the medium run. Instead of thinking of the inflation targeting policy as a success or a failure, we

Figure 5.2 Inflation Rate (Consumer Price Index) and Nominal Exchange Rate, 1999–2005

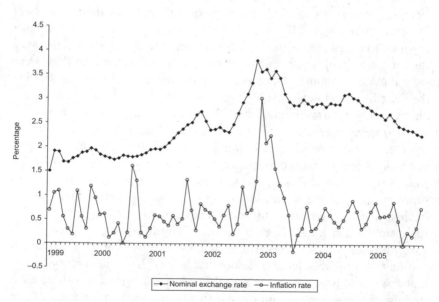

Source: Instituto de Pesquisa Econômica Aplicada (Institute for Applied Economic Research), www.ipeadata.gov.br.
Note: R$/US$ for 1999 = 1; for 2005 = 10.

should understand that it is now the main instrument whereby the conventional orthodoxy keeps the Brazilian economy in the trap of a high interest rate and an uncompetitive exchange rate. Instead of committing to a strategy meant to lower the interest rate, which, by implying a higher exchange rate, might lead to a small and temporary increase in inflation, what we have been doing is clinging to targets for the next year that prevent any better coordinated strategy to lower the interest rate of the type I discuss in Chapter 11.

We have seen that in 1999, Brazil was unprepared to adopt an inflation targeting policy, given that such a policy is intended to manage monetary policy, not to change the monetary policy regime. At that time, to evade the high interest rates that push down the exchange rate, a regime change was needed, as was a strategy to lower the interest rate. If the economic authorities believed that an inflation targeting policy was a good way to go, they would have first had to face the interest rate and exchange rate trap. A regime change naturally involves abandoning the equilibrium interest rate that the managers of the inflation targeting policy have been using, as a real annual rate of 9 percent is incompatible with the new regime.

An obstacle that loses importance as the inflation rate drops, but still needs to be faced, lies in utilities contracts with price-indexation clauses. The managed prices basket amounts to as much as 30 percent of the IPCA. In terms of economic policy, the actions of policymakers have a clear and substantial effect on price-index variability because of monitored prices. As a consequence, the targets may be hit, but at the expense of high social costs, low economic growth, and high interest rates. Monitored prices vary regardless of demand factors and, as Figure 5.3 shows, the inflation of monitored prices has risen far more than the other two indexes.

Therefore, managed prices in Brazil cause a series of problems for its economy. First, the Central Bank's actions through its monetary policy instrument can affect only free prices, which force the monetary authorities to work with demand shocks that may not take place. Second, expected inflation generates a vicious circle for interest rates and makes them extremely high. Managed prices, in turn, are indexed to the Índice Geral de Preços (General Price Index; IGP)[8] and, therefore, to the exchange rate, which magnifies the effects of exchange devaluation on prices. The end result is a very restrictive and severe monetary policy.

In sum, the 1994 Real Plan was a successful reform that deindexed the Brazilian economy and therefore neutralized inflationary inertia. But it was incomplete insofar as managed prices and the public debt remained

Figure 5.3 Monitored Prices and IPCA: 1999–2006

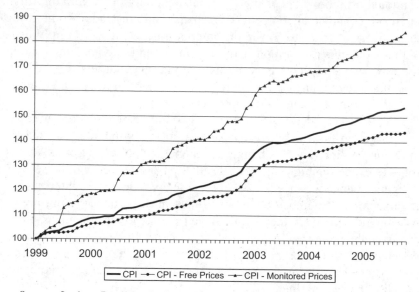

Sources: Instituto Brasileiro de Geografia e Estatística (Brazilian Institute for Geography and Statistics; IBGE), www.ibge.gov.br; Central Bank of Brazil, www.bcb.gov.br.

indexed. Instead of working toward this objective, however, Brazilian monetary authorities accepted the IMF's recommendation of adopting an exchange rate anchor between 1995 and 1998, with catastrophic results. Even so, the inflation targeting policy was introduced in Brazil in 1999 as a substitute for this exchange rate anchor. This monetary reform should have been preceded by reforms to eliminate all forms of indexation. But instead of developing a strategy to reduce the interest rate, involving these reforms and a reinforced fiscal adjustment, the government continued to cast inflation as the main problem to be addressed and adopted a formal inflation targeting policy. The consequence was that, since 1999, the real interest rate has remained extremely high: the Brazilian economy has been unable to escape the interest rate trap.

Perhaps the best strategy might have been to pursue a long-term inflation convergence. Chile, for example, followed this course of action before beginning its inflation targeting policy. The Chileans first promoted the necessary trade openness and sought to balance their accounts, reaching acceptable interest and exchange rates, and then introduced an inflation targeting policy. In other words, Chile, which has been a model of competent macroeconomic policy, allowed inflation to converge smoothly, resulting in a lower social cost than Brazil has experienced. The entire strategy started to be considered as early as 1991. But a light form of inflation targeting policy was fully adopted only in 2000, when the Chilean Central Bank started to release inflation reports. The Mexican case is similar, although in a different time frame.

In Brazil, the economy was not properly prepared for the inflation targeting policy. The authorities should have prepared the economy's several key variables, so that they could converge more smoothly. If they had first focused on escaping from the interest rate–exchange rate trap, they could have adopted an inflation targeting policy later. Instead, overly concerned with inflation, the authorities were quick to adopt a new nominal anchor. As a consequence, the exchange rate remained highly unstable and the economy was unable to hit its inflation target in certain years. Worse, the real interest rate on public debt remained abnormally high—which entailed severe fiscal and development costs. Consequently, Brazil urgently needs to change its priorities concerning monetary policy. The high interest rate, not inflation, is the main problem to tackle. Only by addressing this problem and lowering the interest rate to levels compatible with its sovereign risk will Brazil attain international inflation levels, instead of keeping it at around 5 percent a year. Success in this endeavor, however, will require the involvement of the whole of society and the government.

Notes

1. For example, Bogdanski, Tombini, and Werlang (2000); Figueiredo, Fachada, and Goldestein (2002); and Minella, Goldfajn, and Muinhos (2003).

2. We talk about a "parameter," not a target, because it is not explicit but tracked conventionally by the Central Bank and acknowledged by the financial market. It is not enough to simply explicitly include the exchange rate in the model and select a long-term inflation target, as proposed by Ball (2000), assuming that the foreign exchange movements at this time will be offset.

3. Between January 2003 and September 2005, the Brazilian government paid around R$300 billion in debt service. In US dollars, GDP per capita rose from US$3,235 in 2000 to US$3,325 in 2004.

4. The theory of credibility is either obvious or wrong. It becomes wrong when policymakers advance the "credibility" of their policies in lieu of economic fundamentals. This was the case, for example, in the classic Latin American stabilization experiments of the late 1970s (Diaz-Alejandro 1981) or in the IMF-sponsored Brazilian stabilization program of 1992.

5. After the inflation targets regime was implemented, real interest rates fell, but in 2001, when they were still high in real terms, the rates were again raised.

6. The selected price index—IPCA—is based on a sample of households with incomes of between one and 40 times the minimum wages, with a broad geographical span (Bogdanski, Tombini, and Werlang 2000).

7. Tolerance intervals were expanded to 2.5 percent after 2003.

8. The IGP is a price index calculated by the Getúlio Vargas Foundation that besides taking into consideration consumer prices also includes commodity prices.

6
Overappreciated Currency and the Dutch Disease

I n the previous chapters I criticized the three main causes that the conventional orthodoxy cites to explain poor growth rates in Brazil: the lack of reform, the insufficient fiscal adjustment, and the inflation threat. Moving forward, I concentrate on the real causes: the overvalued exchange rate and the high interest rate. I begin with the exchange rate, which is the most strategic of the five prices that regulate any economic system (the other being the interest rate, the inflation rate, the wage rate, and the profit rate), with direct implications not only for macroeconomic stability but also for savings and investment and, therefore, economic development. Although the exchange rate is the most strategic of the five macroeconomic prices, it is the least studied and the most misunderstood. The interest rate is the key price in every macroeconomic textbook; inflation is the main concern of policymakers; the wage rate and the profit rate are centrally related to income distribution, and the latter also with the investment rate. The exchange rate, however, has always occupied an awkward position in economic theory. John Maynard Keynes well knew its strategic role and probably for that reason opted for building a closed model in the *General Theory* and for a fixed exchange rate in the Bretton Woods agreements. For some time economists were freed from concerns about it. Yet, after the Bretton Woods agreements collapsed in the 1970s and open macroeconomics became a necessity, the discussion of the problem returned.

Neoclassical and Keynesian economists debated for years which exchange rate regime would be more suitable—floating or fixed. The discussion got nowhere, for two reasons. First, rich countries, particularly the United States, were comfortable with their own currencies as international reserve money, and the tendency to recurrent balance-of-payment crises in developing countries, although upsetting, contributed to checking their political demands at international forums and to limiting their international competitiveness. Second, the debate really made no sense: it was a false debate, because the alternative was unrealistic; in practice, countries chose a middle way, pragmatically rejecting either dollarization or full floating. After the major 1990s balance-of-payment crises, the conventional orthodoxy, which had fully supported dollarization and currency boards, changed radically and supported floating exchange rates, maintaining that the crises had been caused by the fixed exchange rate regime. In fact, the crises did not result from the choice of exchange rate regime, but from (1) the fact that countries decided to grow with foreign savings, that is, with current account deficits that caused their currencies to appreciate and foreign indebtedness to grow, and (2) their acceptance of the appreciation of their currencies "to fight inflation." On the other hand, the conventional orthodoxy dismissed the practice adopted by practically all countries of managing their exchange rates as "dirty floating." Only the countries whose currencies are international reserves face limits in managing them because mismanagement would weaken confidence. But even they often interfere in the market price of their currencies. As for the developing countries, there are two options: they either manage their exchange rates, neutralizing their tendency to overappreciation, or leave them to float freely, as the conventional orthodoxy proposes, and as a result fail to grow, or, more precisely, present poor growth performances.

The conventional economics is curiously contradictory in dealing with the exchange rate. On the one hand, it says that it is impossible to manage the exchange rate in the long term. On the other, it criticizes strongly countries that attempt to do so. The conventional economist could argue that there is no contradiction in these two views because one refers to the long term and the other to the short term. But the distinction between the long term and the short term, which is central in microeconomics, makes no sense in macroeconomics and in development economics. The long-term growth of a country is just the sum of many short-term growths. The historical fact is that many countries for many years managed, and continue to manage, their currencies and that this policy has been crucial to avoid the overappreciation that causes recurrent balance-of-payment crises and low growth rates between the crises.

In view of the strategic role played by the exchange rate in the growth process, in this and in the next chapter I discuss a central (and probably new) issue in development economics, namely, the tendency of the exchange rate to overappreciation in developing countries. In this chapter I will discuss this tendency and one of its structural causes, the Dutch disease; in Chapter 7 I will discuss its other structural cause, the attraction that developing countries' higher rates of profit and of interest exert on foreign capitals and its main policy manifestation: the growth-with-foreign-savings policy.[1]

An Obstacle on the Demand Side

The exchange rate is a crucial price on the demand side of economic growth. If developing countries don't neutralize the tendency to the overvaluation of the exchange rate, hoping that markets alone will coordinate the economy, they will see their exchange rate rise above the real equilibrium rate—the rate that makes industries internationally competitive using state-of-the-art technology—and this fact will be a major obstacle to their economic growth. Even if the country has the technological and administrative capacity to diversify its economy and grow by adding industries with increasing value added per capita to its productive system, it will not be able to use this capacity because the overvalued exchange rate will represent a relative bar or a full veto to it: a relative bar if, in the specific country, the overvaluation tendency is moderate; a veto, if it is strong.

There is one basic condition on which the appreciation of a given currency is not overappreciation but a good symptom, is healthy, not a disease: this happens when productivity in the respective country increases faster than in the other countries. All fast-growing economies sooner or later experience such appreciation that makes all effectively richer—able to buy a larger quantity of tradable goods with the same nominal income. Overappreciation is a different matter, because a country with an overvalued currency will have artificially high wages and consumption, combined with low rates of investment and savings. The investment rate that is crucial to economic growth will be kept low because business-people will not have good opportunities for export-oriented investments. Besides this, the country will normally also face a current account deficit and will be threatened by a balance-of-payment crisis, although, as we will see in this chapter, when overappreciation is a consequence of the Dutch disease it will be consistent with long-term equilibrium of the current account.

Overappreciation of the exchange rate is an obstacle to growth on the demand side with serious effects on the supply side insofar as it hinders investment even when business enterprises fully control the respective technology. Conventional economics tends to consider economic growth merely in terms of supply, focusing on education, on a broader improvement of human capital, on scientific and particularly technological development, on innovation, and on investment in machines that increase workers' productivity. Yet, as Keynes classically demonstrated, demand is not automatically created by supply, and therefore it may become an essential obstacle to economic growth. The huge unemployment of human resources that exists in almost all developing countries that have unsatisfactory growth rates leaves no doubt that the main problem is often on the demand side rather than on the supply side. Demand is formed by consumption, investments, public expenditure, and the trade surplus, but the key variables are investments and exports, because they can increase without incurring the cost of households' higher indebtedness as occurs with consumption, or the cost of fiscal imbalance as occurs with public expenditure. Not only do these key variables directly represent demand when there is a positive balance in commercial transactions, but they also encourage investment—the main variable of demand—which operates as much on the supply side as on the demand side.[2] Exports are therefore strategic to solving the problem of insufficiency of demand or of unemployment.

Overappreciation of the currency is a tendency, but it is not inevitable. Developing countries have often been able to develop policies that neutralize it. In fact, although in international economics there is a central distinction between fixed and floating exchange rate regimes, the division between market and managed systems is more relevant. In US macroeconomics textbooks, the exchange rate is not regarded as a variable instrument because, although the US economy is the world's most powerful, the country faces constraints in managing it: the dollar is a market currency. This is essentially a result of its nature as a reserve currency. While the fixed-rate foreign exchange regime prevailed, the ability to manage it was excluded by definition. Since the 1970s, when the US government decided to stop backing its currency with gold reserves and moved to a floating foreign exchange regime, it remained theoretically possible to manage the rate. But because the US dollar is the main international reserve currency, it cannot be subject to entry or exit controls; besides, it makes no sense for the United States to buy or sell its own currency in order to appreciate or depreciate it. The alternative open to other countries whose currency is not a reserve currency—buying strong currencies and increasing reserves when the local currency begins to appreciate due to capital inflows—is practically limited in the case of the United States. By purchasing euros or yens the country would be admitting a weakness inconsistent with its position as issuer of the reserve currency. This is why US textbooks and the conventional orthodoxy regard the exchange rate as an endogenous price whose real value cannot be managed. They generalize from the US experience. As a consequence, it is not rare to overhear Brazilian economists state, from the height of their US Ph.D.'s, that "the exchange rate cannot be managed," ignoring the fact that the statement goes against international experience—that every country, even those whose currencies are relatively strong, attempts to control its rates. Even the United States climbed out of the 1980s crisis only because it was able to persuade the Japanese to appreciate the yen with the Plaza agreements. In the 2000s, faced with massive current account deficits, it is now pressing China to appreciate the yuan. Dynamic Asian countries have a history of permanently managing their exchange rates.

Exchange rate management was already crucial when its scope was basically limited to regulating imports and exports; from the moment international capital flows started to increase to extraordinary levels, such management became even more important. The exchange rate is the most strategic of macroeconomic prices; it is the one with the most powerful, as well as almost immediate, effects on the economy. As we will see in this chapter, the exchange rate does not determine the foreign trade and the financial flow variables alone. It is also a fundamental variable in determining wages, consumption, investments, and domestic savings. For businesspeople, it is crucial that this rate should be stable and competitive—by "competitive" I mean a rate that ensures international competitiveness for firms adopting state-of-the-art technology. Faced with massive international inflows, the exchange rate of a country that represents a small share of the world's economy will, unmanaged, experience great fluctuation. In addition, it is very likely to appreciate, becoming relatively overvalued and losing competitiveness, in times of both prosperity and hardship. In prosperous times, it will attract capital for investment; in normal times the profit rate and the internal interest rate in emerging countries tend to be higher than in rich countries, attracting capital, which exerts downward pressure on the exchange rate. In Brazil, where the interest rate is exceptionally high, the pressure is correspondingly strong. Naturally, in times of crisis the trend reverses itself and, depending on the intensity of the crisis, the foreign exchange depreciation can be both massive and sudden.

The conventional orthodoxy, however, does not think in empirical or historical terms, but in hypothetical-deductive ones. Although experience shows that countries do manage their exchange rates, it deduces, based on the assumption of a floating exchange rate regime, that managing it is impossible. This would not be a problem, however, since—once again contrary to empirical evidence—the floating foreign exchange regime would automatically keep the exchange rate in balance. This view is consistent with the interests of rich countries, for which exchange rate management on the part of developing countries—and particularly medium-income countries—is highly undesirable. What rich countries would prefer is for medium-income developing countries, which are now their competitors in a growing number of fields, to have a relatively appreciated exchange rate. With this, advanced countries would export more and import less, and, also very important, their multinationals would be able, given a certain profit in the local currency, to repatriate more dollars, euros, yen, or pounds sterling than they might if the local currency were competitive. Along these same lines, they do not hesitate to call developing countries' attempts to manage their exchange rates "dirty." Foreign exchange rate regimes are commonly classified as fixed rate, crawling peg, managed floating rate, and floating rate. In fact, in practical terms, given the infeasibility or abandonment of dollarization systems, currency boards, fixed rates, or fixed bands, for countries equipped with domestic savings, and given that only the United States and the euro area do not manage their exchange rates, today's relevant exchange rate regime is the managed floating rate. Through it, with loose capital control mechanisms and not entirely strong monetary policies, countries pragmatically circumvent Robert Mundell's triangle of impossibility.

The Tendency to the Overappreciation of the Exchange Rate

Economic development can happen only with a competitive exchange rate that encourages exports and investment. The empirical evidence for this claim is clear: every country that developed during the twentieth century, such as Japan, Germany, Italy, and, more recently, the dynamic Asian countries, always relied on competitive exchange rates. Recent econometric studies have repeatedly confirmed this.[3] On the other hand, economic theory shows that developing countries should grow faster than wealthy ones, that they should display higher rates of productivity increase. Insofar as this prediction materializes, continues the argument, these countries' exchange rates should appreciate gradually at no loss to their international competitiveness, since the appreciation would just compensate for the productivity increases. Thus, economic theory assumes that developing countries' exchange rates will be consistent with the domestic production of tradable goods made with state-of-the-art technology. My claim is that this assumption is false. A series of factors, some market-related, some arising from strategies proposed by advanced countries, prevents this from happening and makes developing countries' exchange rates remain relatively overvalued. In fact, the problem is more serious: there is a tendency for these countries' exchange rates to appreciate up to the point that a balance-of-payment crisis stops it. This is worse than the well-known and well-analyzed volatility that also characterizes the exchange rate in developing countries.

What are the causes of this tendency of the exchange rate to overappreciate? There are two structural causes for it—the Dutch disease and the attraction that higher profit and interest rates cause on global capitals—and three policy causes that aggravate the second structural cause. The Dutch disease is a particularly lethal cause because, unlike the other factors causing overappreciation, it is compatible with the intertemporal balance of foreign accounts. It is, therefore, a market failure that can be corrected only by managing the exchange rate: only by keeping the exchange rate at a true equilibrium level compatible with the survival of industrial sectors using state-of-the-art technology will the market be able to efficiently perform its resource-allocating role and foster economic growth.

The second structural cause—one that has been widely discussed in the economics literature—is the fact that developing countries usually tend to offer higher profit and interest rates than rich ones, because capital there is relatively scarce. This better return on capital attracts the abundant resources present in advanced countries, thus pushing down the exchange rate as measured in the local currency. This second structural cause (independent of policy) of the tendency to the overappreciation of the exchange rate is aggravated by four economic policies. Three of them are part of the conventional orthodoxy's basic recipe: "financial deepening," the use of the exchange rate as an "anchor" to control inflation, and the policy of growth with foreign savings; the fourth is a malpractice typical of these countries: "exchange rate populism," meaning that with the appreciation of the exchange rate, inflation goes down, real wages increase, and the politician is reelected if the balance-of-payment crisis does not arrive before the election day. Among these causes, the Dutch disease and the policy of growth with foreign savings are the more relevant. Let's begin with the former.

The Dutch Disease

The growth-with-foreign-savings policy is a powerful cause of the tendency to the overappreciation of the exchange rate, and as we will see, it is a "dynamic" cause whereas the Dutch disease is "static." The Dutch disease originated in the production and export of commodities using a cheap and abundant resource that maintains the country's exchange rate at a level consistent with the profitability of the respective industry, but below the level that makes other tradable industries also using state-of-the-art technology economically viable. As Corden and Neary (1982) have stressed, it is a structural phenomenon that provokes deindustrialization. Some authors (Baland and François 2000; Sachs and Warner 1999, 2001; Torvik 2001; Larsen 2004) draw a distinction between the Dutch disease and the curse of natural resources: the Dutch disease would be a market failure, whereas the curse of natural resources would result from corruption or rent-seeking, arising from the abundance of such resources in countries with a backward society and weak institutions. Although the problem of corruption exists in all countries and is more serious in poor countries rich in natural resources, I will not discuss this issue here and will not observe the difference between the two concepts. The Dutch disease is an old problem, but it received this name because it was identified in the 1960s in the Netherlands, when its economists found that the discovery of natural gas and its export were appreciating the exchange rate and threatening to destroy its whole manufacturing industry. It was only in the 1980s that the first academic studies on the subject appeared (Corden and Neary 1982; Corden 1984). Even today the literature on the subject is scarce and inadequate. The Dutch disease causes a chronic or permanent overappreciation and is consistent with current account equilibrium, whereas the growth-with-foreign-savings policy is the main cause of balance-of-payment crises in developing countries: starting from an overappreciated level after a crisis, the adoption of this policy, usually combined with high interest rates to attract foreign capitals, gradually appreciates the national currency. On the other hand, although the market partially controls the negative consequences of the growth-with-foreign-savings policy—a poor control, behind schedule, under the syndromes of the "sudden stop" but anyway a control—this is not the case with the Dutch disease, which is a market failure that no market whatsoever can control.

The Dutch disease is consistent with the intertemporal equilibrium of foreign accounts and may, therefore, produce negative effects indefinitely. It is a market failure because the sector producing natural resource–intensive goods generates a negative externality on the economy's other sectors, preventing those sectors from developing despite their use of state-of-the-art technology.[4] It is a market failure that implies the existence of a difference between the exchange rate that balances the current account (which is the market rate) and the exchange rate that supports efficient and technologically sophisticated economic sectors (which is the rate at which economics predicts that efficient industries will be viable in competitive markets). Only when the Dutch disease is neutralized will the market be able to play its role in effectively allocating resources and in encouraging investment and innovation.

The seriousness of the Dutch disease will vary from country to country, depending on the commodity, its international price, and the cost in the country. In my model of the Dutch disease (Bresser-Pereira 2008), in the countries suffering from it there are two equilibrium exchange rates: the "current" and the "industrial." The current equilibrium exchange rate is the one that balances intertemporally a country's current account and that is therefore also the market rate, the rate on which the market should converge. The industrial equilibrium exchange rate is the one that supports the production of tradable goods in the country without the need for duties and subsidies provided that, on the supply side, the enterprises use the best technology available in the world; in other words, it is the exchange rate that, on average, allows companies using state-of-the-art technology to be profitable or competitive. When there is Dutch disease, this means that the two equilibrium rates are different. If we presume that for all countries the industrial equilibrium exchange rate is equal to 100, the more appreciated is the current equilibrium rate in relation to the industrial equilibrium exchange rate, the more serious will be the Dutch disease. This difference that defines the severity of the disease will depend on Ricardian rents embodied in each commodity, which, in turn, will depend on the difference in productivity between the one in the country and the marginal one that defines the commodity's international prices and also on the other factors that determine variations in this international price.[5]

The Dutch disease leads to an overvalued exchange rate that prevents the production of tradable goods that do not use the resources that give rise to it. For this to occur, a sector that uses a country's natural resources must be substantially more productive than this same sector in other countries in producing a commodity. Given this fact, two consequences result: first, given the fact that the market price of the commodity is defined internationally by the less efficient producer on the margin, the country will realize Ricardian rents; second, since the exchange rate is defined in the market by the less costly commodity on the margin, it will appreciate up to the level at which exports cease to be profitable and producers stop production—a level considerably more appreciated that the one that makes economically viable other tradable industries using technology in the state of the art. In these terms, although the Dutch disease is associated with rents that benefit the country, it is also a market failure representing a major obstacle to the diversification and industrialization of a national economy. In their model, Corden and Neary (1982) supposed an economy with three sectors, two of them related to tradable goods (the "booming" sector or natural resources sector, and the "lagging" sector or the manufacturing industry sector) and a third sector of nontradable goods. Sachs and Warner (2001), summarizing the literature on the Dutch disease, explain it in terms of a wealth shock in the natural resources sector that creates excess demand in the nontradable goods sector, implying a change in relative prices. The appreciated exchange rate is defined by that change in relative prices that results from favoring nontradable goods. In the model I present here those three sectors are present, but the emphasis is placed directly on the exchange rate, and the change in relative prices (which is nothing more than the overappreciation of currency) is related to the Ricardian nature of the rents occurring in the sector that makes use of cheap resources—not only natural resources but also, as we shall see, labor itself.

When Dutch disease exists, even the goods produced with state-of-the-art technology are not viable economically in a competitive market. All other factors of competitiveness being equal, if an advanced technology company sets up in a country affected seriously by this disease, it will probably go bankrupt soon. The corporation would be economically viable only if its productivity were higher than the productivity achieved by the other competing countries—so much higher that it would compensate for the overappreciation of the currency.

In a first stage, while the country is realizing its original accumulation of capital, when it is making the transition from a precapitalist to a minimally capitalist economy, the existence of natural resources to exploit is a positive factor. After this stage, however, the Dutch disease becomes really a disease because, at this time, the country is supposed to industrialize and diversify its economy, and this is made impossible by the overvaluation of the exchange rate. This explains why the countries that commercially exploit their natural resources more were those that developed less. Since World War II, Asian non-oil-exporting countries have grown more than Latin American non-oil-exporting countries, and these latter have grown more than all the oil-exporting developing countries. Mineral-rich African countries to all intents and purposes did not grow. Many factors have certainly contributed to this outcome, but we may generalize by asserting that, the greater the weight of the Dutch disease, the lower is the probability that countries can neutralize it successfully. Evidently, it was easier to neutralize the Dutch disease in non-oil-producing countries than in oil-producing ones, because in the former the disease's severity tends to be milder.

The Dutch disease can be completely neutralized by two measures. First, a tax or levy on the sale of the goods that give rise to it will do the job.[6] This tax should correspond to the percentage difference between the current equilibrium exchange rate provided by its lower cost and the industrial equilibrium exchange rate that opens the way to tradable sectors in state-of-the-art technology. Second, the neutralization is completed by the creation of an international fund with the revenues derived from this tax; the fund will ensure that the inflow of the tax revenues does not revalue the exchange rate. This was essentially what Norway did after it discovered and began to export oil from the North Sea. Britain, which discovered oil at the same time, did not neutralize the Dutch disease, and its economy suffered the consequences (Chatterji and Price 1988). Chile also adequately neutralizes the Dutch disease by heavily taxing copper exports, but this is a partial neutralization, since the revenues from the tax are not directed to the establishment of an international fund. The direct way of neutralizing the Dutch disease is through a tax on sales and exports. The desired effect of the tax is microeconomic: it shifts the supply curve of the good upward in order to move from the level of the current equilibrium exchange rate to the industrial equilibrium exchange rate. The tax increases the commodity's marginal cost to approximately the level required by the other tradable goods to become competitive. If the tax is rightly imposed, it will lead the current exchange rate to become approximately equal to the industrial one, insofar as the producers of the commodity will offer it at this depreciated rate. I say "approximately" because there is no simple way of estimating the necessary rate of this tax.

According to the above-defined terms, neutralizing the Dutch disease appears to be a simple task, but actually it can be very difficult. First, the government will have to face resistance from exporters of the commodities giving rise to the Dutch disease. This resistance is usually great but it is irrational, because the purpose of the tax is not to reduce the sector's profitability but to maintain it and eventually make it even more stable, as long as the revenues from the tax, besides constituting an international fund so that their inflow into the country does not put pressure on the exchange rate, is also used as an exchange rate stabilization fund. In order to maintain profitability, the tax can only be "marginal": it shall be applied only to gains resulting from the depreciation achieved by the tax or, preferably, by temporary measures of inflow control. Second, the tax faces a macroeconomic difficulty since it implies a transitory rise in inflation. Provided that there is no formal or informal indexation of economy, however, prices will subsequently stabilize. A cooling down of the economy during transition may reduce this transitory increase in inflation but will not avoid it. A third and fundamental problem is the decrease in wages caused by the depreciation of the local currency. In developing countries the state should use part of the resources obtained from the tax to increase social services, that is, indirect wages.

In the fourth place, not many countries have political conditions like Norway's for allocating the whole revenue from the tax to setting up funds abroad, as well as a stabilization fund of exportable commodities. In less-developed countries, the tax is generally used for fiscal purposes, since its existence reduces the government's ability to finance its expenses with the direct and indirect taxes used by all countries. This is the case in Chile, for instance. Although we should not confuse this fund with reserves obtained by countries with domestic indebtedness, however, the formation of those reserves is an indication that, after all, the creation of neutralizing funds is not as difficult as we might imagine.

The Dutch Disease in Brazil

We may identify two varieties of the Dutch disease. One is the variety that has always existed and prevented industrialization, as is the case in oil-producing countries. The other represents the situation of the country that, for a while, succeeded in neutralizing the disease and therefore developed but, from a certain time on, in the name of a radical liberalism eliminated the mechanisms of neutralization and began to grow at very low rates, as is the case in Latin American countries that underwent liberalizing reforms without replacing the old system of duties and subsidies by a more rational system of taxes on the sales of commodities giving rise to the disease.

The most important symptoms of the Dutch disease are exchange rate overvaluation, low growth in the manufacturing sector, a rapidly expanding services sector, high average wages, and unemployment (Oomes and Kalcheva 2007). As the Dutch disease is a market failure on the demand side, it limits the investment opportunities in the manufacturing industry producing tradable goods. It exists only when a country's human resources are unemployed, or in other words, when a country has the technical and administrative conditions for investing in the production of goods with more sophisticated technology and higher wages, but the prevailing exchange rate prevents those investments from being made. Notwithstanding unemployment, the sectors where the Dutch disease originates usually pay high wages. Yet, only a few people benefit from this, since the commodities that originate the disease are usually labor saving. Wages may also be low, however, because the workforce is abundant and unorganized in the country.

Countries affected by the Dutch disease either have been exporting a natural resource for a long time but never achieved industrialization or achieved industrialization for a time but later engaged in a process of premature deindustrialization. Brazil and the other Latin American countries except Argentina are in the latter case. From the 1930s on, most Latin American countries industrialized by neutralizing a Dutch disease that they understood intuitively even though they did not know about it. They firmly managed their exchange rates, usually making use of import duties, import administrative restrictions, and export subsidies that made the effective exchange rate much different from the nominal one. In the late 1980s or early 1990s, however, weakened by the foreign debt crisis and by high inflation, under international pressure from rich countries and their conventional orthodoxy, accused of "protectionism" when they were just neutralizing the overappreciation of the exchange rate, these countries abandoned the neutralization schemes. As a consequence of financial liberalization, the countries lost control of their exchange rates; as a consequence of trade liberalization, the effective exchange rate actually appreciated in relation to the nominal one (taking into account, when measuring the exchange rate before liberalization, the duties and subsidies that actually made it depreciate more than the nominal rate suggested). The appreciation is not immediately perceived, since it is disguised by the fact that part of the appreciation results from the elimination of duties and subsidies. Yet the country's manufacturing industry soon begins to suffer the effects of the appreciation, and premature deindustrialization is under way. If the disease is not very intense, as in the case of Brazil, the symptoms of deindustrialization will not be so clear, although they would be reflected in the decreased participation of manufacturing industry in the domestic product and in diminishing net (value-added) exports of manufacturing goods.[7]

Import taxes neutralize the Dutch disease on the import side; export subsidies, on the export one. When the country abandons all export subsidies that neutralized the Dutch disease on the export side, it will lose export capacity—foreign markets gradually close; when it abandons the import taxes that neutralized the Dutch disease on the import side, it starts to lose the domestic market to foreign competitors. Both things happened in Brazil in the early 1990s and gave rise to a deindustrialization process that was not more severe because the Dutch disease in Brazil has not the gravity of the oil-exporting countries. The resistance of the Brazilian manufacturing industry shows how competent and mature it is. But this is not an excuse for Brazil's not having been able to neutralize the disease and make full positive use of its abundant natural resources. The now again overvalued exchange rate (after the sharp depreciation caused by the 2002 balance-of-payment crisis) will gradually compromise the tradable sectors, one by one. Faced with the fact that their foreign sales are no longer lucrative and that the import of competing goods is growing, enterprises will first redouble their efforts to increase productivity; then they will reduce or suspend exports or will increase the participation of imported components in their production, in order to reduce costs; ultimately in this process they will become mere importers and manufacturers of the good they reexport or sell on the domestic market. In other words, the country's manufacturing industry gradually becomes a "*maquila* industry."[8] Deindustrialization is under way. The sales of manufacturing companies and even their exports may continue to show high values, but their value added will decrease, as well as their value added per capita, as we shall see later, because the components with higher technological content will be increasingly imported.

At this point in the analysis, when it is maintained that deindustrialization is taking place and that its cause is the Dutch disease, conventional economists and people associated with short-term interests in maintaining the system refuse to accept the diagnosis—and this predictable refusal constitutes another symptom of the Dutch disease. They begin then to develop empirical demonstrations to deny it. More radical economists will declare that even if deindustrialization is taking place, it does not prevent economic growth. Yet not only the data but also the very logic of exchange rate appreciation without a decrease in the trade balance surplus indicates that the Dutch disease is present and at work.

Another symptom of the Dutch disease and of premature deindustrialization, besides the decreased participation of manufacturing industry in the product, the increase in the imported component in production, and the relative decrease in exports of manufactured goods measured in terms of value added, is the gradual decrease in the export of high value-added goods. This is precisely what is happening in Brazil. As in the participation of exports of manufactured goods in general, the participation of manufactured goods with high technological intensity in imports is misleading, because the gross exports of companies in the process of transformation into *maquilas* remain high; what decreases is their participation in terms of value added, for which data are not always available. The reason why goods with high technological content are more affected by the Dutch disease, however, will become clear only after we present the concept of the extended Dutch disease.

Even though it has the same outcome, we must not confuse this process of transformation of the country's manufacturing industry into a *maquila* industry as a consequence of the Dutch disease with a more general process, which is the division of labor at the international level. This growing division of production at the international level is a consequence of globalization and has been called by several names: *offshoring* when we think of a multinational company producing components abroad (Blinder 2006), *trade in tasks* (Grossmann and Rossi-Hansberg 2006), or *unbundling* (Baldwin 2006, p. 1) when we want to stress the division of labor. These two latter names clearly imply that the division of labor at the international level is essentially a division not between production sectors or between goods and services but between workers. Or, as Baldwin, for whom globalization is a second historical unbundling, states, "this means that international competition—that used to be primarily between firms and sectors in different nations—now occurs between individual workers performing similar tasks in different nations." Through this process, tasks with higher value added per capita and demanding more skilled labor, formed mainly by managers and communicators, are performed in rich countries, which have plenty of this kind of labor, whereas standardized or codified tasks are transferred to low-wage workers in developing countries. This process of division of labor, which gives birth to *maquilas,* such as those that have long been installed along the Mexican-US border, results from the low-skilled labor available in the developing country. When the country begins to increase the quality of its labor, if the exchange rate becomes overvalued on account of the Dutch disease, this workforce will not find employment. And if the country, as was the case with Mexico and the remainder of its manufacturing industry, has already industrialized but has renounced the mechanisms of neutralization of the Dutch disease, the result is that this large group of enterprises will also gradually become *maquila* business firms. As usually happens, the developing country already has the necessary technological conditions to perform more complex activities in its territory, but it does not actually do so or fails to do so because the Dutch disease is causing an overvaluation of its exchange rate. In this case, the country is limited to low technological content processes. Work processes that require more qualifications are reserved for rich countries, on the assumption that developing countries lack this kind of labor, but this is often not true, and high unemployment rates are observed among skilled personnel in those countries.

The Brazilian economy shows today all the symptoms of an industrialized middle-income country that has ceased to neutralize its Dutch disease. Before the Dutch disease was understood, Brazil fought it off pragmatically with protective tariffs that corresponded to currency depreciation on the import side, combined with subsidies to manufactured goods exports that implied a more depreciated currency on the export side. This implied an effective depreciation of the local currency—a depreciation that implied an export tax on the commodities that caused the disease because it was not extended to them. In the 1930–1980 period, products such as coffee, sugarcane, lumber, cocoa, oranges, soy, and iron pushed down on the exchange rate, but the protectionist system put it back in place, albeit clumsily and often arbitrarily. For some time, a system of multiple exchange rates applied, which was replaced with a tariff system in the late 1950s. The government did not levy a tax on exports because it felt it lacked the political capital to do so, but the tax was adopted in practice through the "foreign exchange appropriation" implied in import tariffs and subsidies to manufactured-good exports.[9] Added to this was a series of industrial policy measures of all kinds. These factors came together to determine an effective exchange rate that neutralized the Dutch disease and thereby became compatible with the transfer of labor to industries with higher per capita value added. As Gabriel Palma (2005) showed, the Brazilian economy managed to develop between 1930 and 1980 only because it adopted a structuralist protection policy and an industrial policy that neutralized the Dutch disease. This policy was retained until the 1980s, but that was the decade of the great foreign debt crisis (brought about by another cause of foreign exchange appreciation: the policy of growth with foreign savings) and of the high and inertial inflation that afflicted the country.

In the early 1990s, however, the policy of neutralizing the Dutch disease was radically abandoned. Even in 1990 an accelerated trade liberalization began that implied an appreciation of the effective exchange rate; in 1992, Brazil accepted opening its capital account, which meant giving up managing the exchange rate and preventing its appreciation through controls over capital inflows. To make things worse, after 1994, Brazil formally adopted the policy of growth with foreign savings that even further appreciated the real. A deindustrialization process has since occurred that is very different from that which has been taking place in rich countries. Whereas in the latter, deindustrialization implies a transfer of labor to industries with higher marketing and technology content, deindustrialization in Brazil is regressive, a consequence of the Dutch disease and of the policy of attracting foreign savings; it is a process that transfers labor to agricultural, mining, agroindustrial, and *maquila*-like industrial sectors marked by low per capita value added: "early deindustrialization" therefore becomes the fundamental source of quasi stagnation.

For some time, I have been identifying the relative appreciation of the exchange rate, caused by the combined Dutch disease and the policy of growth with foreign savings, as a root cause of Brazil's quasi stagnation since the early 1980s. But the corporate representatives of the economic activities that give rise to the Dutch disease, connected in particular with mining and agribusiness, as well as, naturally, the representatives of the conventional orthodoxy, deny the existence of Dutch disease— the former because they fear that, once they acknowledge the disease, the government will impose an export tax to neutralize it,[10] the latter because they are permanently interested in appreciated exchange rates in competing countries. In fact, the properly sized tax on the exports of the commodities that originate the disease will only be paid by its producers nominally; actually, they pay nothing because, if the tax were eliminated, the exchange rate would appreciate and their gain would be the same if not smaller. When the government imposes an appropriate tax, who pays is the whole population that will stop buying cheap tradable goods. This low, however, may be compensated by the government, if it uses the tax resources well.

Those who oppose the diagnosis that the Dutch disease exists in Brazil argue that industrial exports remained high despite the foreign exchange appreciation since 2003, but two kinds of considerations are in order in connection with this. First and foremost, in order to determine whether the Brazilian economy has fallen victim to the curse of natural resources, a longer period of analysis must be adopted; the real effective exchange rate must be known prior to the early 1990s, when the trade liberalization implied a reduction of the effective exchange rate, by virtue of the strong reduction of import tariffs and the elimination of export subsidies. If the exchange rate prior to the 1991 commercial and financial liberalization was substantially higher than R$2.10 to the US dollar (which appears compatible with the "current" exchange rate equilibrium (the one that equilibrates intertemporally the current account), the "industrial" equilibrium exchange rate (that makes utilizing the more advanced technology viable) is probably around R$2.70 to the dollar.

The data are clear. Before 1991, in the 1980s, the average real exchange rate was R$3.11 to the US dollar; it dropped to R$2.08 in the 1990s; two balance-of-payment crises (1998 and 2002) sharply elevated this rate, but in late 2006 it was back to around R$2.15, and in middle 2008, R$1.60.[11] These data in and of themselves are indicators of a foreign exchange appreciation caused by the Dutch disease, and also by the growth-with-foreign-savings policy and the high-interest-rates policy. There is no reason to state that the productivity of Brazilian exports of goods with high per capita value added rose by more than it did in foreign competitors. The appreciation between the 1980s and 2008, however, was greater than 19.6 percent because at the rate of R$3.11 in the 1980s, at least 20 percent must be added to the real exchange rate to arrive at the real effective rate, given the substantial reduction in protection following foreign exchange openness.[12] With this correction, the average exchange rate in the 1980s was R$2.73 and the appreciation from that period to 2006 was 42.3 percent.

Second, the Dutch disease does not prevent the maintenance of industrial plants and the export of manufactured goods as long as firms gradually convert into *maquilas,* limited to assembling imported goods with the use of cheap and unskilled labor. This is why the technology content of Brazilian industrial exports is dropping in absolute terms and particularly as compared with the technology and marketing content of the goods Brazil imports.[13] In 2006 Brazil broke its historical trade balance record: a surplus of US$46.1 billion from US$137.5 billion in exports. With this favorable performance, the symptoms of the Dutch disease arise in many forms: the weak increase in Brazil's manufactured good exports, for example, which rose by only 3.3 percent in 2006 against a 9.9 percent increase in manufactured good exports by developing countries.[14] But it is even more important to examine the source of the trade balance: in 2006, 93 percent came from agribusiness.[15] If we were to add the export balance due to ore and related goods such as steel, the percentage would be even greater, leaving none of the balance to manufactured goods with higher value added. The industry's total trade balance (including the industrial aspect of agribusiness) fell from US$30.9 billion to US$29.5 billion; even more significant than this drop, however, is the fact that the high-tech segment's trade balance showed a deficit rather than a surplus and that this deficit rose from US$8.4 billion in December 2005 to US$11.8 billion in December 2006.[16] In 2006, technology-intensive industrial production rose by 8.5 percent—three times as much as the 2.8 percent of the general index—but looking at the sector's trade balance, we see that exports grew by only 6.8 percent, against a 24 percent increase in imports, so that the industry's trade deficit rose by 40 percent over the previous year.[17] The Dutch disease is gradually deindustrializing Brazil, and, as happened also in Mexico, it is gradually transforming the whole Brazilian manufacturing industry into a *maquila* industry: it continues to export manufactured goods but with an ever-decreasing domestic component of high per capita value added. Therefore, Brazil's performance in exports and, more generally, the country's entire foreign trade show signs of a Dutch disease, not as radical as in an oil-exporting country, which prevents the production of any other tradable goods, but of a disease significant enough to keep the Brazilian economy semistagnant.

Another way of looking at the deindustrializing effects of the fact that Brazil stopped neutralizing the Dutch disease in the early 1990s is to examine what happened to the participation of commodities in GDP and to the share of manufacturing industry in the total production of tradable goods. From 1992 to 2007, although the contribution of commodities to the increase in the trade surplus was positive (162.8 percent), the contribution of manufactured goods to this surplus was negative (–62.8 percent). Among manufactured goods, those whose trade deficit increased most were those adopting high and medium-high technology. On the other hand, the share of tradable manufacturing in the total value added of tradable goods fell from 47.3 percent in 1996 to 39.0 percent in 2005, whereas the share of commodities increased from 52.7 percent to 61 percent (Bresser-Pereira and Marconi 2008). Thus, premature deindustrialization is taking place in Brazil. The labor force is not switching from low-productivity manufacturing jobs in manufacturing industry to high-productivity service jobs, as happens in developed countries, but to low-paid commodity jobs.

Notes

1. For a more complete theoretical analysis of the Dutch disease, see Bresser-Pereira (2008).

2. Investment expenditure evidently also depends on other variables, besides increased exports, such as the interest rate and, particularly, business expectations regarding the future, but these latter would be substantially better should the entrepreneurs rely on an exchange rate that stimulates them to export.

3. See, among others, Razin and Collins (1997); Fajnzylber, Loyaza, and Calderón (2004); and Gala (2006).

4. The idea that the Dutch disease implies a negative externality was suggested to me by José Luiz Oreiro. It is thus easier to understand why it constitutes a market failure—a situation where prices do not reflect the (marginal) social cost of production of goods.

5. In this book, these two rates are always conceived in nominal terms: there is no need to talk about a real exchange rate because the important thing is the difference or the relationship between the two equilibrium rates. Yet we will have to distinguish the nominal exchange rate from the "effective-effective" exchange rate, this latter being understood not only as the result of using a currency basket instead of just one hard or reserve currency to calculate it (which would have just one adjective: "effective") but also as the average exchange rate that results from taking into account the import duties and the export subsidies to which the goods are subject.

6. The tax cannot be imposed only on exports because this would imply an artificial diversion of production to the domestic market.

7. For additional information on the Dutch disease, see Bresser-Pereira and Marconi (2008) and Edgard Antonio Pereira (2007). For a dissenting view, see André Nassif (2008).

8. Multinational firms that were established in the frontier of Mexico with the United States just to use cheap labor were called "maquiladoras": they just assembled parts, and involved low value added per capita. From this followed the expression "maquila industry" to designate all industries that tend to behave like that independently of where they are located.

9. Subsidies to manufactured good exports, which completed the system, began only in the late 1960s.

10. This is what is currently happening in Argentina, which has set export taxes on its farming products, which still retain high returns.

11. Federação da Indústria do Estado de São Paulo (São Paulo Industrial Federation; FIESP), www.fiesp.org.br.

12. Tariff protection in the 1980s was close to 45 percent and by 2006 had dropped to about 15 percent, a 30 percent difference. The addition of 20 percent to the real foreign exchange to arrive at the effective rate in the 1980s is, therefore, conservative. It would imply a rate of R$3.73 and, therefore, an appreciation of the real from the 1980s.

13. Since 1990, industries such as chemicals and electronics have been showing a great imbalance between growth in exports and growth in imports; industrial deficit is a clear indication of the relative drop in the technology content in Brazil's foreign trade (Alem, Mendonça de Barros, and Giambiagi 2002). On the other hand, IEDI (2006) shows that in the 2000s the technology content of Brazil's exports continues to fall.

14. *IEDI Bulletin,* December 2006, Instituto de Estudos para o Desenvolvimento Industrial (Industrial Development Studies Institute), www.iedi.org.br.

15. Ministry of Agriculture quoted in *O Estado de S. Paulo,* January 6, 2007.

16. IEDI (2007a).

17. IEDI (2007b).

7
Overappreciation
and Foreign Savings

I n Chapter 6 we saw that the tendency of the exchange rate in
developing countries to become overvalued is caused principally by
the policy of growth with foreign savings and the Dutch disease. The
former factor causes the exchange rate to be cyclically overvalued, al-
ternating long appreciations with sudden depreciations; the latter causes
it to be chronically overvalued. The main negative effect of an overvalued exchange rate, besides instability itself, is to depress the export-
oriented investments that are key to growth. In this chapter, we discuss
how this theory has applied to the Brazilian economy since 1994 and
particularly since 2003. After the Real Plan, the elimination of the mechanisms that neutralized the Dutch disease (tariffs on imports and subsidies on exports of manufactured goods) and the formal adoption of the
policy of growth with foreign savings caused a major appreciation and
two balance-of-payment crises (which involved sudden depreciations).
Thus, the theory worked well in practice. Again, after the 2002 crisis
and exchange rate peak depreciation, as we will see in this chapter, the
exchange rate strongly appreciated, confirming the theory. Yet this appreciation did not cause a balance-of-payment crisis because exports increased explosively after that, and the country was able to build large
international reserves. In 2003 and 2004 the export increase was explained
by the 2002 depreciation and by the sharp increase in commodity prices
reflecting the growth of China. In the following years exports continued
to grow, stimulated exclusively by international prosperity, given the
fact that in 2006 the exchange rate had already come back to the overvalued levels of the 1990s (see Chapter 9). Why so? Essentially because
the aggravation of the Dutch disease that originated in the commodity

prices increase is consistent with balanced and even surplus trade and current accounts, yet it is not consistent with the health of manufacturing industry. On the contrary, it is the cause of increased and premature deindustrialization.

Besides the Dutch disease, however, there is a second structural cause for the tendency to the overappreciation of the exchange rate: the attraction that developing countries represent to foreign capitals owing to the relatively higher profit and interest rates prevailing in these countries as a consequence of capital scarcity. Such attraction causes huge capital inflows that overappreciate the currency. Thus, when we examine the exchange rate in a developing country, we must always take into consideration two components: the Dutch disease and the capital inflows component. In this chapter I will discuss the policies that aggravate such attraction, and particularly the main development policy that, through the World Bank and the IMF, conventional orthodoxy proposes to developing countries: the growth-with-foreign-savings policy.

Growth with Foreign Savings

Foreign savings are the counterpart of current account deficits. A country that has a current account deficit is attempting to grow with other countries' savings: the countries that have current account surpluses. Until the 1960s, the policy of growth with foreign savings remained a theoretical one insofar as advanced countries, since the 1930s, had strictly limited foreign loans to developing ones. But in the 1970s, international banks felt more at ease offering loans and had abundant funds from petrodollars available. Thus, the policy of growth with foreign savings gradually superseded the role of the law of comparative advantage in practically neutralizing developing countries' growth efforts.

Brazil, which had already completed its industrial revolution, had every reason to grow more rapidly than rich countries. Economic theory predicted that after developing an economic infrastructure and a modern class of industrial entrepreneurs, a developing country would show growth in a self-sustained way and would catch up, that is, would gradually converge on its development levels, as economic theory predicts. Brazil completed its industrial and capitalist revolution in the 1970s, but, after that, its growth rate was strongly reduced while macroeconomic instability prevailed. If I were asked why this instability and quasi stagnation occurred and my response had to be limited to a single cause, I would harbor no doubt in stating that it was the attempt to grow with foreign savings—a major cause of the tendency to the overappreciation of the exchange rate—and its three consequences: high rate of substitution of foreign for domestic savings, foreign financial fragility, and recurrent balance-of-payment crises. Every growth period was usually accompanied by increased current account deficits insofar as the policy was to grow with foreign capitals, the exchange rate appreciated, and after the country experienced a high substitution of foreign for domestic savings and increased foreign financial fragility, it ended in a balance-of-payment crisis.

Brazil's first experience in this domain since the 1930s happened in the 1970s and ended up in the great 1980s debt crisis. After 40 years of restrictions to foreign indebtedness, the international financial system changed policy in response to the excess liquidity in the world economy that followed the first 1973 oil shock. Lacking a critique of the policy of growth with foreign savings, developing countries hastily took advantage of this "opportunity" to finance their planned investments, not realizing that a large part of it would go eventually to consumption through the process of currency appreciation and artificially increased wages. When the opportunity offered by the recycling of the petrodollars materialized, it was immediately accepted, since all schools of economic thought believed that growth should happen with foreign savings. During the 1970s, developing countries—Latin American ones in particular—went heavily into debt, and the result was the severe macroeconomic destabilization and major economic crisis in the early 1980s. Nevertheless, after the crisis of the 1980s, international loans to developing countries came back in force in the 1990s, with the full support of the conventional orthodoxy, which formally adopted the policy of achieving growth with foreign savings. It is not surprising that the new foreign debt became a fundamental factor making for macroeconomic instability and missed growth.

The critique of this policy only began in the early 2000s. Whereas new developmentalism adopted a harsh attitude toward public indebtedness and foreign indebtedness, the conventional orthodoxy, which is supposedly "strict," remained faithful to its strategy of using foreign loans as a means of neutralizing medium-income countries' international competitiveness. In fact, new developmentalism is more demanding than the conventional orthodoxy concerning the intertemporal equilibrium of foreign accounts, despite the "tough" rhetoric that the orthodoxy has dressed itself in. The conventional orthodoxy sees it as "natural" that a developing country should have high public and foreign debt, as long as such debt levels remain stable, and likewise regards it as "natural" that the interest rates on these two kinds of debt should be high and that the exchange rate should be relatively appreciated (consistent to the level of current account deficit) but not appreciated to the level that would make the country unable to start paying off the debt with revenues from exports. For the conventional orthodoxy, a current account deficit means that the country is receiving foreign savings, which it assumes to be necessary to growth. New developmentalism rejects this loose view—compatible with exchange rate populism and with the capture of the public wealth by rentiers. For macroeconomic stability to be achieved, the foreign debt must be small and under control. Highly indebted nation-states are financially fragile nations constantly subject to the "advice" of the conventional orthodoxy and prone to balance-of-payment crises. Besides, the growth-with-foreign-savings policy implies increased indebtedness without a corresponding increase in the investment rate insofar as the ensuing appreciation of the national currency causes a high rate of substitution of foreign for domestic savings. When a nation-state has a high level of foreign debt, its citizens must achieve extraordinary savings just to pay the interests on the debt.

Actually the 1970s growth-with-foreign-savings policy promoted by rich countries, besides being a form to use the abundant petrodollars originated in the 1973 first oil shock, was useful in neutralizing medium-income countries' competitive capacity. Until then, the law of comparative advantage, in addition to being one of the landmarks of economics, was the ideological instrument with which imperialism exerted its domination in order to neutralize late-developing countries' attempts to protect their infant industries. Britain was first to use it, against late-developing European countries. Rich countries then used it against developing ones. In the 1940s, Raúl Prebisch, Celso Furtado, and Hans Singer criticized this theory. Paradoxically, however, the pioneers of development economics also believed in the need for growth with foreign savings. The big push theory of the 1940s is nothing other than this.[1] The same thesis is embedded in Latin American structuralist theory, which defended protecting infant industries but did not realize the strategic nature of the exchange rate. It is central to the "associated dependency" theory of the late 1960s.[2]

On the part of the North, until the 1970s, its central banner in relation to economic growth was trade liberalization. Yet, as developing countries demonstrated competitiveness in producing even sophisticated manufactured goods, it became increasingly clear that commercial globalization would be advantageous to rich countries only in combination with financial liberalization and a series of steps to reduce the policy space open to medium-income countries. This was achieved within the framework of the WTO Uruguay Round of trade talks (Wade 2003; Chang 2006). On the other hand, after the foreign debt crisis was relatively resolved by the Brady Plan (which got its name from US secretary of the Treasury Nicholas Brady), another form of neutralizing medium-income countries' international competitiveness was formulated: the policy of growth with foreign savings combined with opening the capital account. In the early 1990s, after the collapse of the Soviet Union and the unfettered hegemony the United States achieved in this decade, new times were beginning with the administration of Bill Clinton. Under the orientation of the US Treasury, the IMF and the World Bank ceased to be concerned with developing countries' foreign debt and announced what they should now do was to grow. The prescription was simple: they just had to grow with foreign savings; they should compete for the foreign savings of rich countries. For that, they were supposed to add to their list of reforms an additional one: the opening of the capital account. Foreign savings became the central concept of the new times: instead of the "development *cum* debt" of the 1970s, or "structural adjustment" of the 1980s, developing countries should now engage in a great competition to obtain foreign savings. In fact, the rich countries were merely returning to a classical form of making profits and neutralizing the growth capacity of developing countries, by getting them indebted.

Like any successful ideology, the policy of growth with foreign savings has a simple—and apparently reasonable—formulation in the sentence "capital-rich countries are supposed to transfer their capital to capital-poor countries." Because poor and medium-income countries believed in this proposition, they became highly indebted in the 1970s and faced a major debt crisis in the 1980s, returned to current accounts deficits in the 1990s, saw their currencies appreciate, and again fell into balance-of-payment crises: Mexico in 1994, four Asian countries in 1997, Brazil and Russia in 1998, and Argentina in 2001. This unintentional but effective means of neutralizing the competition of countries equipped with cheap labor had almost been forgotten in the great debt crisis of the 1980s, in which rich countries felt threatened. But it would become clear again in the early 1990s, with the beginning of another wave of capital flows to developing countries, now called "emerging markets." The idea was born in the US Treasury and immediately embraced by the IMF and the World Bank.[3]

Naturally, the stated objective of the new policy was not to neutralize medium-income countries' competitive capacity but to contribute to their growth; in practice it was the natural, and largely unconscious, way that the powerful countries define what is "good" for the others. For rich countries' governments, represented by Washington's international agencies, and mainly for those countries' financial and commercial multinational enterprises, the idea of competition among medium-income countries for getting the capitals (loans and direct investments) was attractive because it gave them additional power. For multinationals, the idea of being wooed instead of subjected to political constraints was even more attractive because it made them more secure. For advanced countries, that their medium-income competitors appreciated exchange rates brought only benefits.

At that time, in the early 1990s, soon after the fall of the Berlin Wall, the United States was at the acme of its prestige and power. Developing countries, in turn, found themselves weakened by the foreign debt crisis and by the high inflation that many, Brazil in particular, were experiencing. As such, developing countries widely accepted financial globalization, which even appeared to be a natural complement to trade globalization; that is, opening the capital account seemed like an obvious step to follow the trade liberalization that had already taken place. The more dependent a country was, the more quickly it adopted the tempting proposal from the North of growth with foreign savings, that is, with current account deficits. Some sounder or more prudent Asian countries did not let themselves be fooled. Others bowed to the ideological hegemony, accepted the strategy, incurred heavy current account deficits, and finally experienced the severe balance-of-payment crisis of 1997. But they learned fast, devaluing their currencies and immediately returning to current account surpluses. On the other hand, Brazil, like almost every Latin American country, plunged with determination into the competition for foreign savings, faced balance-of-payment crises, and did not develop.

Under the nineteenth-century British ideological hegemony and its core argument, namely, the law of comparative advantage, developing countries always knew that protecting their infant industries was essential in the first stage of their industrialization. Many of their leaders knew of the role Alexander Hamilton had played in the United States in the early nineteenth century. Friedrich List's book (1999 [1846]), in which he defended protecting infant industries and identified the use of the law of comparative advantage as a "kicking away the ladder" practice against countries in the position of Germany, whose economic development was late, had been read by many politicians, economists, and business leaders in Latin America.[4] Still, although the combined adoption of open capital accounts and growth with foreign savings has been disastrous for middle-income countries, it seems that their elites were not able to adapt List's reasoning to the present: criticism of these two policies has been slow to surface.

There has been some criticism of financial liberalization. Deepak Nayyar (2003, p. 74), for example, notes that "financial liberalization . . . has been associated with the emergence of a new rentier class and the inevitable concentration of financial assets has probably contributed to worsening income distribution." But the critics of opening the capital account did not extend their criticism to the policy of growth with foreign savings, because it continued to appear "obvious" that the capital-rich countries should transfer funds to capital-poor countries. But nothing is more important for developing countries than to cast the most strategic of macroeconomic prices—the exchange rate—in a key role in economic development and to criticize this policy of growth with foreign savings. Although countries such as China and India keep financial flows and the exchange rate under control and grow sustainably, in the 1990s in Brazil, as in other Latin American countries with the exception of Chile, the exchange rate remained relatively appreciated because of the excessive and uncontrolled inflow of capital. Only after the balance-of-payment crises late in the decade did some of them change their policies. Before, it was precisely after the opening of the capital account and the formal adoption of the policy of growth with foreign savings— in the early 1990s—that the exchange rate began its appreciation. There is an enormous surplus of poorly compensated capital around the world in search of more investment with better returns. Developing countries that open their capital accounts and adopt the policy of growth with foreign savings that creditor countries propose see their small economies flooded with capital of all kinds that appreciates their currencies. To prevent foreign exchange overvaluation, developing countries have no choice but to create barriers against incoming capital or to buy reserves.

Asian countries, including those that dropped their guard for a while and faced crisis, have been using one or the other mechanism to prevent their currencies from gaining value. Their better-balanced income distribution enables them to avoid foreign exchange populism, unlike Latin American countries.[5] Among these latter, only Chile consistently adopted a policy of controlling incoming capital through the 1990s. In 2005, however, it capitulated to US pressure and the short-term interests of exporters, entering into a bilateral free trade agreement with the United States. The first condition the agreement stipulates is the prohibition of controls on capital inflows. That is, Chile has agreed to cease managing its exchange rate. As a result, and because the price of copper has risen, the exchange rate has been appreciating dangerously in Chile. It would be no surprise if its economic performance should worsen in the coming years.

The extension of financial globalization to developing countries, or, more specifically, their adoption of the policy of growth with foreign savings and opening the capital account, brings into existence the unintentional but effective process of neutralizing the competitiveness of countries with access to cheap labor. This process can be divided into three stages. First, current account deficits cause a process of substituting foreign savings for domestic savings. As repeated current account deficits occur, the country's financial or equity (resulting from direct investment) foreign debt increases so that, at the second stage, the country becomes indebted, financially weakened, and, therefore, financially dependent on others: any inability to roll over debt can lead to a balance-of-payment crisis; as a consequence, the country is or feels compelled to embrace confidence building, that is, to adopt creditors' recommendations without subjecting them to the due criticism based on the national interest criterion. The third stage is crisis: whether because foreign debt–to–GDP or foreign debt–to–exports levels have become excessive or because they gather dangerous speed, creditors, who have already been downgrading the debtor's risk rating, suddenly decide to suspend rolling over the debt; the country starts bleeding reserves, and finally is left with no alternative other than a debt moratorium.

There is, however, a situation in which foreign savings do contribute to economic development instead of hampering it. In the rare cases where a country is already growing fast and, for this very reason, offers investors high profit opportunities, resorting to foreign savings may be a valid choice for a while, as the wage increases deriving from foreign exchange appreciation will not flow entirely to consumption. The marginal propensity to consume drops and the middle class invests a substantial share of the national income, attracted by the particularly favorable returns. This, however, is a rare occurrence. The last time it was clearly manifested in Brazil was during the 1968–1973 "miracle."

The early and mid-1990s were the times of the policy of growth with foreign savings; in the late 1990s, these times were over. In this moment, the conventional orthodoxy again underwent correction, such as the shift from dollarization, that is, from a fully fixed exchange rate to a floating rate, but orthodoxy remained loyal to its proposed policy of growth with foreign savings. Developing countries, however, changed. Developing countries learned from the financial crisis in Asia, Brazil, and Russia: they practically rejected growth with foreign savings and started achieving large current account surpluses. Whether for this reason or because the world is experiencing a period of great prosperity, the crises have disappeared and the IMF's loans portfolio has dropped by more than two-thirds: from US$70 billion in the late 1990s, it had fallen to around US$20 billion in 2006.

Foreign savings is a curious expression in the national accounts: the savings are, by definition, the current account deficit. The term *foreign savings* is used because the deficit will have to be financed by a reduction of international reserves or by foreign finance. If there were an assurance that the net results of direct foreign investment would be used to increase the rate of capital accumulation, there would be some justification for the policy of growth with foreign savings, but no such assurance exists. Yet, as with loans, the direct investments that finance current account deficits almost always end up financing consumption rather than investment. Rich countries do receive direct investments, but, as these countries' direct investments are mutually offsetting, the goal is not to finance the current account deficit or even to increase investment but rather to increase competition and absorb technology. In addition, these countries know the pitfalls of growth through foreign indebtedness. In the nineteenth century Britain often used debt as a strategy to reduce countries to colonial status.[6] Rich countries themselves never used foreign savings to grow or did so marginally at most. The story that this is how the United States grew in the nineteenth century is a myth. Yet, repeating the classic strategy of "do as I say, not as I do" (Ha-Joon Chang 2002), the conventional orthodoxy doesn't hesitate to counsel developing countries to use direct investments and loans to finance their current account deficits: that is what it calls the "growth with foreign savings" strategy.

The balance-of-payment crises that took place in the 1990s and culminated with the Argentine crisis in 2001 induced advocates of the policy of growth with foreign savings to become more cautious. But the assumption that capital-rich countries should transfer their funds to capital-poor ones still stands as one of the conventional orthodoxy's pillars. My criticism is aimed precisely at this assumption, which is as misleading as it is obvious. Economics, like other sciences, is full of such cases where one must reject what appears to be common sense. It is important not to confuse this with criticism of opening the capital account.

A debate has emerged among economists on the topic of financial openness and capital flows: some criticize liberalization, whereas others are enthusiastic proponents. The latter embraced the neoclassical assumption that all liberalization is beneficial and argued that financial liberalization is as necessary for development as trade liberalization and that both should take place simultaneously. Among the critical studies, one of the most significant is by Rodrik (1998), who showed that there is no evidence that countries without capital controls enjoy greater growth. A significant work, in view of its place of conception, was by Prasad, Rogoff, Shang-Jin, and Khose (2003); in it the four economists connected with the IMF found that no evidence exists that financial globalization had helped developing countries grow any faster.[7] Many economists have discussed the destabilizing nature of the open capital account as a result of the increased exchange rate volatility it causes. Opening the capital account, however, is not enough for bad results to emerge. One must, at the level of development economics, add the criticism of growth with foreign savings, of which, to the best of my knowledge, there is nothing of significance to be found in the literature. After outlining this criticism in 1999 and 2001, in 2002 I began a series of papers on this topic.[8] There are now significant studies on the subject, especially the research undertaken by Gala (2006), who has recently shown that dynamic Asian countries maintained a competitive exchange rate and grew mostly with domestic savings; Berr and Combarnous (2007), in turn, studying Latin America and the Caribbean, showed that between 1990 and 2003 the countries that adopted the policy of growth with foreign savings became weaker.[9] Within the framework of open capital accounts, it is the policy of growth with foreign savings that pushes the exchange rate down or up. My criticism is therefore aimed at the very heart of the conventional orthodoxy, whose assumption is that developing countries need foreign savings in order to grow. On the contrary, under normal circumstances the countries that did adopt this policy lagged behind.

Countries that adopt the policy of growth with foreign savings undergo three perverse stages. There is no need to criticize this strategy once it has come to the second or third stage, as the damage done to the country becomes obvious. I will therefore limit my analysis to stage one, at which the country has not yet suspended international payments, or even gotten deep enough into debt to become dependent on creditors and therefore compelled to adopt the alienating practice of confidence building, but has fallen victim to the perverse process of substituting foreign savings for domestic savings because, through appreciation of the exchange rate, a sizable share of the foreign funds that should hypothetically increase investment ends up as increased consumption.[10]

The policy of growth with foreign savings has a complementary policy, namely, fiscal deepening policy. Financial deepening is just an elegant name to justify high interest rates that will attract capital inflows; it was introduced by McKinnon (1973) and Shaw (1973) in the 1970s, when many developing countries controlled their interest rates and often kept them negative. Besides, "capital deepening" should convey earnestness in terms of economic policy, whereas "administered interest rates" conveys economic populism. Another complement to the policy of growth–*cum*–foreign savings is the use of the exchange rate and particularly the use of an exchange rate "anchor" to control inflation. This policy became popular in the 1990s, after Argentina in 1991 controlled hyperinflation by fixing the exchange rate in relation to the US dollar. The disastrous consequences of such a policy are well-known even by the conventional orthodoxy, which after the late 1990s abandoned it in favor of a floating exchange rate. Yet, the practice of using exchange rate appreciation to control inflation remains central to the conventional orthodoxy. We saw in Chapter 5 that most of the success of Brazil in reducing inflation since 2002, when the depreciation of the real pushed it to around 10 percent, is due to the subsequent appreciation. On the other hand, when the exchange rate becomes overvalued, the acceleration of inflation that depreciation will cause easily prevents such depreciation from taking place. This acceleration is temporary in an open, competitive, and nonindexed economy; the inflation bubble will soon subside. But the stigma of high inflation can be so significant, as it is in Brazil, that—faced with any acceleration of inflation rates, however temporary—people fear the return of high inflation, legitimizing the Central Bank's interest rate hikes, even in the absence of excessive inflation, simply to appreciate the exchange rate and make sure that the exchange rate goes back down.

Exchange rate populism is also a cause of the tendency to the overappreciation of the exchange rate. For some years, I have been using this expression to define the malpractice of populist politicians who use the appreciation of the exchange rate to get reelected. An appreciated exchange rate is attractive in the short run as it implies higher real wages and higher profits than an exchange rate competitive rate would provide. The rich, who measure their wealth in dollars, see it grow every time the foreign exchange rate increases in value. The wage of the middle class, with its relatively high component of imported consumption, rises when the local currency gains value. Even the poorest benefit from real wage increases with uncompetitive exchange rates, as a portion of the products in their consumption basket becomes cheaper. Members of the government have an interest in an appreciated exchange rate because it pleases voters, and as a result, they do not hesitate to practice what I have been calling *foreign exchange populism*. And the government's economists who accept the conventional orthodoxy's single mandate for the Central Bank—controlling inflation—also have an interest in an appreciated exchange rate because they can say—as has become usual in Brazil recently—that the appreciation of the real was "good" because it increased wages. In fact, we have two types of economic populism: fiscal populism, when the state spends more than it receives, and exchange rate populism, when the nation-state spends more than it receives. The conventional orthodoxy criticizes the former but is sympathetic to the latter because exchange rate appreciation is consistent with its central proposal to developing countries (growth with foreign savings). Let us, then, first examine this policy, and then discuss the Dutch disease—the two main factors behind the tendency to the overappreciation of the exchange rate.

Foreign Savings and No Growth: 1994–2002

The quasi stagnation that has prevailed for so many years in the Brazilian economy is directly related to the acceptance of the policy of growth with foreign savings. From 1930 up to the late 1960s, Brazil's industrialization and growth were essentially financed by domestic savings. In the early 1970s, when foreign indebtedness again became a possibility for developing countries, Brazil used it to finance the "Brazilian miracle" (1968–1973). This was a classic moment in which foreign savings played a positive role in growth: since investment opportunities were very good, the increase in wages and salaries did not flow into consumption but into investment. After that, however, in this same decade, particularly in 1979 and 1980, Brazil was one of the countries that resorted most irresponsibly to foreign finance. This explains why the 1980s debt crisis had such a negative impact on the Brazilian economy. After the crisis Brazil opened its capital account in 1992 and, based on the Real Plan's success in stabilizing prices, again engaged in the policy of growth with foreign savings, but now with added gusto. Then began a massive inflow of speculative capital drawn by the apparently good prospects of the Brazilian economy and by the high interest rates. The immediate consequence was the explosive appreciation of the real. This appreciation turned the foreign trade surpluses that the country had been reporting since 1983 (when it depreciated the currency) into high current account deficits that matched perfectly the policy of growth with foreign savings that the North was then prescribing for the South. The combined effects of these two policies were disastrous for the economy of Brazil and other Latin American countries. The only exception was Chile, which, like the Asian countries, was able to control incoming capital and defend its exchange rate from the appreciation associated with current account deficits. The last time the Brazilian economy showed high growth rates was in the 1970s. Since then (as Table 1.3 showed), it has remained semistagnant. Although income per inhabitant rose by 6.1 percent a year in the 1970s, in the 1990s and the first seven years of the 2000s it grew only 1.09 percent and 1.84 percent respectively, notwithstanding the influence of foreign savings in the 1990s.[11]

After 1995, Brazil openly and firmly adopted the policy of growth with foreign savings. The Brazilian elites were convinced that the country would develop only by resorting to foreign savings. President Fernando Henrique Cardoso had held this belief since the late 1960s when, with Enzo Faletto, he formulated his "theory of associated dependency."[12] As Cardoso took office at the peak of a neoliberal and globalist ideological wave from the North, whose core thesis was precisely this, it is easy to understand why his administration gambled all of its chips on this strategy. Thanks to the abundant loan and venture capital available from the globalized system and to the good prospects for the Brazilian economy that accompanied the price stabilization achieved in 1994, Cardoso had no trouble putting into practice a policy that seemed the epitome of reason, and the country showed ever-increasing current account deficits. The result, however, was not increased investment and growth rates, but semistagnation.

In his first four-year term (1995–1998), the Cardoso administration fully adopted the policy of growth with foreign savings and incurred large current account deficits, converting a surplus of 0.9 percent of GDP in 1992 into a deficit of 4.73 percent of GDP in 1999 (see Table 7.1), ending in a severe balance-of-payment crisis. This crisis, whose immediate cause was the suspension of the rollover of Brazil's public and private debt by foreign creditors, was clearly related to the country's high indebtedness level. By late 1998, the debt-to-exports ratio had increased more than fourfold. Reelected, in January 1999 the president immediately allowed the exchange rate to float, the real depreciated by around 30 percent in real terms, and the country seemed to move again in the direction of macroeconomic equilibrium and, possibly, resumed development. Soon after that, however, in July 1999, when the short-term interest rate was still astronomical, the government decided to implement an inflation targeting policy. Having lost the exchange anchor, it wanted, with support from the IMF, to replace it with a monetary anchor

Table 7.1 Foreign Savings, Domestic Savings, and Investment as Percentage of GDP, 1992–2006 (selected years)

	Foreign Savings[a]	Domestic Savings	Investment[b]
1992	−0.92	19.35	18.42
1994	0.44	19.83	20.75
1996	3.15	16.12	19.26
1998	4.32	15.37	19.69
1999	4.73	14.17	18.90
2001	4.45	15.02	19.47
2003	−0.62	18.41	17.78
2005	−0.49	16.43	15.94
2006	−2.86	19.36	16.50

Sources: Instituto de Pesquisa Econômica Aplicada (Institute for Applied Economic Research), www.ipeadata.gov.br; and Instituto Brasileiro de Geografia e Estatística (Brazilian Institute for Geography and Statistics), www.ibge.gov.br.
Notes: a. Foreign savings = current account deficit.
b. Investment = gross fixed capital formation.

(Blanchard 2005). It was the wrong time to implement such a policy, as it had been conceived to manage a certain monetary policy regime, not to change it, as we will see later in this chapter.

Brazil, caught since 1994 in a trap of high interest rates and uncompetitive exchange rates, needed to change its regime, to develop a strategy to lower the basic interest rate that weighed on the public debt, and thereby threw the state's finances out of balance. But this was not done. Because the inflation targeting policy was adopted in 1999, when the short-term interest rate was still very high, the equilibrium interest rate that became part of its macroeconomic model was around 9 percent; as a result, the country itself became formally caught in the trap of high interest rates and uncompetitive exchange rates into which it had already fallen. The 1998 crisis notwithstanding, the government was still convinced that the policy of growth with foreign savings was appropriate. This strategy, combined with the high interest rate, caused the exchange rate to appreciate again after the 1999 depreciation, so that the foreign debt–to–exports ratio remained above 4. Given such indebtedness levels, given a stagnant economy, and, since the second half of 2002, given a new threat as perceived by creditors in the form of the probable election of a Workers Party presidential candidate, Luís Inácio Lula da Silva, it is no surprise that the country should face a second balance-of-payment crisis.

As Table 7.1 shows, the current account deficit or foreign savings Brazil received increased steadily between 1994 and 1999: in 1994 the deficit was 0.92 percent of GDP and in 1999 it was 4.73 percent. Still, as predicted by the theory behind the critique of the policy of growth with foreign savings that I am proposing, the investment rate did not rise; in fact, going beyond what the theory predicts, it dropped a little, from 20.75 percent of GDP in 1994 to 18.90 percent in 1999. In the 1995–2002 period, the current account deficits were financed by loans and direct investments. Direct investments rose dramatically, as we can see from Table 7.2: in 1995, direct investments were limited to 0.62 percent of GDP, but exceeded 5 percent of GDP in 1999 and 2000, thus fully financing the current account deficit.[13] Nevertheless, as can be seen from Table 7.1, the economy's total rate of investment did not grow in this period but fell, indicating that the rate of substitution of foreign for domestic savings was higher than 100 percent! What did rise was net income transferred abroad and foreign indebtedness. How to explain why the high level of direct investment did not increase the country's rate of capital accumulation? The critique of the policy of growth with foreign savings provides an explanation.

In much the same way, the investment rate did not decrease as exports and foreign savings decreased after 1999. As we can see from Table 7.1, between 1999 and 2006, foreign savings fell by 7.59 percentage points of GDP, whereas the investment rate decreased just 2.4 percentage points.

Table 7.2   Direct Foreign Investment and Net Income Transferred Abroad as Percentage of GDP, 1995–2007

	Direct Foreign Investment	Net Income Transferred Abroad
1995	0.62	1.6
1996	1.39	1.5
1997	2.35	1.9
1998	3.66	2.4
1999	5.33	3.7
2000	5.44	2.9
2001	4.41	3.8
2002	3.61	3.8
2003	2.00	3.5
2004	3.00	3.3
2005	1.91	—
2006	1.69	—
2007	2.43	—

Sources: Instituto de Pesquisa Econômica Aplicada (Institute for Applied Economic Research), www.ipeadata.gov.br; and *Conjuntura Econômica* [Economic Conjuncture], www.fgv.br/ibre/cecon.

How to explain this? How were domestic savings able to grow so fast and replace the foreign savings? We might argue that the explanation lies in the same criticism offered against the policy of growth with foreign savings, but this would be true only by virtue of the fact that, with depreciation, real wages and domestic consumption dropped, thus increasing domestic savings. In fact, the two depreciations caused a change in the prices of tradable goods relative to the prices of nontradable ones. As a consequence, the average wage, that is, the price of the nonmarketable good par excellence—labor—dropped in this period. The resulting drop in worker income—which, according to the PNAD for 2004, the latest information available, amounted to 18.8 percent between 1996 and 2003—allowed a reduction of consumption and an increase in domestic savings.

The other main reasons why increased domestic savings offset the drop in foreign savings were the 2.5 percentage-point reduction in the budget deficit (and, therefore, the relative increase of public savings) between 1999 and 2003 and the increase in the investment needed to enable increased exports. Thus, a foreign accounts bonanza began in 2003, when the Lula administration was inaugurated. In fact, the period has been a bonanza for the economies of almost every country, boosted by growth in China and the United States. In 2004, Brazil's GDP grew by 5 percent as a result of increased exports, but the Central Bank's decision to increase an interest rate that was already at absurd levels limited growth in 2005 to a mere 2.4 percent. During the first three years of the Lula administration, the Brazilian economy grew at a slightly brisker pace than under the preceding administration, but at about half the rate achieved by medium-development countries similar to Brazil. Most seriously, however, thanks to the increased exports, the exchange rate gradually began to appreciate again and, in early 2006, it was already close to R$2.00 to the US dollar. Exports remained strong in 2005, but there were many indications that manufactured goods exports were beginning to lose momentum, whereas imports were rising. In other words, the country, trapped as it was by high interest rates and an uncompetitive exchange rate, slowly returned to the policy of growth with foreign savings.

Substitution of Foreign for Domestic Savings

We can now determine what happened in Brazil after the Real Plan. Between 1994 and 1999 the current account deficit rose sharply and, therefore, so did the foreign savings received, whereas the investment rate remained practically unchanged. Then, as predicted by the model, domestic savings were replaced with foreign savings. After 2000 or, more accurately, after the 1999 depreciation of the real, the process started to go into reverse: a structural shock transformed a current account deficit of 4.73 percent of GDP in 1999 to a 2.86 percent current account surplus in 2006 (see Table 7.1), implying a foreign adjustment of 7.59 percent of GDP. Table 7.1 also showed that with the drop in foreign savings the investment rate decreased but in a much smaller proportion: in fact, if we compare the average 2006 investment rate with the same figure for 1999, the investment rate fell just 2.4 percentage points as domestic savings substituted for foreign savings. This happened because, as the model predicts, wages dropped and so did consumption, thereby increasing domestic savings on the supply side, whereas on the demand side exports grew (more than doubling between 2002 and 2006, as Table 7.4 shows), leading to increased investment in the tradable goods sector and, therefore, to increased domestic savings as well. In Brazil, the reverse substitution process was amplified in the period by the fiscal adjustment that began in 1999, which reduced the size of the negative public savings, and by improved trade ratios since 2003. If the model we introduced is accurate, the first period should show a high rate of substitution of foreign for domestic savings and the second should show an equally high, if not higher, rate of substitution of domestic for foreign savings.

The rate of substitution of foreign for domestic savings in a given period is just given by the division of the negative change of domestic savings (in percentage points of GDP) by the positive change in foreign savings (ignoring the signals and multiplying by 100); in its turn, the substitution of domestic for foreign savings in another period is given by the division of positive change of domestic savings by the negative change of the domestic savings. Table 7.3 summarizes the measurements of the two substitution rates. To measure the rate of substitution of foreign for domestic savings in Brazil in the period that this book is addressing, I chose the period when foreign savings were clearly on the rise (1994–1999) and, to measure the reverse process of substitution of domestic for foreign savings, I selected the period when foreign savings were declining (1999–2006). The basis adopted for measuring the change was the initial year of each period. The results are not surprising on its direction or on its dimension; the two rates are very high, one of them superior to 100 percent. In the first period, the substitution of foreign for domestic savings was 131.9 percent, since the decrease in domestic savings was bigger than the increase in foreign savings. In contrast, in the second period the rate of substitution of domestic for foreign savings was 68.4

Table 7.3 Rate of Substitution of Foreign for Domestic Savings (1994–1999) and of Domestic for Foreign Savings (1999–2006)

Years	Foreign Savings, Sx (% of GDP)	Domestic Savings, Si (% of GDP)	Period	ΔSx	ΔSi	$\Delta Si/\Delta Sx$ (%)
1994	0.44	19.83	—	—	—	—
1999	4.73	14.17	1994–1999	4.29	−5.66	131.9
2006	−2.86	19.36	1999–2006	−7.59	5.19	68.4

Source: Compiled by the author with data from the Instituto de Pesquisa Econômica Aplicada (Institute for Applied Economic Research). www.ipeadata.gov.br.
Note: Data on foreign savings and domestic savings are from Table 7.1.

percent since the increase in domestic savings was smaller than the diminution in foreign savings but still a very high increase.

Other researchers, although unequipped with a theory to explain the phenomenon, measured the shift in domestic savings caused by foreign savings in various countries and periods, and most come up with a figure of around 50 percent.[14] I am not aware of studies showing the opposite substitution when foreign savings are falling. Instead of falling strongly, investments fell moderately with the fall of foreign savings—which explains the 75 percent substitution. It would have been 100 percent if the substitution had been full; 0 if no substation had occurred. The increase in domestic savings that occurred in the period could be predicted by the model: when the exchange rate depreciates, wages and salaries fall and consumption also falls. But it was not the drop in real wages alone that enabled this outcome; the fiscal adjustment the government had promoted since 1999 and the increase in exports since 2002 pushed by a major increase in the prices of the commodities the country exports also explain the good behavior of domestic savings.[15]

In this chapter I have reexamined, from a critical perspective, the policy of growth with foreign savings that after the early 1990s became part of the conventional orthodoxy, that is, of the set of diagnoses and recommended reforms and economic policies for developing countries. I have shown that countries that accept such strategies see their development neutralized in a three-stage process, from the substitution of foreign for domestic savings, through indebtedness and financial fragility, to a balance-of-payment crisis. The latter two stages imply that the country has exceeded its foreign debt threshold and require no criticism. The first stage, however, must be criticized because in it the rate of substitution of foreign for domestic savings tends to be high inasmuch as the inevitable foreign exchange appreciation that coexists with the current account (which defines the strategy itself) artificially raises wages and increases consumption while reducing export-oriented investments. This means that the country goes into debt, whether financially (through financial instruments) or in terms of equity (through direct investment), theoretically in order to increase its investment capacity, but in the end, a significant portion of the resources received substitutes for domestic savings or, in other words, is diverted into consumption. This will not happen only in the exceptional case that the recipient country's economy is growing at a fast pace, offering extraordinarily high profit opportunities, because at such times the fee-earning middle class and the capitalists will show a greater than normal propensity to invest. On the other hand, when the country decides—is forced, that is, by crisis—to give up the strategy of chronic current account deficits, the reverse should happen, with the substitution of domestic for foreign savings.

I assume that the model applies to all economies that decide to accept the recommendation of growth with foreign savings and do not have great profit opportunities to show, but since I have formulated it based on the Brazilian experience, I applied it directly to Brazil's case. I have defined the rate of substitution of domestic savings as the change in domestic savings relative to foreign savings and have seen in Table 7.3 that in the period when foreign savings were rising (1993–1999) the rate was 68.4 percent. On the other hand, when current account deficits fell and became a surplus (2000–2005), the rate of substitution of domestic for foreign savings was 131.9 percent.

Brazil developed extraordinarily after 1930 and completed its capitalist revolution in the 1960s, or the 1970s at the latest. It was therefore to be expected that its development should become relatively self-sustained, as predicted by development economics. But this was not the case. The Brazilian economy has been semistagnant since then. Why? Based on the model and on the findings, I have concluded that the main reason why economic growth failed to become self-sustained was that, starting in the 1970s, the country became involved in the policy of growth with foreign savings that ended in unprecedented crisis in the 1980s; in the 1990s the policy was repeated, again with disastrous consequences. As such, criticizing the growth-with-foreign-savings policy is crucial if medium-income countries are to achieve what economics predicts: once industrialized, equipped with a state and a business class that arises with the capitalist revolution, to converge gradually to rich countries' development levels.

State Exports and Some Growth Since 2003

The strong appreciation of the real that has been taking place since early 2003 confirms the trend of the exchange rate to become overvalued, discussed in the previous chapter. (This appreciation will be shown in part in Figure 7.1.) With the Real Plan, the increased confidence of foreign investors and speculators in the Brazilian economy, combined with the rising interest rate and the establishment of the policy of growth with foreign savings, caused huge capital inflows and a marked foreign exchange appreciation beginning in the second half of 1994. The consequence was the disastrous 1995–1998 period, with high exchange appreciation and a greatly increased foreign debt, ending with the balance-of-payment crisis of the second half of 1998 that led to the introduction of the floating exchange rate regime and the sharp depreciation of January 1999. The conventional orthodoxy prefers the term *financial crisis* to *balance-of-payment crisis,* but the fact is that financial crises in developing countries are almost always related to creditors' refusal to roll over foreign debt. In line with the ideology of the conventional orthodoxy that has prevailed since the early 1990s, namely, that growth must come from foreign savings or current account deficits, creditors say they are concerned only with public debt; foreign debt would be unimportant according to the twin deficits hypothesis and the Lawson doctrine,[16] which assumes that the market will provide a satisfactory resolution for private debt. But this is mere rhetoric; in fact, creditors are chiefly concerned with foreign debt and the current account deficit, as they know that in certain cases the state may be able to meet its commitments internally, but the nation-state may lack the wherewithal to settle its debts should foreign creditors suddenly decide not to continue rolling over the foreign debt, as they did in 1998 and, again, in 2002. This second crisis, besides having economic causes, also had a political cause: the Lula candidacy. After the election, the new government revealed its willingness to continue its predecessor's orthodox economic policy, and the market calmed down.

After the 2002 balance-of-payment crisis and after a black 2003, the performance of the Brazilian economy clearly improved as GDP increased in the following three years by, respectively, 3.6, 3.75, and 5.2 percent. These rates were substantially inferior to those of most developing countries but represented an improvement. Yet they were not the outcome of a policy change but were caused principally by increased demand for and prices of the commodities exported by Brazil as a result of world prosperity, especially China's, which enabled Brazilian exports to double over a period of five years (Table 7.4). In a few years the large current account deficit changed into a reasonable current account surplus (Markwald and Ribeiro 2006; Bauman 2006). In 1999 the current account deficit amounted to 4.73 percent of GDP (see Table 7.1); by 2003 the country had found balance in its current account and in the two subsequent years achieved a current account surplus in excess of 1 percent of GDP. From 1999 to 2005, therefore, an enormous foreign adjustment took place, amounting to 6.4 percent of GDP.[17] As a consequence, the country's foreign debt–to–exports ratio fell dramatically, as seen from Table 7.5, and, in March 2008, Brazil was elevated to "investment grade"

Table 7.4 Exports, 1999–2007

	Exports (US$ billion)	Index (2002 = 100)
1999	55.2	79
2000	64.6	92
2001	67.5	97
2002	69.9	100
2003	83.5	120
2004	109.1	156
2005	134.4	192
2006	137.5	197
2007	160.6	230

Source: Instituto de Pesquisa Econômica Aplicada (Institute for Applied Economic Research), www.ipeadata.gov.br.

Table 7.5 Foreign Indebtedness Ratios and Brazil Sovereign Risk

	Foreign Debt/ Exports Ratio[a]	Foreign Debt/GDP (%)[a]	Brazil Sovereign Risk (EMBI+)[b]
1995	3.42	22.58	933
1997	3.77	24.76	521
1999	5.03	45.00	640
2001	3.88	44.34	870
2002	3.77	49.56	1,439
2004	2.28	36.40	383
2005	1.58	28.30	305
2006	1.23	15.82	192
2007	1.20	13.59	222

Sources: Data from www.bloomberg.com and indebtedness rates computed based on the database of the website of the Instituto de Pesquisa Econômica Aplicada (Institute for Applied Economic Research), www.ipeadata.gov.br.
Notes: a. Foreign debt in December each year.
b. Sovereign risk as measured by J. P. Morgan's Emerging Markets Bond Index Plus (EMBI+).

by Standard and Poors. Public foreign debt, which was 29 percent of GDP in 2001, became zero in net terms in the following years, as the Central Bank swapped US dollar–denominated federal bonds for domestically indexed securities and bought dollars in an attempt to prevent exchange rate appreciation.

After this export shock, the Brazilian economy faced the classic paradox involved in the natural resources curse or Dutch disease: the disease was aggravated by the price increase since it made exports of commodities profitable with an even more appreciated currency, but the economy prospered, pushed by commodity exports. Even the manufacturing industry sector performed reasonably well because, as it lost foreign markets, it gained domestic ones owing to the increase in real wages and salaries. This increase in exports, together with an interest rate kept at very high levels, ensured an inflow of currency (which confirmed the tendency to the overvaluation of the national currency), causing the US dollar to fall against the real to a highly appreciated level by mid-2008.[18] As Pastore and Pinotti (2006) noted, "the cycle of increased international commodity prices that began in the early months of 2002 led to a 50 percent growth in the average prices of Brazilian exports, which allowed the real exchange rate to appreciate without hurting exports." From a rate of almost R$4.00 to the dollar, Brazil went to R$1.70 to the dollar at the end of 2007, notwithstanding the Central Bank's large (but still insufficient) dollar purchases. At the same time, as Figure 7.1 shows, the real exchange rate had not yet reached its 1995–1998 levels but was clearly at a level inconsistent with the country's need to increase exports, investment, and domestic savings—and therefore inconsistent with a reasonable average annual growth rate of 5 percent. At these exchange rates, exports and the trade balance remained high, but there were clear signs already of reduced manufactured goods exports. On the other hand, the increase of imports at a pace substantially brisker than that of exports through 2006 is another indication that the exchange rate cannot be sustained in the medium run.[19] Consider, in addition, that the industrial sectors that are least affected by the foreign exchange appreciation are those with a high share of imported inputs, operating, therefore, under a model similar to Mexico's *maquilas*.

Concerned with foreign exchange rate appreciation, the Brazilian authorities have been trying to manage it in practice, even though they claim that the inflation rate is their sole target. They are therefore in contradiction with the conventionally orthodox thesis that the long-term real exchange rate cannot be managed. But they have not met success because they must purchase reserves to prevent appreciation, acquiring funds in the domestic market. Yet they are unable to buy as much as they would need to prevent appreciation because the high domestic interest rate implies a brutal fiscal cost that a state already deep into debt cannot afford. Whereas Asian countries pay 1–2 percent real interest rates, Brazil, through its Central Bank, pays 9–15 percent real annual interest rates when the country buys reserves. The Central Bank has been buying since 2004, so that in early 2007 Brazil's international reserves exceeded US$100 billion; in addition, it has traded US dollar–denominated debt for real-denominated debt at an almost equal amount, in an attempt to prevent the currency's appreciation; these figures are high, but the Central Bank should have bought far more, as dynamic Asian countries do, in order to contain the drop of the US dollar. The alternative would be to impose controls on incoming funds, a choice the country renounced when it opened its capital account in 1992, and to levy

Figure 7.1 Real Exchange Rate and Accumulated Exports Since 1993

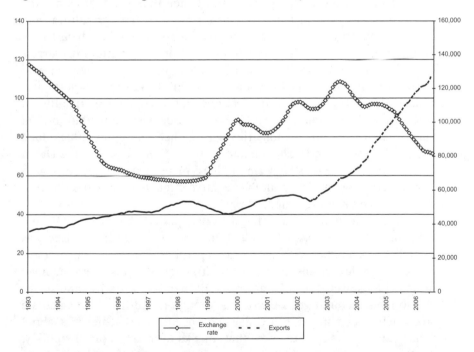

Source: Fundação Centros de Estudos de Comércio Exterior (Center of Studies of Exterior Commerce, Funcex).

Notes: Measurements are made in January of each year. Deflators: FGV = Fundação Getúlio Vargas; IPC = consumer price index; DI = internal availability.

FGV IPC-DI and CPI for 13 countries (trade current-weighted average); 2003 average = 100. Exports accumulated over 12 months.

taxes on Dutch disease–causing goods. Sooner or later, the country will have to adopt a combination of these three policies if it is to resume growth.

The conventional orthodoxy camp always has optimists who, in much the same way that they claim that resumed development is just around the corner, vow that structural changes are beneficial to Brazilian exports and make the current exchange rate compatible with growth. This is a mistake made by economists who have apparently abolished the law of supply and demand. There is no reason to believe that the Brazilian economy has undergone a structural shock capable of changing its equilibrium exchange rate. Structural shocks do happen, but they require that the country's productivity increased at a substantially higher rate than that of the other competing national economies; they require a change in productivity levels in industries with high per capita value added relative to other countries' competing industries—which has not occurred in Brazil. Had it taken place in a large number of farming industries, we would have a generalized Dutch disease. This is not the case either; it is not just manufacturing but also the agricultural and livestock industries that are being hit by the appreciated exchange rate. True, certain export goods benefit from the country's natural resources, such as sugar and ethanol, iron and steel, and oil, and their international prices are currently very high and contribute to keeping exports at a high level.[20] The very low cost of these goods leads to an artificially appreciated exchange rate compatible with a trade balance in equilibrium, but stifles or jeopardizes industries with higher per capita value added that produce with the latest technology. It is a "mild case" of the Dutch disease, limited as it is to a small share of the export of goods with higher technology content; but the negative effect it already has on them should not be underestimated.[21]

During the national-developmentalist period, between 1930 and 1980, one of the reasons why Brazil grew at an extraordinary pace was its ability to keep the exchange rate competitive. This was done by indirect and complex means, through a multiple-exchange system or, since the late 1960s, based on a combination of high import tariffs and subsidies to manufactured good exports. Although it is difficult to calculate how much of a competitive effective exchange rate was achieved, Gabriel Palma (2005) managed to show that, thanks to the structuralist policy, the Brazilian economy behaved over this long period as if it were an economy poor in natural resources. It was thus able to maintain a competitive effective exchange rate, avoiding the Dutch disease—which the country has been unable to do ever since it liberalized its trade account and, above all, its capital account.

Given the Brazilian authorities' submission to the Washington Consensus, expressed in this case in the refusal to introduce temporary controls on capital inflows and in the maintenance of exceedingly high interest rates that prevent the purchase of reserves at the levels needed, what we see is the Brazilian government's inability to control its exchange rate. This allows us to predict the resurgence of severe balance-of-payment problems in the not too distant future. All it will take for the Brazilian economy to get into trouble again at the foreign accounts level is a reversal of the present highly favorable situation of the global economy and a fall in commodity prices.

Notes

1. Development economics, since its founding paper (Rosenstein-Rodan 1943), has been supported on this thesis: see the paper by Lewis (1958 [1954]) and the two-gap model of Chenery and Bruno (1962), which are fundamental; the Latin American structuralist theory, a version of development economics, was also adopted since Raúl Prebisch (1963); for Keynesian economics, see McCombie and Thirlwall (1994), McCombie (1997), and Porcile and Tadeu Lima (2006), who take up the structuralist concept of higher income elasticity in imports than in exports.
2. Cardoso and Faletto (1970 [1969]), although admitting that Latin America had grown with domestic savings until the 1950s, claim that from the 1960s onward it could grow only with foreign savings; for a recent discussion of the problem, see Bresser-Pereira (2005c).
3. The US undersecretary of the Treasury was at this time Lawrence Summers, who had previously been head economist of the World Bank.
4. Roberto Simonsen, for example, who was probably the first articulate advocate of national industry, used this book repeatedly in his studies (Cepeda 2004).
5. The Asian Tigers themselves lowered their guard in the early 1990s, which led them into the crisis of 1997. Faced with the crisis, though, these countries, which had reserves of about US$200 billion at the time, devalued their currencies, and now their accumulated reserves amount to nearly US$1 trillion. They clearly purchased reserves to prevent the exchange rate from appreciating again owing to the inflow of funds not only from increased exports but also from resumed capital flows. China, whose growth rate has long been exceptional, keeps capital movements under control and its exchange rate relatively devalued.
6. In 1882, for example, bankers from Britain and other European countries, with their governments' cooperation, offered loans to Viceroy Ismail of Egypt intended to finance his sumptuous and grandiose projects, at high rates that made repayment impossible. When default was confirmed, Britain saw it as an excuse to intervene. Egypt remained under the domination of the British Empire until Gamal Abdel Nasser led the country's independence in 1952.

7. This IMF discussion paper shows that there is a difference between what its analysts state in papers and the institution's officially recommended policies. Despite the pressures they endure, some economists are able to say more in their work than their superiors would like to read. It is easy to imagine that this paper, despite not quite making any direct criticism, was not welcome. And it is no surprise that in 2006 the four authors published a "reappraisal."

8. See Bresser-Pereira (2001a [1999], 2001b, 2002a, 2004b), Bresser-Pereira and Nakano (2003), Bresser-Pereira and Varela (2004), and Bresser-Pereira and Gala (2008).

9. According to Berr and Combarnous (2007, p. 541), "although the discourse has evolved [due to balance-of-payment crises], the practices nevertheless remain strongly linked to a growth strategy oriented toward foreign savings that is denounced by Bresser-Pereira [2002a]. Our results confirm that such an approach weakens Latin American and Caribbean economies and holds them under the supervision of IFIs."

10. For a discussion of balance-of-payment crises or foreign exchange crises, see Alves, Ferrari Filho, and Paula (2004). In their review, the authors distinguish first-, second-, and third-generation models; these models invariably cast the public deficit in a leading role in explaining the crises. A postgraduate student of mine, Lauro Gonzáles, is writing a thesis to show that the roles of the policy of growth with foreign savings and, therefore, current account deficits are truly the deciding factor.

11. Data from the website of the Institute for Applied Economic Research: http://www.ipeadata.gov.br.

12. Cardoso and Faletto (1970 [1969]). My criticism of this theory can be found in Bresser-Pereira 2005b.

13. In 1999–2000, direct investments exceeded the current account deficit, which means that the country paid off some of its financial debt.

14. Gala (2006) provides a survey of this research.

15. Although the primary surplus was around 0 percent of GDP from 1995 to 1998, in the 1999–2002 period it was around 3.5 percent and, in the following four-year period, around 4.5 percent. Fundação Centros de Estudos de Comércio Exterior (Center of Studies of Exterior Commerce; Funcex), www.funcex.com.br.

16. The thesis was so named because it was adopted by British finance minister Nigel Lawson in the 1980s.

17. Given the current account deficit in 1999 (4.73 percent) and 2005 (−1.65 percent), the adjustment was exactly 6.38 percent of GDP.

18. In October a sharp depreciation of the real took place; in a few days the exchange rate moved from R$1.60 per dollar to R$2.30. It was triggered by the global financial crisis, but its cause was the overappreciation of the real and the perspective of a rapidly increasing current account deficit.

19. Here is one sign among many: whereas the exports quantum rose by 4.7 percent in the 12 months ending in June 2006, the imports quantum rose by almost twice as much, 8.1 percent, in the same period. Data from the website of the Institute for Applied Economic Research: http://www.ipeadata.gov.br.

20. In the period between 2002 and the first half of 2006, exports (12-month accumulated) in the sugar industry rose by 107 percent, those in the

extraction and minerals industry by 163 percent, steel by 128 percent, raw oil and coal by 228 percent, and refined oil by 170 percent. In total, exports increased by 107 percent in the period. Sugar exports rose by the same amount as the total. Data from the website of the Institute for Applied Economic Research: http://www.ipeadata.gov.br.

21. The exports of technologically intense products (according to the OECD categorization) rose by 30.3 percent in 2004, 34.3 percent in 2005, and just 7.2 percent in the 12 months ending in June 2006: www. funcex.com.br; Ministry of Development, Industry, and Commerce [MDCI]; and IEDI 2007a.

8
High Interest Rates

In the previous chapters I discussed, first, the alleged causes of low growth rates in Brazil, namely, lack of reforms and a continuing inflation threat; second, a cause of low growth rates correctly identified by the conventional orthodoxy, namely, insufficient fiscal adjustment; and, third, the Dutch disease and the policy of growth with foreign savings, which cause, respectively, the exchange rate to be chronically and cyclically overvalued. In this chapter I discuss the high interest rate prevailing in Brazil. Together with the overvalued exchange rate, it is a constituent of the macroeconomic trap that has ensnared countries adopting the conventional orthodoxy. Between 1980 and 1994, high and inertial inflation was the most severe symptom of Brazil's macroeconomic imbalance; since then, the most severe symptom has been the high interest rate. In much the same way as it was impossible, back then, to contemplate economic growth with monthly inflation rates of between 10 percent and 20 percent, since 1995 it has been impossible to resume economic development with real short-term interest rates of between 8 percent and 15 percent. Real interest rates were already stratospheric before 1995 but were masked by high inflation. After high inflation was brought under control in 1994 and after the 1999 exchange rate devaluation, it became increasingly clear that the great problem the Brazilian economy still faced in achieving macroeconomic balance and, thus, the conditions to resume development was the Central Bank's high real short-term interest rates.

These rates have varied over time but have remained gargantuan since the late 1980s. In the 2000s, the average real short-term interest rate has been 11 percent—and rarely less than 8 percent. Although the high interest rate is repeatedly blamed on public indebtedness, other countries with development and indebtedness levels similar to Brazil's have much lower interest rates, as seen from Table 8.1. A comparison of the Brazilian short-term interest rate with those of other countries leads to the realization that this is a Brazilian problem that neither characterizes other developing countries nor is related to the country's public indebtedness level. Márcio Holland (2006b, p. 1) computed Brazil's real interest rate between 1996 and 2004 at 14 percent and, drawing a comparison with other countries, concluded that "the domestic interest rate should be, on average, eight percentage points below that level."

As it weighs directly or indirectly on the entire public debt, the high short-term interest rate present in Brazil is incompatible with fiscal adjustment itself. As it sets the levels of long-term loans, this short-term rate—the Selic—should also be incompatible with the investment needed to resume development. The inconsistency, however, is partially compensated by government subsidies to the investments of large corporations and farmers: in the first case, through the long-term interest rate (TJLP); in the latter, through subsidized farming credit. The TJLP has been lower than the Selic itself and provides no spread to the Banco Nacional de Desenvolvimento Econômico e Social (BNDES), which, however, has access to a significant amount of almost cost-free funds and

Table 8.1 Public Debt and Short-Term Real Interest Rate, 2006 (selected countries)

	Public Debt (% of GDP)	Real Interest Rate[a]
Brazil	57.4	11.06
Turkey	74.4	5.60
Mexico	24.4	3.82
Russia	34.8	2.00
South Korea	15.8	1.96[b]
China	29.6	1.30
Philippines	71.5	1.03
Chile	14.8	1.22
India	62.2	0.68
Thailand	46.6	−0.90[b]
Argentina	64.0	−1.79

Source: The Economist, www.economist.com.
Notes: a. 2006 data computed by subtracting the April 2006 consumer price index from the short-term interest rate.
b. For these countries, the May 2006 consumer price index was used.

can therefore bear this vast subsidy. Yet, knowing very well that subsidies are necessary for minimal investment to occur, Brazilian business-people and economists shy from the term—aware as they are of the pathetic oxymoron of a policy based on the conventional orthodoxy, as Brazil's has been since 1995, embracing massive compensating investment subsidies. In fact, these subsidies prove the irrationality of the Central Bank's basic interest rate: they would not be needed if the rate were reasonable.

The Selic is equally incompatible with fiscal adjustment. We saw in Chapter 7 that the continuing fiscal imbalance in Brazil is mainly the result of the extraordinary weight of the interest rate on public expenditures. Alan Blinder (1999, p. 70), referring to the short-term real interest rate, says that "this rate is relevant to practically no economically interesting transaction." He has in mind, of course, the United States and other "normal" countries. In Brazil, however, the rate is relevant to a transaction of immense interest to rentiers: it is the interest rate on a large share of public bonds. This is a legacy from the high inflation period that central bankers and Brazilian governments more generally have shown no inclination to solve or courage to address.

A major fiscal effort was made in the early 1990s, and the country achieved fiscal balance: for four years the budget deficit was zero. After 1995, however, public deficits returned because of the state's high spending in the social area and the maintenance of the interest rate at a very high level.[1] Despite a massive increase in the tax burden that began at the time, public deficits remained relatively high. Then, and under the new logic of the conventional orthodoxy, *budget deficit* was deleted from the lexicon and was replaced with *primary surplus*—a variable that interests the state's creditors and disregards interest expenditure. In practice, with the Central Bank's absurd interest rate and the massive public debt, all attempts at adjustment were self-defeating, insofar as the weight of interest expenditure as a share of public expenditures rose extraordinarily. The primary surplus target agreed upon with the IMF and demanded by domestic and foreign owners of the public debt, however, was reached and so was the goal of the privileged creditors of the Brazilian state, namely, a stable public debt–to–GDP ratio consistent with a high interest rate.

Finally, the interest rate the Central Bank of Brazil has been enforcing since 1995 is incompatible with capital accumulation and development because, besides requiring high profit rates to make investments viable, it exerts pressure on the exchange rate and causes the real to appreciate. In this manner, the interest rate strengthens the trend of keeping the exchange rate at a relatively appreciated level, a result of the Dutch disease, of the abundance of capital in the world, of the lower profit rate usually encountered in developing countries, and of the policy of growth with foreign savings. An overvalued exchange rate will defeat any development strategy.

Economics regards a policy of interest rates as high as those in Brazil for so many years as aberrant. The interest rate is inevitably a controversial topic, as it involves the interests of businesspeople, workers, and rentiers. In the Brazilian case, however, except for rentiers and their associates, the Central Bank's interest rate causes only losses. Businesspeople lose because they are discouraged from investing; workers lose because the employment level is reduced. The only winners are rentiers and the financial industry, which collects fees from rentiers. But, except for the financial industry, this policy is perhaps already becoming a negative-sum game in which everybody loses, as such high interest rates mean an immeasurable loss of GDP, which allows one to assume that everyone would be better off today had such high interest rates not prevailed in Brazil since the stabilization achieved with the Real Plan.

But for many years Brazilians accepted this curse as something "natural." The laws of economics, however, are not natural, and there is nothing natural about a short-term interest rate of between 8 percent and 15 percent in real terms, when it ranges from 0 to 3 percent elsewhere. It is a disease that results from other economic variables or from variables that are not necessarily economic (structural, cultural, or institutional) or from hidden interests and the economic policy that embodies them. In this chapter I attempt to show that it most likely results from the last of these possibilities. This demonstration is central because, if true, the Brazilian economy can be rid of this malaise far more easily than the parties interested in high interest rates lead us to believe.

The Short and Long Terms and Brazil's Sovereign Risk

Why is the short-term interest rate so high in Brazil? The simplest answer one may be tempted to offer is that it is high because the Brazilian state lacks credit. Because of the severe fiscal maladjustment, the answer seems reasonable. But why is it so severe? Not because the public debt–to–GDP ratio is too high, but, as we have seen, because the state interest expenditure–to–GDP ratio is astronomical relative to that of other countries. Therefore, it is not the fiscal imbalance that determines the interest rate, but the interest rate that determines the chronic fiscal crisis. Of course, this is a two-way process (the interest rate causes fiscal imbalance, which reinforces the high interest rate), but the evidence allows no doubt about the main causal direction.

For the conventional orthodoxy, this answer is unacceptable because it would remove one of its main excuses for not seeking a lower short-term interest rate. Apart from a few more sophisticated economists aligned with the orthodoxy, conventional economists choose to argue that the cause of the absurd level of Brazil's short-term interest rate lies in fiscal maladjustment. What they find most attractive in this thesis is that it allows conditioning any reduction of the short-term interest rate on "resolving the fiscal maladjustment" and, as a result, such a reduction is indefinitely delayed. "First," they claim, the fiscal problem must be addressed, and only "later" can the interest rate fall. No matter that these conventionally orthodox economists have been at the helm of the Brazilian economy since 1993 and are, therefore, responsible, wholly or partly, for any fiscal maladjustment. No matter, either, that since 1999 the fiscal goals set—primary surplus targets as defined by the IMF—have been strictly met. From this one might logically conclude that the fiscal maladjustment has been overcome, and the short-term interest rate could start to fall in earnest. But these contradictions are irrelevant. What matters is keeping the interest rate high and, to this end, the need for additional fiscal adjustment—which, by the way, is in fact needed—becomes an armor-clad excuse.

Before 2002 another—simpler and even more mistaken—explanation was cited for the high interest rate. Whenever anyone asked why the interest rate was so high in Brazil, the almost deadpan answer was "because Brazil's sovereign risk is very high." That is, the interest rate was high because Brazil's international credit was low, because Brazil's sovereign risk as assessed by rating agencies such as Moody's and Standard and Poor's was high.[2] The thesis seemed reasonable because, at the time, Brazil's sovereign risk was in fact high, at around 700 points; add to this the interest rate on US Treasury bonds and expected inflation in Brazil, and the result was, on occasion, close to the nominal Selic rate. And so, through the confusion between short-term interest rates, which do not depend directly on *ratings,* and long-term interest rates, which do depend on them in the presence of foreign debt, the matter was "solved."

But since the beginning of 2002, with the publication of a paper on a strategy of development with stability (Bresser-Pereira and Nakano 2002), it has become clear that Brazil's sovereign risk cannot be held responsible for high interest rates. Contrary to the generalized belief that had prevailed until then, there is no correlation between long-term interest rates or sovereign risk and the base, or short-term, interest rates adopted by the central banks of various countries; the correlation, which exists by definition, is between risk ratings and long-term interest rates. We showed this with a simple table containing 2001 data, which is reproduced here as Table 8.2. It clearly shows that countries with risk ratings equal to or lower than Brazil's have much lower interest rates. If the same table were built with current figures, the numbers would naturally differ, but the lack of correlation would remain. Bresser and Nakano's arguments on interest rates, made public in early 2002, had great and generally very favorable repercussions. The text included new ideas that would subsequently become the topic of several academic papers and broad public debate. The topic of interest rates finally entered the country's agenda.[3]

The argument that Brazil's high sovereign risk explained the high short-term interest rate involved confusion between short-term and long-term interest rates. The confusion begins with the indexation of public bonds to the Selic, so that it is not the long-term interest rate but the short-term one that weighs on Brazilian public debt bonds. The Central Bank's interest rate policy thereby affects public debt directly, instead of in a merely indirect manner as is the case in normal countries. In those countries, short-term interest rates are determined by central banks in their attempts to influence the long-term interest rates on public

Table 8.2 Risk Ratings and Short-Term Real Interest Rate, 2001

	Risk Rating[a]	Real Short-Term Interest Rate
Argentina	CCC+	33.47
Indonesia	CCC+	4.39
Turkey	B–	–2.97
Russia (July IPC)	B	4.08
Venezuela	B	2.18
Brazil	BB–	10.95
Peru	B–	4.10
Colombia	BB	3.28
India (August IPC)	BB	1.71
Mexico	BB+	0.87
Philippines	BB+	7.27

Sources: Bresser-Pereira and Nakano 2002. The country ratings were obtained from Standard and Poor's; the real interest rates were obtained from *The Economist,* www.economist.com.

Note: a. October 2001 data except where noted. IPC = consumer price index.

bonds, whereas in Brazil it is the Central Bank that defines the long-term interest rate that is here institutionally confused with its short-term counterpart.

There is a long-term interest rate in Brazil, but it is not internally determined as there is no domestic market for long-term loans other than the public bonds market; it is defined externally by the interest rates that leading Brazilian companies pay abroad and, therefore, by Brazil's sovereign risk. It doesn't matter, therefore, that the Selic is not coupled with the long-term interest rate, that is, the market rate that depends on Brazil's sovereign risk. For those interested in high compensation for those holding public bonds, it is the short-term interest rate that matters. The conventional orthodoxy and financial market players, who do not hesitate to lean on market fundamentalism when it comes to the interest to be collected from the state, prefer this interest to be set by a captured Central Bank rather than defined by the market.

The indexation of the interest rate on public bonds to the Selic implies the absence of a true long-term interest rate in Brazil. Yoshiaki Nakano (2006b), quoting Arnold Harberger (1996), notes that, according to this University of Chicago economist, the Central Bank's true independence depends on banking reserves not being used to finance the state. This is not the case in Brazil, where banking reserves are mixed up with capital market funds in financing the public sector. Therefore, Nakano concludes: "Brazil does not have a market for long-term bonds at pre-set rates, nor a true interest rate framework. The Brazilian public debt's profile is short-term, with an average maturity of little more than two years. This means that we must refinance almost half of the public debt within a year. As a result, public bonds have a twofold grip on the bonds market, through their volume and their high interest rate."

Given that public bonds are oddly compensated at the short-term interest rate, the long-term interest rate does not exist in practice, unless understood as the interest rate on international loans taken out by the government and top-tier Brazilian corporations. How is this rate determined? If the likelihood of default as estimated by creditors is zero, the rate will equal that on US Treasury bonds. As the expected risk increases or drops, so does the interest rate demanded by creditors. The effective likelihood of default is always connected with foreign debt, whether public foreign debt, where the state is the debtor, or total foreign debt, where the debtor is the nation-state. This likelihood varies depending, respectively, on the size of the public deficit and of the public debt and, mainly, on the size of the current account deficit and of the foreign debt. In the case of the nation-state's foreign accounts, where foreign debt is already at high levels, creditors will understand that the country's risk is high and demand a high long-term interest rate. The long-term interest rate remains high in Brazil because the country still has relatively high levels of foreign debt; only public foreign debt has been overcome.

When we showed, in 2002, that no correlation existed between countries' risk ratings and the short-term interest rate, the demonstration was surprising for those who had explained the high level of this interest rate in Brazil by reference to the country's then-high sovereign risk. In fact, there was nothing surprising about this, given the theoretical and practical disconnect between the two variables. Still, one might expect a drop in Brazil's sovereign risk to bring about a corresponding drop in the short-term interest rate, because some correlation, even if not perfect, certainly exists between the short-term and the long-term interest rates. But what we have seen in Brazil since the export boom of 2002, which allowed the government to pay off its foreign debt, was that Brazil's sovereign risk dropped vertically during the 2002 crisis from 700 points to little more than 200 points without a fall in the Selic—the rate on public bonds, the rate set by the Central Bank (Figure 8.1); there was only a nominal drop in 2006 made possible by reduced inflation. As Nakano notes (2006a), "because of a perceived drop in Brazil's sovereign risk and no expected exchange-rate devaluation, the domestic interest rate should have dropped." But that did not happen in Brazil. The explanation lies in the empirically verified behavior that the Brazilian interest structure systematically displays: an anomalous and inverted inclination, that is, the Central Bank's very short-term interest rates are, as a rule, higher than long-term ones determined "freely by the market." The uncoupling of the two variables has proved radical. The exogenous character of the long-term interest rate in Brazil is clear, because, as we will see later, the Selic directly indexes 50 percent of Brazil's public bonds and, indirectly but closely, 100 percent, so that, oddly (differently from all other countries), the interest rate that remunerates state creditors is not the long-term but the short-term interest rate.

The assumption that the short-term interest rate was also determined by Brazil's sovereign risk included the additional assumption that the risk ratings that determine sovereign risk and the long-term interest rate would also determine the short-term interest rate. The argument we offered in 2002, based on Table 8.2, was based not on the lack of direct relationship between the risk ratings and either the short- or the long-term interest rate in Brazil but on the fact that making a cross-country comparison, we could not find a relationship between the short-term interest

Figure 8.1 Brazil's Sovereign Risk and Real Interest Rate

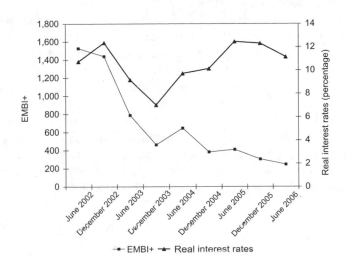

Sources: J. P. Morgan for the Emerging Markets Bond Index Plus (EMBI+) or Brazil's sovereign risk; Instituto Brasileiro de Geografia e Estatística (IBGE) for the Índice de Preços ao Consumidor Amplo (Extended Consumer Price Index; IPCA); and Central Bank for the short-term interest rate, or Selic.
Notes: Data for June 30 and December 31 of each year.

rates and sovereign risk ratings. Thus, we concluded, the explanation that the interest rate in Brazil is high "because the risk of Brazil is high" is false. When Brazil's sovereign risk dropped and the short-term interest rate failed to follow suit and a large gap opened, the lack of connection between the two variables then became clear. The Selic is high in Brazil not because the sovereign risk is high (it is not so anymore) or because of the "need to fight inflation," but to compensate generously and directly rentiers—the state's creditors. Since public bonds in Brazil and specifically the return on Letras Financeiras do Tesouro (Treasury Financial Bonds; LFTs) pay directly the Selic or short-term interest rate decided by the Central Bank, this rate plays a role that in other countries is attributed to a market rate of interest: the long-term interest.

To see how long-term interest rates can be substantially lower than short-term ones, one must have a clear understanding of the difference between the two—a distinction that the conventional orthodoxy always leaves unclear when discussing interest rates in Brazil, failing to point out that one is endogenous and the other exogenous. The long-term interest rate is endogenously defined by the market. In a country that still has foreign debt (only the public foreign debt has been paid off), the real long-term interest rate depends on the risk foreign creditors perceive. Risk as perceived by domestic creditors is irrelevant to the determination of the long-term interest rate because long-term financing is almost nonexistent in Brazil, except for what BNDES offers, and because Treasury bonds pay the short-term interest rate, Selic. This, however, pushes up the international rate inasmuch as domestic creditors' mistrust can spread to foreign creditors. True, this contagion has lost momentum in recent years, as can be seen in Brazil's falling sovereign risk while the short-term interest rate remained stratospheric.

The Wolf and Sheep Story

As seen in Chapter 7, the fact that the state is excessively indebted is not the main cause of the high interest rate because the index that most clearly depicts fiscal imbalance—the state interest expenditure–to–GDP ratio—is precisely the one that depends on the very interest rate we want explained. The short-term interest rate, as discussed above, is not high because the Brazilian state lacks credit: the rate that might be high because of this is the long-term interest rate, which is now much lower than the short-term interest rate. What, then, is the reason? When Bresser and Nakano (2002) made it clear that this explanation lacked substance, the old fable of the wolf and the sheep in a stream was repeated. If it is not because of that, it is because of that, or of that, or of that that the wolf eats the sheep. Some economists at the Pontificia Universidade Católica (Pontifical Catholic University, PUC) in Rio de Janeiro immediately came forward.[4] They did not accept that the monetary authorities should assign multiple purposes to the interest rate and gave an assurance that, under the inflation targeting policy, the Central Bank has a single purpose: to keep the inflation rate under control. Not one of them sought to defend the conventional wisdom of the time, according to which interest rates in Brazil were high because of the country's high sovereign risk. They insisted that the problem of inflation remained, and controlling it required high interest rates.

Why does the Central Bank need a real basic interest rate of between 8 percent and 10 percent to keep inflation under control, when other countries achieve the same results with much lower rates? Is it not true that what matters for controlling demand is the *change* in the interest rate, not its level? How to explain that Brazil's base real interest rate is much higher than those in other countries with similar risk ratings? And why does it not fall when sovereign risk does? Or even when inflation does? The interest rate is certainly an appropriate instrument to fight demand-side inflation and smooth out the economic cycle. But when there is no excess demand, why keep the interest rate at such high levels? In addition, why not make the real basic interest rate float, not between 1 percent and 3 percent as rich countries do, but between 0 percent and 5 percent, as other countries do with risk ratings similar to Brazil's? Given the cyclic nature of capitalist economies, the real short-term basic interest rate in Brazil should vary as a countercyclical mechanism, as is the case with monetary policy elsewhere. Therefore, when the economy heats up and the risk of inflation rises, the Central Bank raises the interest rate; when a deceleration of the economy can be foreseen, the rate is reduced. In rich countries, the short-term interest rate used as a monetary policy instrument hovers in the vicinity of 1 percent; it is often negative in real terms, and there is nothing surprising about this. In developing countries, it would be reasonable to consider a slightly higher short-term rate. But in Brazil, as we have seen, it is stratospherically higher.

To determine whether the short-term interest rate is high as a means to fight inflation, an early test is to compare the short-term real interest rate and the inflation rate. In principle, using annual means, it would be reasonable for the short-term interest rate to fall after the inflation rate fell. If a high interest rate were needed to control inflation, a lower inflation rate would signal to the Central Bank when to lower the Selic. This is not, however, what Figure 8.2 shows. The inflation rate drops, but the real interest rate remains high, even when the inflation rate is compared with the subsequent year's interest rate.

When Bresser and Nakano published their 2002 article, which included what I believe was the first consistent criticism of the interest rates used in Brazil, some illustrious conventionally orthodox economists tried to refresh our memories: "You have forgotten inflation!" We had not. We simply understood that the high and inertial inflation had been tamed by the Real Plan in 1994 and that there was no reasonable economic argument to justify a real equilibrium interest rate of 8 percent in real terms in Brazil, when such a rate is around 1 percent in developed countries and around 3 percent in developing ones. Is this really the chosen equilibrium interest rate? The rate that the Central Bank's

Figure 8.2 Real Interest Rate and Inflation (2002–2006)

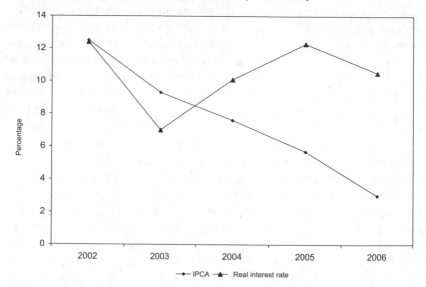

Sources: Instituto de Pesquisa Econômica Aplicada (Institute for Applied Economic Research), www.ipeadata.gov.br; and Central Bank, www.bcb.gov.br.
Note: a. 2006 data are forecasts.

inflation targeting model uses is not in the public domain, despite all of the institution's rhetoric of "transparency" in the context of the targeting policy. But this figure is confirmed by the inflation and interest rate forecasts produced not only by the financial market but above all by the Central Bank itself: in these forecasts 8 percent acts as a floor for the real interest rate. Are there any scientific "grounds" to determine such a high equilibrium interest rate? I don't think so. Muinhos and Nakane (2006) calculated the equilibrium interest rate in the 2000–2004 period at 10 percent, using the method of filtering the high-frequency movements of observed real interest rates. It was probably by using a similar method, based on recent past performance, that the economists who formulated the Central Bank's targeting model reached an 8 percent real equilibrium interest rate. This is obviously a limited method that assumes that the interest rate in force in the economy is a "normal" rate and that only high frequencies must be eliminated from it. With this method, the same authors estimated the equilibrium interest rate in Argentina in the same period at 7.6 percent. The method's limitations were then made evident: we know that the real interest rate in Argentina has been around zero since 2006.

When the interest rate drops, inflation does rise in Brazil, not because of increased demand but mainly because the reduced interest rate leads to a rise in the exchange rate, and this rise temporarily pushes up inflation. "Temporarily" because inflation in Brazil is no longer runaway; the runaway component has been substantially reduced. The equilibrium interest rate is related to Taylor's rule, which lies at the base of inflation targeting models, including the model adopted in Brazil since 1999. As we saw in Chapter 5, this rule states that the interest rate, *i*, is equal to the equilibrium interest rate, *i**, plus the difference between the expected inflation rate, *p*, and the inflation target, *p**, plus the product gap *j* (*Y* – *Y**), plus an exogenous shock factor, *d:*

$$i = i^* + \varphi\,(Y - Y^*) + \gamma\,(\pi - \pi^*) + \delta.$$

According to the practice in rich countries, their central banks, on reacting to changes in the inflation rate or the product gap, could decouple *i* from *i**, but only moderately. Therefore, our conventional economists conclude, it must be the same in Brazil. If the equilibrium interest rate is 8 percent, the real Selic cannot be below this level so as not to bring inflation back. When the interest rate reaches this level, it means that the economy has achieved full employment or, as conventional economists put it, its "natural rate of unemployment" or that the product growth rate has equaled potential GDP growth. And what would this growth rate be? This was also calculated when the inflation targeting policy was defined: it could be no higher than 3.5 percent, given the capital accumulation rate of a little less than 20 percent that has been prevalent in Brazil. Might this not be a very low ceiling rate, implying an average rate no higher than 2.5 percent and, therefore, a per capita income growth rate four times lower than in the 1950–1980 period? "No," says the conventional orthodoxy, "it's fine like this. This is the rate that ensures macroeconomic stability."

In fact, in much the same way that the conventional orthodoxy does not really want to lower the short-term interest rate, it has no interest in seeing the country grow at a reasonable pace. Supported by misguided calculations that define potential GDP growth as a projection of past growth, it accepts a rate that, acting as a ceiling, automatically sentences the country to quasi stagnation. As noted by Delfim Netto (2005), this is "pedestrian statistics." The conventional orthodoxy naturally maintains rhetoric in favor of both things, but neither meets the immediate interests of the political coalition that sustains it. In Brazil, therefore, after it became clear that the real interest rate would not go lower than 8 percent in real terms, the most sophisticated explanation that was forthcoming was that this very high rate was the equilibrium rate, i^*. But there is no justification for such a high i^*, preventing the Central Bank from reducing the Selic to levels used in countries with similar risk ratings as Brazil (a real rate of between 2 and 3 percent).

Given the obvious lack of a basis for this second explanation of the high short-term interest rate, a third one emerged. The interest rate was high to increase Brazil's low savings levels, or offset them by attracting capital, as suggested, for example, by Claudio Haddad (2003). The country would not be able to lower the interest rate because Brazil's savings rate is low, so that it requires foreign savings (or current account deficits) to secure complementary funding for its investments. Therefore, Brazil needs a high interest rate to attract capital, as well as a high domestic savings rate, independent of the foreign exchange rate and interest policy and dependent only on fiscal adjustment. This is, therefore, a return to the notion that fiscal adjustment is necessary, which is not contested; but the idea that in order to achieve it, lowering the short-term interest rate is not a consequence but a condition to be met even as the state's current spending is reduced, certainly is contested. And this is a return to the thesis of growth with foreign savings, whose negative effects on developing economies such as Brazil's I have already discussed.

A fourth explanation can be found in Arida, Bacha, and Lara Resende (2005). Until 1994 these economists, who played a decisive role in the formulation of the Real Plan, were critical of the conventional orthodoxy because it ignored the theory of runaway inflation. After 1995 they embraced the theses of the conventional orthodoxy. When, in 2002, criticism of the Central Bank's interest rate and exchange policy gained currency, they reacted by justifying the high interest rate with the argument that the problem was inflation. To neutralize runaway inflation, these economists had developed a brilliant, almost miraculous strategy—the strategy of the index currency URV—to be used temporarily to allow the conversion of all prices into this interim currency, which neutralized the lag in price adjustments that characterized runaway inflation. They understood that they could do the same with the problem of the interest rate.

The first attempt in this regard came from the group's most active economist, Persio Arida, who in June 2002 came up with the thesis that the problem of the high interest rate could be solved with a reform that allowed full convertibility of the real. In his words, "Brazil has lived with very high interest rates for a very long time. I suggest that we need to make the real a fully convertible currency to consolidate macroeconomic stability."[5] The argument lacked the clarity of a runaway inflation-neutralizing index currency; it was nothing but a reflection of the economists' tendency to turn the wondrous institution that is the market into a myth capable of infinite market arbitration: through convertibility, the short-term and long-term interest rates would align. At the same time, this would deprive us of a foreign exchange rate policy, in addition to reducing Brazil's ability to exogenously define its own short-term interest rate, as it would be determined by the "natural" interest rate—or equilibrium interest rate. Arida (2003, p. 8) acknowledged that this equilibrium rate was much higher than what would be reasonable: "Estimates may be somewhat inaccurate, but we are talking about 'natural' real rates of between 8 percent and 10 percent a year, against a world where the natural rate is somewhere between zero and 3 percent a year." Because, however, this rate was "structural" in addition to being "natural," the great challenge Brazilian economists would face was to lower this rate. But how?

In 2005, in association with Lara Resende and Bacha, the answer appeared. The problem lay in the lack of institutional reforms. More specifically, the short-term interest rate was high because of "jurisdictional uncertainty." The Brazilian legal and court system was incapable of providing sufficient protection for long-term loan agreements—driving up the interest rate. In addition to lacking any originality, the hypothesis does not bear analysis. Two questions suffice to demolish it: first, if the interest rate is stratospherically high in Brazil because its institutions fail to sufficiently protect loan agreements, how to explain the fact that interest rates were much lower in the past? Despite all the reforms, have institutions deteriorated in Brazil? Second, why do other countries whose institutions are clearly more backward or less advanced than Brazil's sport much lower interest rates? With this explanation, there is a return to the state's lack of credit to explain the high short-term interest rate. But this lack of credit now depends on more than just fiscal adjustment and also requires institutional reforms that, by definition, demand time to be outlined and implemented and to take hold. Therefore, the country would have to live with a real short-term interest rate of more than 8 percent a year for a long period, until such time as a set of institutional reforms creates "jurisdictional certainty." In the meantime, interest rates can and should remain as they are.

Of course, a country such as Brazil needs institutional reforms—every country must make reforms on an ongoing basis, and some need reforms more than others. I have addressed this topic in Chapter 3. But the lack of reforms cannot be blamed for the prevalence of an excessive

Selic interest rate: there always are imperfect institutions, but this is not a new fact, whereas high interest rates are. In the past, Brazilian institutions were less developed, and, even so, the interest rate was much lower. Besides, the country's institutions, if not better than, are quite similar to those found in countries with similar (or lower) risk ratings but much lower interest rates. In fact, the argument of "jurisdictional uncertainty" makes no logical sense and neither does it hold water empirically. Holland, Gonçalves, and Spacov (2005, p. 25) tested the hypothesis with an econometric model and found that "the results are largely unfavorable not only to Arida, Bacha and Resende's conjecture, but also to variants on their argument." Certainly a single econometric study is not enough to reject a hypothesis, but because the hypothesis lacks the requirement of a new fact (to explain how interest rates could be much lower in the past), as well as of the nature of an exclusive fact (to explain how other countries with less developed institutions and, therefore, greater jurisdictional uncertainty can show lower rates), there is no choice but to reject this explanation, too.

Finally, this series of mistakes has a last conventional explanation that is not just false: it is a half-truth. The interest rate is so high because the fiscal problem has not been solved. I have discussed this argument in Chapter 7. It can be summarized as follows: "Ours is a fiscal problem. The government spends more than it takes in, forcing the Central Bank to keep interest rates high in order to inhibit private demand and fight inflation. The government spends a lot and this is why the tax burden is high and spawns heterogeneous tax rates leading to distortions." This position is a way to take up the problem of the Brazilian state's lack of credit. As seen earlier, the state does not deserve the credit a fiscally sound state must have; this, however, occurs not because the public debt–to–GDP ratio is high but because the state interest expenditure–to–GDP ratio is exceedingly high. The interest rate is not, therefore, a consequence of the negative indebtedness index, but a fundamental cause thereof. But saying that the short-term interest rate is high because the fiscal problem has not been solved is easy for the conventional orthodoxy because this gives it an excuse to maintain the extortionate rates now found in Brazil.

As long as the necessary fiscal adjustment "does not materialize," the short-term real interest rate will remain stratospherically high as it is today. Because, since 1999, the Brazilian government has been meeting the IMF's fiscal targets and the fiscal problem has not been solved, one can reasonably expect that it never will be. And, as a result, the high interest rate may remain high permanently. Sure, conventional orthodoxy invariably assures us that "the interest-rate fall is just around the corner," but it is doubtful that this mythic "corner" exists since it does not serve the domestic and international political coalition that sustains it.

Better Causes

After all, why has the interest rate in Brazil been so high for so many years? Out of all the causes the conventional orthodoxy cites, only the Brazilian state's fiscal imbalance is partly true, as creditors tend to demand higher rates from heavily indebted debtors, but this cause is prejudiced because the most important factor behind the state of fiscal imbalance is the interest rate itself. I understand that the main reason why the short-term interest rate is so high in Brazil is the fact that the conventional orthodoxy, which has prevailed since 1990 or 1993, has no interest in lowering it and in keeping the exchange rate competitive, and is also not truly determined to face the fiscal imbalance. I know that I will be accused of being a "conspiracy theorist" (a classic defense used by the powerful) for the assertion that conventional orthodoxy is really not interested in reducing the public debt or lowering the interest rate to a moderate level. But no conspiracy is actually needed for a political coalition to informally succeed in achieving ideological hegemony in relation to the set of values and beliefs that serves its interests. All that is needed is that the domestic and international classes or sectors that make up the coalition be powerful, that they control the media and are capable of employing strategic academics to exert ideological hegemony,[6] that they put the Central Bank at their service, and subjugate the rest of society. Of course, there may be resistance from part of society, such as has been going on mainly since 2002, so that the dominant groups are not always able to impose their will.

I do not assign all the blame for high interest rates and high public indebtedness, for overvalued currency and high foreign debt, to economic authorities and the values and belief system to which they subscribe, but it seems clear to me that economic policymakers following conventional orthodoxy precepts are not interested in lowering the short-term interest rate because doing so would be directly opposed to the interests of rentiers and the financial industry, who profit from high interest, and of multinationals and foreign competitors, who benefit from the uncompetitive exchange rate. They are not interested in solving the fiscal imbalance problem but simply in retaining an indebtedness level that its creditors find comfortable, even though, according to the conventional orthodoxy, this is the main cause of the high interest rate. This statement will bother the representatives of the conventional orthodoxy, who honestly wish for an adjustment, but my analysis is not about the intent, motivations, and objectives of these representatives, which I assume to be sincere, but about their observed behavior, which often contradicts their stated objectives. What matters is determining what is in fact taking place, what economic policy is being implemented. If economic policymakers were truly determined to solve the problem of fiscal imbalance and in reducing the interest rate, they would not select as a fiscal target a primary surplus that keeps the public debt–to–GDP ratio stable but would strive to achieve a zero nominal budget deficit and, thus, cause that ratio to drop substantially. Therefore, they do not set a more ambitious nominal budget deficit target, as proposed by Delfim Netto (2006),[7] because they know that this would be justified only if, at the same time and to attain the same goal, they were willing to reduce the short-term interest rate. This second step is not part of their actual plans. In fact, stating that fiscal balance must be attained so that interest rates can then drop is mainly an excuse to delay lowering interest to reasonable levels. It is a classic delaying tactic. Fiscal adjustment is not achieved, they argue, because the government, although dominated by the conventional orthodoxy in the monetary area, is populist when it comes to public spending. The conventional orthodoxy is inevitably rational and faultless; the fault lies, by definition, with politicians.

Monetary authorities' lack of motivation to solve the interest-rate trap problem is also related to the "confidence building" practice: in usually high-indebted developing countries, policymakers are supposed to adopt the policies that rich countries and their financial institutions recommend in order to build confidence (policies that often do not correspond to the national interest of the developing country).

The first two explanations of why the short-term interest rate remains so very high are, therefore, the unwillingness of those who have been in charge of Brazilian economic policy since 1995 (1) to adopt the fiscal shock needed to reestablish fiscal balance and, at the same time, (2) to take steps to lower the rate and make the exchange rate competitive. The two reasons are ultimately just one: the fiscal imbalance is left unchallenged not only owing to fiscal populism but also because attacking it would imply lowering the short-term interest rate—an outcome that is not congenial to either public debt holders or those who benefit from the appreciated exchange rate. The Central Bank's behavior leaves no room for doubt in this respect. It is always willing to raise the interest rate and resists lowering it as much as possible; any increase in inflation, any hiccup in the domestic or foreign economy, justifies interrupting a reduction process or beginning a hike. And let it not be said that this kind of "conservatism" is typical of all central banks. Central bankers elsewhere are, in fact and rightly, relatively conservative, but they do not act as their Brazilian counterparts do. Márcio Holland (2006a) shows that the coefficient of the function of the Central Bank's reaction to an increase in expected inflation is two or three times higher than in economies such as the United States, France, Germany, Britain, South Korea, and Japan, to name a few.

In addition to this basic cause, there are other, more economic and institutional causes that explain the high interest rate and hamper the monetary authorities' efforts to lower it. The main one has to do with a strange monetary institution that has been created in Brazil and which I began discussing in Chapter 7: indexation of the interest rate to the interest rate itself, of the Selic to the Selic itself, or, in other words, the use of the Selic, which is the interbanking or short-term interest rate to index the interest rate itself. Strictly speaking, the Selic is not a rate but a system—the Clearance and Custody System for public bonds. Now, however, it is also a rate. As defined by the Central Bank, "it is the rate found at Selic." According to Nakano (2006a, p. 7), "the first anomaly is the use of the Central Bank–determined Selic rate, an operational instrument for monetary policymaking in the open market, to directly compensate post-fixed 'long-term' public bonds, the LFTs."

When the system was created in 1979, public bonds became almost perfect substitutes for the reserves that banks were supposed to keep, whether mandatorily or voluntarily. Bank reserves started providing the same yield as public bonds—which in itself made the Brazilian financial system sui generis. As noted by Fernando de Holanda Barbosa (1996, pp. 88–89), "the fact that the sale of public bonds immediately converts into bank reserves made the demand for surplus reserves independent from the interest rate." As a consequence, "if the Central Bank provided reserves at a volume below demand, the interest rate would rise unimpeded; should it inject excessive reserves into the system, the interest rate would equal zero. As a result, the Central Bank has no choice, under the circumstances, but to control the interest rate." The situation was strange, but all would be well if the Central Bank managed the interest rate properly.

But a serious problem arose in 1986. Faced with the failure of the Cruzado Plan and the ensuing inflationary boom, the Central Bank needed to raise interest rates, but this would lead to bankruptcy among the appropriately leveraged banks. The creative solution adopted was to create the LFTs, indexed to the short-term interest rate itself, the Selic. As a result, when the interest rate rose, bonds would not lose value, and the financial industry, which must always be protected at such times, would be kept safe. But the Real Plan should have done away with this kind of bond. After high inflation was brought under control, the Central Bank and the Treasury failed to take firm steps to eliminate debt indexation; they merely outlined actions that were always aborted for fear of inability to refinance the debt, even though players—banks in particular—had no choice but to invest their short-term funds in government bonds. Consequently, as Barbosa (2006, p. 236) noted, this indexation of the interest rate to the interest rate itself explains why the short-term interest rate in Brazil is so much higher than in other emerging economies. "The answer is quite simple: we have created in the past and continue to use today a rather peculiar government-issued asset that is indexed to the inter-banking interest rate. This bond adds the public debt's risk premium to the inter-banking interest rate."

Furthermore, with the maintenance of such a bond, any difference between the short-term and the long-term interest rates ceases to exist in the Brazilian domestic financial system.[8] Bank reserves, which already provided returns, now offer the same yield as the public debt. As a consequence of this indexation, which exists nowhere else in the world, rentiers and the financial industry have nothing to lose, and much to win, from increased interest rates: contrary to the general rule, the amount of bonds does not drop as interest rates increase. This indexation, in addition to casting the short-term interest rate in the role that belongs to the long-term interest rate in normal countries, poses an obstacle to reducing the short-term interest rate. In other countries, the monetary or interest rate policy selected by the Central Bank has no direct effect on the long-term interest rate on public and private bonds. In the absence of this separation, the government can claim that it does not lower the short-term interest rate because it would be unable to roll over its debt, thus continuing to grace rentiers with an interest rate that is set not by the market but by the government itself.

Another less important, but still significant, cause of the high interest rate is the policy of increasing the average maturity of the public debt that the Central Bank has long adopted. On the surface, it is a reasonable policy, but in fact it drives up the interest rate because it encourages the Central Bank to decide on interest rate hikes. Stretching out public debt is desirable but cannot be accomplished with artificial steps that only add severity to the problem at hand, the interest rate levels: it will be accomplished by making the required fiscal adjustment, which includes reduced, rather than increased, short-term interest rates. The mistaken assumption of the stretching-out policy is that, in the absence of indexation and of a high interest rate, the market will stop funding the bonds, when we know that the major banks that dominate the market have no choice for short-term investment other than rolling over public bonds.

Another way of explaining the high interest rate is to say that the Central Bank, in the absence of an alternative instrument, uses it to excess, assigning so many purposes to it that it becomes difficult to lower. In addition to controlling inflation, it is used to stretch out the debt's maturity profile, to cap exchange rate devaluation to prevent cost-based inflation, to attract foreign capital to fill the balance-of-payment gap, and to ensure the rolling over of public debt. The interest rate was used to lure foreign capital chiefly in the years subsequent to the Real Plan, when no one doubted that growth would come from foreign savings and foreign funds were limited. Since 2003, when foreign resources became abundant, this reason to raise interest was all but forgotten, but, in yet another sign that their goal was not to lower interest, economic authorities failed to realize that this abundance was an opportunity to do so.

The short-term interest rate is also high in Brazil because Brazilians have long become used to living with high interest rates since the coup of 1964. This makes it difficult for them to resist the existing rates. To encourage popular savings and fund the national housing system, the government chose to establish "savings accounts" that should, by law, pay 6 percent interest per year: a very high interest rate on a safe investment, until governments began to "skim off" depositors, adjusting accounts indexation as a means to reduce their yield. This very high rate ultimately failed to serve the poor for very long, but it set a psychological floor for the real interest available to the rich.

It is also legitimate to argue that the interest rate that firms and individuals pay in Brazil is high for an additional reason besides the high Selic: because the bank spread is very high. I have not discussed this point, however, because my point has been to determine why the short-term interest rate is so high. To discuss the problem of spreads I would have to discuss a whole series of reforms, including the drastic reduction in mandatory reserves—which is beyond the scope of this book. On the other hand, as Oreiro, Paula, Ono, and Silva (2006) showed, the main cause of the high margin banks charge on their loans is the high level and great volatility of the Selic itself.

One way of summarizing this entire analysis would be to say that the Brazilian interest rate is high because the Brazilian economy is caught in a trap made up of a high interest rate and an uncompetitive exchange rate—a trap that is defined at two levels: first, every time the interest rate drops, the exchange rate appreciates and inflation rises; second, insofar as the exchange rate is kept artificially valued, the economy tends to exchange imbalance and balance-of-payment crisis. I will, however, leave the discussion of this problem for Chapter 9, where I discuss the implied model of the macroeconomics of stagnation.

Natural Rate and Contradiction

In this wide-ranging debate on why the short-term interest rate is so high, the conventional orthodoxy shows a fundamental contradiction. It regards the short-term interest rate as the sole economic policy instrument available to economists, an instrument that is viable, within the triangle of impossibility, thanks to the floating domestic currency. For the conventional orthodoxy, exchange policy does not exist; only interest rate policy does. But throughout the debate on Brazil's high short-term interest rate, the conventional orthodoxy in practice treats this rate as if it were endogenous—as if the monetary authorities were unable to intervene, except to bring it closer to an equilibrium interest rate that, as we have seen, has been very inaccurately computed. It is an obvious contradiction.

For the new-developmentalist economists, lowering the interest rate would be easier in the presence of an increased effort at fiscal adjustment, but Brazil's fiscal crisis itself will be overcome only when a strategy agreed upon between the government and society manages to reduce interest rates and the state's unnecessary spending at once. Conventionally orthodox economists, however, espouse neoclassical economics, which assumes that the market determines every price. This applies not only to the short-term interest rate but also, and chiefly, to the real interest rate, which orthodox economists do not hesitate to say that the government is unable to influence via economic policy. The fact that it also applies to the Selic is strange, at least. Brazil's economists are not so clear on this connection because they realize the contradiction: if the main economic policy instrument available to central banks is management of the short-term interest rate, how can it not be managed? But the behavior of conventionally orthodox economists leaves no doubt that they understand that this rate is endogenous and, therefore, unmanageable. Whenever they can, they forget the difference between the long-term interest rate, which is in fact determined by the market, and the short-term interest rate, or the Central Bank's base rate. Then they insist that "the interest rate will fall as soon as the fiscal adjustment is accomplished."

Finally, when devoid of arguments, they point out that, according to the Taylor rule, the short-term interest rate cannot drift too far from the "natural" or equilibrium rate. Indeed it cannot, but neither is there any justification for assuming an equilibrium interest rate of around 8 percent in real terms. This makes no economic sense. The econometric studies that led to this figure are biased as a result of the high interest rates present in the Brazilian economy when the calculations were made, in much the same way as the calculation of potential GDP: they reproduce the Brazilian economy's weak performance in recent years. In this connection José Luís Oreiro (2006) notes that the domestic equilibrium rate (which Knut Wicksell called the "natural rate" and John Maynard Keynes referred to as the "neutral interest rate") is the real interest rate level capable of ensuring a stable inflation rate and the full use of the country's productive capacity (in terms of IS-LM, it is the intercept of the IS curve and the potential product), whereas the foreign equilibrium interest rate is the rate that ensures a balanced balance of payments (equal to the sum of the real foreign interest rate and the sovereign risk premium).

The foreign equilibrium rate, in contrast, is inversely dependent on the Brazilian economy's foreign vulnerability level, that is, on the foreign debt as a share of exports, of the level of foreign currency reserves, of the current transactions balance in the balance of payments, and so on. When sovereign risk was 800 basis points and the foreign rate was 2 percent, a domestic interest rate of 10 percent seemed reasonable. Today, however, Brazil's sovereign risk, added to the real interest rate on US Treasury bonds, produces an interest rate of around 5 percent in real terms because, in 1999, Brazil unwittingly broke away from the model of growth with foreign savings by making a necessary adjustment to the exchange rate. Yet the global economy's demand for Brazil's products has risen extraordinarily since 2002. But despite this foreign adjustment, the short-term interest rate has not dropped. Why? Oreiro understands that, in addition to the Central Bank's conservatism, another reason is the fact that the domestic equilibrium rate failed to keep up with the fall in foreign rates, for which two explanations exist.

The more conservative hypothesis is that, from 1994 to 2005, there was a great increase in nonfinancial government spending (mainly current consumption) as a share of GDP. This increase in nonfinancial expenditures shifted the IS curve upward, raising the level of the real interest rate compatible with stable inflation and the full use of the productive capacity. For the purposes of this argument, it is irrelevant whether or not the government is running a deficit; what matters is the level of government spending as a share of GDP. The developmentalist explanation is that, with the elimination of public investment from 1994 onward (today the government invests barely 0.5 percent of GDP), there was a reduction in the economy's potential growth, so that the low growth of potential product (and, therefore, of aggregate supply) keeps the domestic rate at a high level.

Because I regard fiscal imbalance as a real cause of the high short-term interest rate, I accept this explanation in part. We have seen, however, that it is not sufficient because the interest rate itself is an essential and prior cause of increased public expenditures. In fact, we have no choice but to consider the explanation based on hyperconservatism or the capture of the monetary authorities. This policy naturally has the support of government politicians. Why? In essence, because, like the society they represent, they fear a return of inflation and submit to hegemonic thinking and to the conventional orthodoxy that expresses it. On the one hand, they are afraid to confront the political coalition that sustains the Washington Consensus—a coalition that is certainly strong, as we will see in Chapter 10; on the other hand, they are flattered by the compliments that Washington and New York are always ready to pour on politicians and economic authorities willing to accept their wise recommendations.

To return to the conventional orthodoxy's contradiction, the one thing to be said in its favor is that it is more reasonable than neoclassical "macroeconomics" after Robert Lucas, who takes the problem of endogeneity to its limit. Although the Washington Consensus stands divided and admits that economic policymakers enjoy some freedom, the macroeconomics that embraces a radical form of the rational expectations hypothesis fails to acknowledge the legitimacy of any economic policy. I placed macroeconomics between quotation marks because, in my opinion, Lucas never wrote on macroeconomics: he just extended to macroeconomic variables the neoclassical hypothetical-deductive model of general equilibrium. To really discuss macroeconomics, one must proceed from Keynes and Michael Kalecki. The economist must employ a historical-deductive method instead of the hypothetical-deductive and work with open—and, therefore, contingent—models that are practical and make it possible to conceive of and draw up competent economic policies (Bresser-Pereira 2005d).

Notes

1. Note, also, that after the Real Plan the state could no longer rely on revenues from the inflation tax. On the other hand, tax revenues rose significantly thanks to improved tax collection.

2. Garcia (2004), for example, embraces this thesis.

3. Some papers were published in the July 2002 issue of *Brazilian Journal of Political Economy;* the debate was intense in newspapers and can be found on my website, at www.bresserpereira.org.br.

4. Edmar Bacha's criticism was expressed in a letter addressed directly to me (Bacha 2002), and Francisco Lopes's appeared in his January 2002 *Macrométrica* (Lopes 2002).

5. See Arida (2002). This newspaper article was followed by a paper (Arida 2004) on the same topic. Criticism of this thesis can be found in Oreiro, Paula, and Silva (2004); Ferrari Filho, Jayme, Lima, Oreiro, and Paula (2005); and Ono, Silva, Oreiro, and Paula (2005).

6. This has been the role of neoclassical economics with its general equilibrium model and its macroeconomic and growth models: to act as a meta-ideology justifying neoliberalism.

7. The proposal was actually submitted in 2005.

8. Because Brazil no longer had a market-defined long-term interest rate, it was able to set this term aside to designate a rate defined administratively by BNDES to foster major investments financed by this institution.

9

A Macroeconomic Model

After examining in the previous chapters the failure of the conventional orthodoxy to ensure satisfactory growth rates and relating this fact principally with an overvalued exchange rate and a high interest rate, I can now sum up what has been presented so far and relate the variables discussed so that they form a whole: a system—a perverse economic system, but nonetheless one with its own logic.

After the Real Plan of 1994, a new macroeconomic framework established itself whose general outline has remained the same since then. Concerning the three macroeconomic prices analyzed, the following characteristics can be distinguished: (1) a low inflation rate, (2) a high short-term interest rate (Selic), and (3) an overvalued exchange rate. I might also add the two other macroeconomic prices I did not deem it necessary to analyze in depth here, namely, the profit rate and the wage rate. In regard to them, it is enough to point out two factors. The first is that the spread between the expected profit rate and the interest rate has not been sufficient to encourage businesspeople to invest beyond what is necessary to keep their plants modern and competitive, which is, therefore, not sufficient for major autonomous investment to occur or for the investment rate to grow above 20 percent of GDP. The second factor is that the wage rate has remained basically stagnant despite the increase in productivity, because in addition to the continued presence of an unlimited supply of labor that prevents average wages from rising, the high unemployment levels have the same effect in the short term.

The macroeconomic policy, in turn, is conventionally orthodox. It is characterized by (1) control of the public debt by means of a fiscal policy based on high primary surpluses, not on the fiscal deficit, and on maintaining minimal public investments; (2) control of inflation by means of an extremely high short-term interest rate; and (3) the absence of a true exchange rate policy that really neutralizes the tendency of the real to overappreciation, even though since 2003 the government has been buying US dollars to prevent the rate from falling further.

The combination of the macroeconomic framework described through macroeconomic prices with a conventional monetary policy has produced the following results: (1) low growth rates of income per inhabitant and of wages, (2) a high unemployment level, and (3) a high tax burden. Since 2005 the per capita growth rate has improved owing to a major increase in exports, which doubled over five years. Yet this improvement arose not from a change of policy but from extremely favorable international conditions caused by China's high growth rate. Thus, the interest rate remained very high and the exchange rate, which had sharply depreciated in the 2002 crisis, again appreciated strongly in the following years.

In this chapter, although acknowledging that a real macroeconomic system cannot be described by a closed mathematical model, I present as simple a macroeconomic model as possible, summarizing the previous chapters. I adopt the methodological assumption that macroeconomics is an essentially historical-deductive branch of economics; that is, when new relevant historical facts occur, the macroeconomic model must adapt.[1] As such, an absolutely general macroeconomic model makes no sense, even though John Maynard Keynes spoke of a "general theory." There are general macroeconomic concepts, as well as a few principles and trends that are part of the Keynesian model. Thus, we know that consumption depends on income, saving depends on investment, investment depends on the marginal efficiency of capital and on interest, and interest depends on liquidity and the supply of money. To this we must add that today the interest rate is essentially a exogenous variable defined by the Central Bank and, principally, that the exchange rate, which in principle is a market rate that is in equilibrium when the current account is balanced intertemporally, actually must be, and often is, managed not only because of its high volatility but because there is in developing countries a tendency of the exchange rate to overappreciation. We must add that the exchange rate determines not only imports and exports but also expected profits, investments, and, thus, savings. Besides, the model will vary depending on a country's stage of economic development, size, and autonomy from or dependency on more developed ones.

The Brazilian macroeconomic model can be defined in terms of a series of variables that I categorize as structural variables, economic policy variables, flow result variables, and stock result variables, as follows:

1. Three structural variables: (1.1) low wages; (1.2) high income concentration, with the resulting trend toward fiscal and exchange rate populism; and (1.3) a tendency of the exchange rate to overappreciation
2. Four institutional or economic policy variables: (2.1) absence of fiscal policy aiming to truly eliminate fiscal imbalance; (2.2) high short-term interest rate; (2.3) lack of exchange rate policy aiming to neutralize the tendency of the exchange rate to overappreciation caused by the Dutch disease and by large capital inflows; and (2.4) survival of several forms of indexation, particularly in privatized public services
3. Seven flow result variables: (3.1) negative public savings and nominal and relatively high budget deficit, despite the high primary surplus (given the size of interest payments by the state; (3.2) a low investment rate in relation to GDP, especially in public investment; (3.3) near-stagnation of income per capita; (3.4) high unemployment and informal-economy levels and low wages; (3.5) a profit rate unable to meet the interest rate, except in the case of subsidized loans; (3.6) current account deficits as the exchange rate appreciates, leading the country gradually to balance-of-payment crisis and sharp exchange rate depreciation; and (3.7) a high tax burden, which, in addition to funding a welfare system or a social state, finances the high interest paid to rentiers
4. Three stock result variables: (4.1) high public indebtedness; (4.2) high foreign private and public indebtedness;[2] and (4.3) a high level of economic denationalization, including of monopolistic public services

Most of the data on and discussions of these variables have been provided in previous chapters. The variables exist within a social and political framework characterized by radical income concentration and the loss of the concept of nation. Low wages are an indication of the inequity that prevails in the country and of Brazil's underdevelopment, characterized by low average productivity and unlimited labor supply. High unemployment is an indicator of the productive potential that is not realized; emphasizes that personal accomplishment is impossible for a large number of citizens, in particular youths just entering the labor market; and is a clear sign of a macroeconomics of stagnation. The formal indexation of contracts and the informal indexation of wages are an inheritance from the high inflation that the Real Plan eliminated; their presence suggests that inflationary inertia is still an important phenomenon. The high basic interest rate found in Brazil is characterized by a radical decoupling between the Brazilian interest rate and that found in other countries with similar or worse risk ratings. The tendency of the exchange rate to overappreciation is connected, on the one hand, to structural factors (the Dutch disease and the attraction that higher interest and profit rates exert on foreign capital) and, on the other, to policies, particularly to the policy of growth with foreign savings associated with the open capital account and to exchange rate populism. Because of these characteristics, the Brazilian economy has for many years been reporting growth rates typical of semistagnation.

Despite the primary surpluses, the high budget deficit keeps public indebtedness at a high level, particularly as concerns the interest on this debt. The current account deficit turned into a surplus after 2003, not because of any economic policy adopted but because of a great increase in Brazil's exports caused by international prosperity and by two balance-of-payment crises that depreciated the exchange rate. Thanks to the growth of exports, the economic growth rate increased somewhat. This created an opportunity for the monetary authorities to lower the interest rate, as the increased rate of capital accumulation and resumed development could then depend on this decrease alone. But the opportunity was mostly missed; the Central Bank reduced the interest rate much less than it should have when the conditions were favorable, in 2006 and 2007; in 2008, with inflation rebounding, the bank immediately increased it. Finally, the more serious problem that the Brazilian economy faces is, again, an extraordinarily overvalued currency. The exchange rate was in mid-2008 around R$1.60 per dollar—a rate definitively inconsistent with Brazil's long-term growth.

The Perverse and the Benign Frameworks

In the introduction to this book I argued that the economic system in force in Brazil does not follow the logic of economic development. Its logic since 1994 has been that of high interest rates and an uncompetitive exchange rate. In fact, the prevalent macroeconomic framework after the Real Plan can be summed up in a macroeconomic equation defined by high interest rates and an uncompetitive exchange rate, preventing an increased capital accumulation rate and resumed economic growth. No sophisticated arguments are needed to understand the difference between this equation and its opposite, the benign equation defined by a moderate interest rate and a competitive exchange rate. Countries that developed in the twentieth century, such as Japan, Germany, Italy, the Asian Tigers, and, more recently, China, did so based on such an equation. Brazil itself developed in the 1970s only as long as the effective exchange rate stayed low enough to stimulate the export of manufactured goods or the substitution of imports with domestic goods.

Figure 9.1, made up of six quadrants numbered clockwise, attempts to capture the essence of the post-1994 Brazilian macroeconomic model that is characterized by a perverse framework and compare it with the benign framework used by developing countries that do grow. The present Brazilian model is defined by a high interest rate, i_1, Quadrant 1, an overappreciated exchange rate defined by the position of the curve interest-exchange rate in Quadrant 3, and the corresponding four in the four other graphs, whereas the benign model is defined by i_2 and its corresponding points. As Quadrant 1 shows, the high interest rate, i_1, results in low investment, I_1, given the negative incentive to invest caused by the high cost of capital. It also results (Quadrant 2) in high public spending, D_{G1}, given the high level of the interest rate and the equally high public debt. It also contributes to keeping the exchange rate, e_1, uncompetitive or overvalued as a result of international arbitrage in open economies: the theory of uncovered parity (Quadrant 3). Quadrant 4 is a 45-degree line to transfer the exchange rate from the X-axis to the Y-axis. The appreciated exchange rate that corresponds to the high interest rate defined along the i-e_1 curve, in turn, determines jointly a high current account deficit (foreign savings), S_{x1} (Quadrant 5), and, a low level of exports, X_1 (Quadrant 6), and a low level of investment (Quadrant 1).

It is important to point out, however, that it is not the high interest rate alone, or even chiefly, that exogenously determines the uncompetitive exchange rate and the perverse framework. Given the tendency of the exchange rate to overappreciation that we discussed in Chapter 6, and particularly the Dutch disease, even though this tendency is not neutralized by economic policy, the exchange rate that intertemporally balances the current account remains appreciated in relation to the "industrial exchange rate equilibrium" (Chapter 6), which makes viable tradable state-of-the-art industries other than the commodities that cause the disease. The model does not overlook this fact. The curve i-e_2 relating the interest rate and the exchange rate in Quadrant 3 is to the right

Figure 9.1 One Macroeconomic Model, Two Frameworks

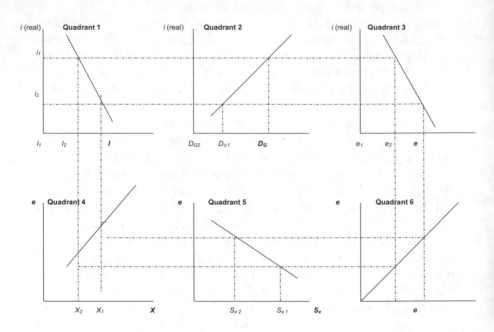

of the curve $i\text{-}e_1$, because the latter reflects an overvalued currency, whereas the former indicates a competitive one, consistent with the industrial exchange rate equilibrium. If the overappreciation increases because, for instance, the prices of commodities exported by Brazil have increased, the curve $i\text{-}e_1$ shifts still farther to the left. When the country is able to neutralize the tendency of the exchange rate to overappreciation, the curve $i\text{-}e_1$ (which is part of the perverse framework) changes into the curve $i\text{-}e_2$ (which is part of the benign one).

Investment, however, increases not just because the interest rate is lower in the benign framework but also because the expected profit curve $i\text{-}I_1$ or marginal efficiency of capital curve shifts to the right to $i\text{-}I_2$. Thus, investment is increased because the interest rate goes down and because the expected profit curve shifts to the right as a consequence of the increased opportunities to make export-oriented investments.

The perverse framework is defined by the high exogenous interest rate, i_1 (which is a point in Quadrants 1 to 3), and by an overvalued currency that is represented by the exogenous position of the $i\text{-}e_1$ curve, whereas the same two exogenous variables, i_2 and $i\text{-}e_2$, are respectively a moderate interest rate and a competitive exchange rate. The conventional orthodoxy views these two variables, especially the exchange rate, as endogenous rates, but the benign framework consistent with new developmentalism acknowledges one fact that is observable in the practice of high-growth developing countries, namely, that both rates are exogenous—within certain limits, they can be managed.

In this model there are several partial equilibrium points, but the overall equilibrium is reached only when the interest rate is low enough and the exchange rate competitive enough to allow the economy to achieve reasonably full employment. Among the partial equilibrium points, the more dangerous is the "market exchange rate equilibrium," which makes the current account equal to zero intertemporally (a necessary reminder is that it is more appreciated than the industrial equilibrium exchange rate given the existing Dutch disease).

The Interest and Exchange Rate Trap

Throughout this book, I have argued that the Brazilian economy is caught in a trap of a high interest rate and an uncompetitive exchange rate. It is now time to add detail to the argument. Despite its high levels, the basic interest rate in Brazil moves in a way that is naturally similar to those of other countries, that is, it increases when the economy expands and decreases when it contracts. But our monetary authorities have been unable to make consistent reductions to the rate or to prevent the real from appreciating. The outcome is what we call the "interest rate and exchange rate trap." The fact that the very short-term interest rate fluctuates between 8 percent and 15 percent in real terms, when in other countries this fluctuation range is four to five times narrower, is in and of itself a trap. This can be easily perceived in graphic terms. As in any other country, the Brazilian basic interest rate moves up and down—it is higher when the economy is heated, and lower when the economy loses steam—but this variation, unlike that in other countries, takes place at much higher levels: higher not only than in developed countries but also higher than the basic interest rate variation levels in intermediate development ones.

We can begin our discussion of the trap by focusing first on the interest rate and then on the exchange rate: we have to consider both variables because they are strongly related. To begin with the interest rate, the simplest way to explain the trap is to remember the 9 percent real equilibrium interest rate that the Central Bank uses in its inflation target model. To accept this as the equilibrium rate means that the monetary authorities are unable to bring the short-term interest rate below this level, except for very brief periods of time, since inflation would pick up from that point onward. This is, in fact, a self-imposed trap by the Central Bank that reveals its unwillingness to lower the interest rate. I will not repeat my previous criticism of how this equilibrium interest rate was calculated, or of the government's inappropriate timing in implementing an inflation targeting policy—a policy that can manage, but not change, a monetary policy regime.

The basic operating mechanism of the interest rate trap is quite simple. Whenever the Central Bank begins reducing the interest rate, the exchange rate depreciates and the consequent changes in relative prices, with tradable goods increasing in price relative to nonmarketable ones, cause inflation to rise. This threatens the inflation targeting policy, and the Central Bank reacts by again raising the interest rate. Therefore, and paradoxically, supply-side inflation is fought with a policy intended to contract demand. With such premature interruption of interest rate cuts, it is no wonder that the Brazilian economy is marked by growth that ends soon after it begins.

The exchange rate trap is even more lethal than its interest rate counterpart, as it can easily end in a balance-of-payment crisis, whereas the former may end in a fiscal dominance crisis, although this is unlikely. Let us first imagine this trap in the absence of inflation. The exchange rate overvalued by the Dutch disease, the policy of growth with foreign savings, and the high interest rate policy reduce exports and increase imports. The country's foreign indebtedness indexes deteriorate, downside prospects at the margin worsen, and, suddenly, creditors decided to suspend foreign debt refinancing, as was the case in 1998 and 2002. At this point, as noted by Luís Nassif (2003), "the 'market' no longer analyzes countries based on whether their fundamentals are good or bad, but on whether the country is 'cheap' or 'expensive.' Whatever a country's situation, if it depends on speculative capitals, a time will come when it reaches its upside ceiling. At this point, there is no miracle capable of making the capital stay there." A balance-of-payment crisis becomes inevitable—and foreign aid merely mitigates its effects.

Let us now put the interest rate and the exchange rate together to illustrate the trap in its entirety. What should the Central Bank do when the aggregate demand is weak and there is an opportunity for lowering the interest rate? The obvious decision would be to lower the interest rate in response to a softening economy. When the interest rate falls, aggregate demand responds slowly, whereas the inflow of capitals and the exchange rate do so much more quickly: the local currency soon begins to depreciate. Exchange rate depreciation means a change in relative prices leading to more expensive tradable goods, and inflation rises to accommodate the change in relative prices inherent in any exchange depreciation. Yet, this rise is a temporary rise: as soon as the accommodation occurs, prices again stabilize in the absence of other causes pushing them upward and, naturally, in the absence of indexation. But the Central Bank sees it differently; the bank continues to reason as if inertial (fully indexed) inflation still persisted in Brazil. Thus, in the Brazilian inflation targeting policy there is no room for *temporary* rises of inflation. When a cost and price increase caused by devaluation looms over the inflation target, the interest rate is raised again, without taking account of the fact that this is an inflationary "bubble" that will soon calm down.

We have seen that this trap ended in balance-of-payment crises twice recently, in 1998 and 2002, as the high interest rates attracted unnecessary foreign capitals and the real appreciated. In both cases, the increased inflation caused by the sudden depreciation of the real was moderate—far lower than expected by the advocates of the conventional orthodoxy—and temporary. Inflation dropped again as soon as the exchange rate stopped rising: as, in fact, good economics would have it. But because the government was then already raising the interest rate and lowering the exchange rate, it attributed the drop in inflation to its interest policy targeting demand-side control when, in fact, it was just the good old law of supply and demand at work. Before 1994, inflation did not recede when the exchange rate stopped rising because the entire economy was indexed at the time; with indexation almost extinct, as soon as the exchange rate stops rising, the inflation rate will drop back again, not necessarily to its former level, but to one that makes it possible to accommodate the relative prices unbalanced by the depreciation.[3] With the higher interest rate, however, the exchange rate again appreciated, restarting the cycle.

I wrote that a crisis is more unlikely to occur owing to fiscal dominance than to the balance of payments. In fact, the two types of crisis are closely connected, as in either case it is creditors who suspend debt refinancing: either the state's creditors prevent public debt from being rolled over, or the nation-state's creditors prevent foreign debt rollover, or both. The crisis of 2002, which ended up as a balance-of-payment crisis, was almost a fiscal dominance crisis as well. When the interest rate remains very high for very long, the country finds itself in a perverse equilibrium. Lending may continue to appeal to creditors because of the high interest received, but at the same time they realize that the risk of lending increases and may demand even higher interest rates or suddenly suspend the country's or the state's refinancing. This was the case in Brazil in 1988 and 2002. Given this second perverse equilibrium, revealed by the fact that the increased interest rate not only fails to expand loan supply but also increases the debtor's likelihood of default when already heavily into debt, creditors may suddenly suspend their loans. This amounts to a case of fiscal dominance if the main debtor is the state itself. When one creditor makes such a decision, others follow, in what is known as the "herd effect." The country then faces a balance-of-payment crisis. This was the case in both 1998 and 2002, but only foreign creditors were affected; domestic ones are unable to suspend public bond refinancing for lack of alternatives. Foreign creditors, however, did not stop at preventing public debt from being refinanced: they interrupted private foreign debt as well.

We can now see how two economies with similar macroeconomic fundamentals can have very different interest rates, or how countries with similar credit ratings can have different interest levels. Countries such as Brazil, which adopt very high basic interest rates to attract capital or maintain debt refinancing, end up at the perverse equilibrium point. In other words, creditors can easily perceive the continued raising of the basic interest rate—from an already high level—as an increase in sovereign risk. As a result, countries with low interest rates and inappropriate macroeconomic fundamentals may be perceived by their creditors as lower risks than countries with better macroeconomic fundamentals but a high basic interest rate. The latter situation holds for Brazil.

Equilibrium Interest Rate

We have seen that the definition of the equilibrium interest rate plays an important role in the interest rate and exchange rate trap. A central issue in inflation targeting policy is determining the equilibrium interest rate. This rate is defined as the interest rate at which the potential product equals the real product, or at which a critical installed capacity level is reached; it is, therefore, the interest rate for which the unemployment rate would be nil (or equal the natural unemployment rate, according to neoclassical ideology) and the inflation rate does not accelerate. Determining the equilibrium rate is essential because central banks today adopt, whether formally or informally, inflation targeting policy in lieu of monetary target policy. And they no longer make monetary policy—

to be understood as a policy whereby monetary aggregates are controlled—but interest rate policy.

When Keynesianism was the hegemonic paradigm, monetary and fiscal policies were used together. With the hegemony of neoclassical monetarism since the mid-1970s, central banks started to employ monetary targets. In less than ten years, however, central bankers realized that the theory had nothing to do with reality and abandoned monetary targets for the far more pragmatic policy of inflation targets. The fact that neoclassical economists then co-opted the practice with rational expectations and "credibility theory" is irrelevant at this point. What matters is that central banks started working with formal—or preferably informal—inflation targets, using a neutral or reference rate as a basis to manage the two instruments, or the two macroeconomic prices, over which they had any influence: the short-term interest rate and, to a lesser degree, the exchange rate.[4]

In addition to not using monetary targets, central bankers ceased to make monetary policy (properly so called) to influence the interest rate and started determining the interest rate directly. Textbooks still mention open-market operations to increase or reduce money supply, but these transactions became secondary insofar as central banks make short-term interest rate policy in the hope of influencing the long-term interest rate. This rate, however, is not completely exogenous because, as we have seen, central banks, including Brazil's Central Bank since 1999, adopt a response function shaped like the Taylor rule, where a neutral or equilibrium interest rate plays a key role.

We have seen that, according to the Taylor rule, the central bank must react to shocks and minimize losses (that is, differences between real and potential product, $Y-Y^*$, and between the inflation rate and the inflation target, $p-p^*$), but must take into account the fact that it cannot drift far from i^*, or the equilibrium interest rate. A fundamental variable in any inflation targeting policy model, therefore, is the equilibrium interest rate. In developed countries, this rate is about 2 percent a year in nominal terms—and, therefore, close to zero in real terms. In the Brazilian model, however, it hovers near 9 percent in real terms. That is, the model and the Brazilian central bankers who put their faith in it assume that the inflation rate would start rising as soon as the interest rate fell beneath this point. How the Central Bank arrived at this number remains a mystery. No historic data exist in Brazil to allow such an inference, nor are there any logical arguments to sustain such odd behavior on the part of the Brazilian economy. A vast and inexplicable distance exists between 0 and 9 percent—a distance whose explanation is found not in strictly economic arguments, based on the behavior of individual economic agents, but in political economy, based as it is on group interests.

Figure 9.2 allows a better understanding of the problem of the equilibrium interest rate in Brazil. In this graph, the equilibrium interest rate depends on the position of the Philips curve, which relates inflation, *pi,* and variation on employment, *n.* The equilibrium interest rate that the Central Bank assumes by not letting the real interest rate, *i,* drop below 8 or 9 percent is probably curve pi_1, where this interest rate corresponds to 5 percent inflation—approximately the 2005 interest rate. Therefore, we have a Philips curve with a marked shift to the left, indicating that the country would achieve full employment or potential product at this rate of 9 percent. Now, not even the loosest definition of unemployment or the most elastic NAIRU would allow anyone to claim that a country is at full employment with a real short-term interest rate of 9 percent or even 8 percent. Such an equilibrium interest rate makes no sense, therefore. And the argument that it was obtained by means of econometric calculation does not hold, as historical interest rates and inflation data since the high runaway inflation was brought under control are short-lived and distorted by two foreign exchange shocks (1999 and 2002). Keynesian structuralist economists have always claimed that the Brazilian economy has certain uniqueness; this book, in discussing Brazilian post-1994 macroeconomics, adopts this assumption. But, in this case, those claiming a uniqueness that borders on the absurd for the equilibrium interest rate of the Brazilian economy are the advocates of the conventional orthodoxy.

On the other hand, I do not believe that a real interest rate equal to zero is reasonable as the equilibrium interest rate in the Brazilian economy today. The equilibrium interest rate is probably at around a real 3 percent, compatible with reasonably open full employment.[5] Therefore, the relevant Philips curve for the Brazilian economy, which, for the sake of simplicity, I assume to be vertical, is in 2006 probably pi_2 rather than pi_1. According to this curve, a 3 percent real interest rate is compatible, at first, with a real inflation rate and an inflation target of, say, 5 percent. Later on, however, in order to lower the inflation rate to zero at the theoretical limit, the Philips curve consistent with an inflation targeting policy would have to shift to pi_3. Consistent and cautious inflation targeting policy may gradually achieve this shift. In fact, zero inflation is not ideal, as, at this rate, relative price adjustments may become deflationary: experience in developed countries suggests that 2 percent is an ideal inflation rate.

Figure 9.2 Interest Rate, Employment, and Inflation

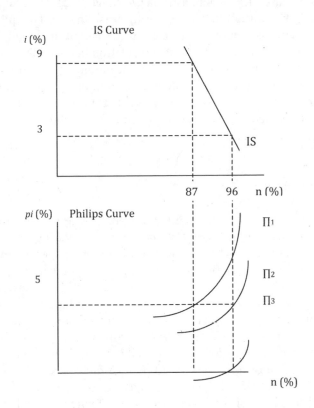

At the moment, however, with such a high real interest rate, the country's economy is entrapped. When the interest rate drops, the exchange rate rises, producing cost inflation, not demand-side inflation. A cost shock should not force a reaction from the Central Bank. According to proper inflation targeting policy, monetary authorities are not to react to temporary shocks. But this is not what goes on in Brazil. In addition, the Central Bank considers only the gap between the inflation forecast and the target, after the practice of the European Central Bank, instead of adopting the US Federal Reserve's more competent practice of making a compromise between the two gaps.

A policy of raising interest rates to fight inflation is justified only if an economy is near full employment and based on a short-term logic. Under these two conditions, the Philips curve–based analysis makes pragmatic sense. When we take longer periods into consideration, however, we see that inflation is more a consequence than a cause of economic crisis (a defense mechanism, as Ignácio Rangel taught); resumed growth tends to reduce inflation levels, not increase them.[6] This phenomenon has been witnessed more than once in the Brazilian economy, but the Rangel curve, that is, the negative correlation between the inflation rate and growth that Rangel proposed, is not unique to the Brazilian economy. One of its most remarkable manifestations occurred in the United States in the 1990s—a period of true full employment while the inflation rate remained incredibly low.[7] In Brazil, too, this possibility should be kept in mind at all times.

Economic Policy

This macroeconomic framework I am presenting is made up of interlocking market variables and economic policy variables. But we can still single out some of the central traits of the orthodox and conventional economic policy Brazil has been pursuing since 1995. The minister of finance and the Central Bank follow the IMF's prescription and pursue two targets only—primary surplus and inflation—and use the interest rate to hit the former, even where inflation is not caused by demand but is inertial or a temporary result of a higher exchange rate. This policy, in addition to being unsuitable for fighting either inflation or the acceleration of inflation caused by cost increases, has a negative effect on the fiscal target, since the budget deficit increases as the interest rate neutralizes fiscal constraint efforts by affecting the high public debt.

Economic authorities regard the Selic rate, although it is formally set every month by the Central Bank, as an endogenous variable, as if it were a market price over which they have no effective control. By defining this rate, the monetary authorities would simply be sanctioning what the "market" authorizes. This "market" is a curious "personalized," "subjective" market that "thinks," "opposes," "likes," or "disapproves." It is not the true market—a competitive institutional space for the exchange of information and the purchase and sale of securities according to certain rules. This market is known in its own environment as the market's "sell side," dominated by security-selling organizations.[8] It is an invention sanctioned by the economist- and dealer-oriented media, which rely on conventionally orthodox economics and take advantage of the speed of communication that information technology affords to disseminate their information, opinions, and interests. Even though this "market" juxtaposes and partly melds with the true market, which it purports to referee, this other market, the "buy side," made up of those who truly buy and sell, even if not always driven by rationality (this is the "herd effect"), is the one that really counts. Making economic policy in Brazil means using decisions and arguments to confront this personalized "market" that makes judgments and represents interests. Many believe that the financial markets are unbeatable, but that is not true. The personalized market is itself a pragmatic institution: when it sees policies it opposed starting to work, its leaders quickly switch positions. This market is often wrong, but it is not dogmatic insofar as its agents are not interested in the value of ideas (this is the domain of ministers and scholars) but motivated by the interests that those ideas legitimize or delegitimize.

Model Summary

The open-ended macroeconomic model I have just described naturally draws some characteristics from macroeconomics textbooks, but it also contains others that are not addressed in them or are approached only in advanced texts, such as unique cases. Essentially, what we have before us is a macroeconomics of stagnation. Its most important characteristics are:

1. The high public debt and a high tax burden; budget deficit and negative public savings despite a high primary surplus. The main explanations are: (1.1) a high basic interest rate itself, weighing on a high level of debt and implying high fiscal spending; (1.2) high social spending to honor a commitment made during the democratic transition to reducing inequality; (1.3) a relatively inefficient state apparatus; and (1.4) fiscal economic populism.
2. The high short-term interest rate. The main explanations are: (2.1) the Central Bank's policy of responding to important interests involved in high rates; and (2.2) an insufficient fiscal adjustment state.
3. A volatile and usually overvalued exchange rate. Volatility is expressed in a cycle characterized by chronic appreciation, balance-of-payment crisis, and sudden appreciation. Overappreciation's main explanations are: (3.1) Dutch disease, which is the most important one, as it is compatible with a balanced current account; (3.2) adoption of the policy of growth with foreign savings and an open capital account that necessarily implies a relatively appreciated exchange rate; (3.3) a high interest rate that attracts foreign capital and thereby appreciates the local currency; (3.4) the

appreciated exchange rate that is used as a tool to control inflation; and (3.5) high income concentration that favors exchange
rate populism or the artificial inflation of wages and consumption
that an appreciated exchange implies.
4. A tendency for a low investment rate; an increase in the rate is
crucial for the economy to grow at a satisfactory pace. Its main
explanations are: (4.1) the overvalued exchange rate that reduces
expected profits or investment opportunities in export-oriented
industries; and (4.2) the high interest rate that requires a high
profit rate to make investments viable, despite low wages.
5. A low inflation rate, but not quite at international levels. Its main
explanations are: (5.1) the Brazilian economy remains partially
indexed; and (5.2) the recurring crises caused by the high interest
rate and the uncompetitive exchange rate, which lead to sudden
depreciations of the real and renewed but temporary inflation.

These characteristics define a chronic crisis for Brazil that has kept
the country semistagnant in terms of income per inhabitant since 1980—
a crisis whose main characteristics are the high short-term interest rate
and an overvalued currency. Beginning in 2004, growth rates increased,
pushed by the sharp depreciation of the real that occurred at the end of
2002, and principally owing to major increase of commodity prices. The
country moved from current account deficit to current account surplus:
instead of receiving, it began to offer foreign savings. Yet, this positive
situation was short-lived. The exchange rate that overshot to R\$3.95 in
December 2002 fell steadily after that, confirming the tendency to the
overappreciation of the exchange rate. As I show in Figure 9.3, in the
first half of 2005, the real overcame the threshold of the industrial equilibrium exchange rate, e_1 (which I believe to be around R\$2.70 per dol-
lar), and industrial enterprises using technology in the state of the art
began to face increasing difficulties to compete internationally. One
year later, the real surmounted the threshold of the current equilibrium
exchange, e_2, in which the current account is intertemporally in equilibrium (which I believe to be around R\$2.10 per dollar). In July 2008 the
current account was already US\$14.7 billion, and the estimated current
account for the year would be almost 3 percent of GDP. The reduction
of the trade surplus and a sharp increase in remittances by the multinational enterprises explained the large deficit. The prediction for 2009
is that this deficit will reach US\$60 billion. Given its high foreign re-
serves, this does not mean that in the next two years the country will
face another balance-of-payment crisis. But it shows how precarious is

Figure 9.3 The Successive Thresholds of Brazil's Exchange Rate

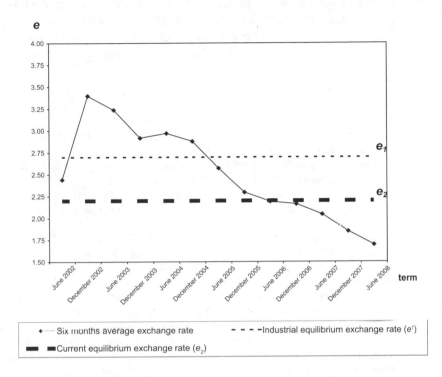

its economic situation, how false is its macroeconomic stability, and it also shows how wrong are conventional economists and journalists who—given the good behavior of Brazil according to the Washington Consensus standards—do not cease to praise present and future feats of Brazil.

In 2008, new and major oil reserves were discovered, and now Brazil is expected to be in the next ten years a major oil exporter. In addition, the excellent conditions existing in Brazil for the production of ethanol from sugarcane, combined with the sophisticated technology that the country was able to develop in this area, open new and positive perspectives for the country. But this also means that the Dutch disease will aggravate the situation—and that the appreciation of the real may be a long-term overvaluation. If this is true—if Brazil continues to follow conventional orthodoxy precepts—the perspectives for it are bleak unless we believe that Brazil can limit itself to be the farm and the mine of the world, leaving the factory business to Asia and the cognitive business to the rich countries. The alternative to this conventional ortho-doxy model is not industrial policy, as old developmentalism would have it (although some industrial policy is always required), but a more competent, exported-oriented macroeconomic policy—a policy that a national development strategy such as new developmentalism endorses.

Notes

1. On this, see Bresser-Pereira (2005d); on the use of open-ended systems in economics, see Dow (1996) and Chick (2004).

2. The fact that the public foreign debt is today very small derives not from policy but from the huge increase in commodity prices. It is not a sustainable situation since the country is already back to current account deficit.

3. Productivity gains caused by depreciation will also have a role to play in the accommodation.

4. The interest rate is not the "only" instrument available to central banks, as the conventional orthodoxy argues; every central bank also tries, with more or less success, to manage the exchange rate. See Bofinger (2001) and Bofinger, Mayer, and Wollmershäuser (2002).

5. Or the equilibrium interest rate is compatible with a "time varying NAIRU" (TV-NAIRU), as the NAIRU proper is fictional.

6. The classic explanation for this kind of behavior can be found in Rangel (1963, 1985). The 1985 paper offers the Rangel curve, showing a negative relationship between growth and inflation.

7. I say "true full employment" because the unemployment rate was around 4 percent, which should correspond to frictional unemployment—and, therefore, full employment—instead of substantially higher rates compatible with the theory of the "natural rate of unemployment."

8. The term *sell side* concerns brokerage houses that mediate transactions, as opposed to the *buy side,* the funds that actually buy securities. The sell side becomes more notorious because brokers produce research reports with opinions on prices and assets, thereby expressing the market's "expectations" in writing.

10
Political Coalitions

In preceding chapters, I have criticized the macroeconomic policy that has been adopted in Brazil since 1995. Thus, I criticized the conventional orthodoxy not principally because it rejects industrial policy, that is, state intervention in the economy, but because, in terms of development strategy, it supports financial markets opening and growth with foreign savings, and, in macroeconomic terms, because it favors high interest rates and noncompetitive exchange rates. Although I believe that it is always necessary to control or coordinate markets, I believe that in a middle-income country such as Brazil, where the industrial revolution has already been completed, the market is supposed to allocate resources. But to do that, the market needs an effectively stable economy, where the exchange rate is competitive, the interest rate is moderate, inflation is low, and reasonably full employment prevails. Of these four conditions of real macroeconomic stability, only one—low inflation—exists in Brazil.

In this book, I tried, as objectively as possible, to depict how the Brazilian macroeconomic system is articulated, choosing as key variables two fiscal variables—public deficit and public debt—and three macroeconomic prices—the exchange rate, the interest rate, and the inflation rate. At the same time, I analyzed fiscal and monetary policies in an attempt to show how these policies are mistaken insofar as they fail to either stabilize or expand the Brazilian economy. I could blame these mistakes mainly on the submission of the economists in charge of the Brazilian economy to the conventional orthodoxy, to the diagnoses and recommendations emanating from the North. This is an appropriate means to analyze economic policies, but the political economy explanation, associated with

221

the identification of interest groups, is more relevant. Inability and cultural mimesis are certainly there, but the political coalitions formed to uphold certain interests are more relevant to understanding the perverse logic of the conventional orthodoxy's macroeconomics of stagnation. The two factors are difficult to separate because right and wrong convictions and private and group interests always meld together. Where economic policymakers lack a republican spirit, that is, the ability to take positions opposite to their own interests but aligned with national interests, their economic assessments will always follow the interests of the groups they represent. Therefore, the Brazilian economic authorities often make decisions that run counter to national interests, whether because they believe in what they are doing or because these decisions are made in consultation with those interests the authorities informally represent.

Interests play an important role in the definition of economic policies, which usually have behind them political coalitions or political pacts. In Brazil, as we can see in Table 10.1, the industrialization and fast growth between 1930 and 1980 took place first under a National-Popular Pact that had Getúlio Vargas as the leading figure; this was followed by a Bureaucratic-Authoritarian Pact. Both of these were nationalist and developmentalist pacts where the industrial bourgeoisie and the public bureaucracy played the major roles. In the late 1970s, a Democratic-Popular Pact became the main collective agent of the transition to democracy. This was probably the more socially encompassing political pact Brazil experienced. The industrial bourgeoisie made its own transition from an authoritarian to a democratic approach and again led the coalition politically. This pact was born out of the indignation of society with President Ernesto Geisel's highly authoritarian "April package" of 1977. The new Democratic-Popular Pact resulted in the Diretas

Table 10.1 Political Pacts Since 1930

	Political Pacts
1930–1959	National-Popular
1960–1964	Political crisis
1964–1977	Bureaucratic-Authoritarian
1977–1985	Democratic-Popular, outside government
1985–1989	Democratic-Popular, as government
1990–2006	Neoliberal-Dependent

Já campaign, the 1985 democratic transition, and the constitution of 1988. The administration of José Sarney (1995–1999) was the first expression of this pact at the government level. Led by Ulysses Guimarães, Congress was able to pass a new, democratic, and social constitution that reflected the consensus of the time, in particular the notions of democracy and social justice, and was imbued with a national character that confirmed the equally national nature of the Democratic-Popular Pact. Yet, President Sarney and the administration's minister of finance, industrialist Dilson Funaro, were unable to address the major crisis of the 1980s. The dramatic failure of the Cruzado Plan of 1986 took Brazil to a major economic and political crisis that would open room for the neoliberal ideological wave from the North to find domestic allies and finally to take control of the country and for a new political coalition to form: the Neoliberal-Dependent Pact. The moderate but effective nationalism that had dominated Brazilian politics since the 1930s was replaced by a globalist or dependent view of the country. In the framework of the neoliberal wave, the new political coalition combining rentiers, the financial sector, and multinational and rich countries' interest became dominant and claimed the monopoly of "universal" values.[1]

As seen in the Introduction to this book, this surrender received a boost from the fact that the dominant political parties, after redemocratization, had been born out of what I have termed the Democracy and Justice Cycle, which left the problems of nation and development in the background. PMDB, which had been the party of democratic resistance; PT, which stands as an early schism of the unions and the lower-middle class in 1981; and PSDB, a second schism of the professional middle class in 1988, are all parties for which the idea of a nation is practically absent. Having appeared during a cycle of ideas and values that denied the possibility of a "national bourgeoisie" and, therefore, of a nation and that assumed that economic development was ensured through foreign savings or multinationals, these parties had no concept of nation. As a result, they did not strongly oppose the new hegemony from the North that came with the neoliberal wave.

The extraordinary economic development Brazil experienced between 1930 and 1980, however, did not occur by mere chance, but as a result of three national political coalitions that attempted to free the country from dependency or carry out its national revolution: (1) the National-Developmentalist Pact, from 1930 to 1960, led by Getúlio Vargas and combining industrialists, "imports-substituting" members of the old landowner oligarchy,[2] government technobureaucrats, and organized laborers; (2) the Bureaucratic-Authoritarian Pact, from 1964 to 1977,

led by the military and with the exclusion of workers; and (3) the Democratic-Popular Pact, which included almost all of the Brazilian society and, despite having been formed in 1977 to spearhead the democratic transition, held office only from 1985 to 1989. During those three
pacts, but mainly the first one, a great national agreement emerged
around economic development. All the pacts endured crises, but the first
two successfully promoted economic development. The third one faced
two crises that took up all of its time: first, the crisis that favored it—the
military regime crisis, which began in 1977 and carried the pact to power
in 1985—then its own crisis, beginning in 1987, with the massive failure of the Cruzado Plan and ending with the 1989 election of Fernando
Collor de Mello as president. This election marked the end of national
pacts, the surrender to conventionally orthodox globalism and neoliberalism, and the formation of the now prevailing coalition, the Neoliberal-
Dependent Pact.

A crucial difference existed between the first two coalitions and the
third in terms of the social cycle of which they were a part. The first
two appeared in the Nation and Development Cycle, which began in the
early twentieth century and ended with the 1975 military coup. In this
cycle, the related concepts of nation and development were so powerful
that, even when the coup of 1964 led to the collapse of the idea of a nation as perceived by society by associating the military and businesspeople with the United States, a limited coalition of industrialists and
bureaucrats within the state continued to lead a national industrialization process for 16 years more. The Democratic-Popular Pact, on the
other hand, although it encompassed almost all of Brazilian society,
emerged in the Democracy and Justice Cycle, which took capitalist development for granted and dismissed nationalism as a necessary condition for development. It is no surprise, therefore, that it failed to prevent
the national revolution from being interrupted and dependency from
growing deeper, as has been the case since 1990. The failure of the
Cruzado Plan was the decisive factor that delegitimized not the ideas of
democracy and social justice but those of the nation and national development that were a part of the Diretas Já ideology. Unable to withstand
the great crisis of the 1980s and to resume economic development, the
Democratic-Popular Pact, undermined by domestic populism, could not
stand up against US hegemony and the globalist ideas that the fall of the
Berlin Wall and the neoliberal ideology of the end of history reinforced.
It was replaced by the Neoliberal-Dependent Pact, devoid of a national
or patriotic character and still prevailing in Brazil, although as of early
2008 its depletion was evident.

For the capitalist class of a developing country such as Brazil, the basic political choice lies in whether to ally with the workers and professional middle classes that make up the domestic market or with the elites of wealthy countries. In the former case, the capitalists must accept higher direct wages and also indirect wages in the form of public education, health, and social security services rendered to workers and the professional middle class. In exchange, it will have a larger and safer domestic market in which to realize profits, and the governments that represent it will enjoy greater political legitimacy. In the latter case, local capitalist elites may accept lower domestic direct and indirect wages and enjoy a friendlier welcome—although never one on an equal standing—from their counterparts in wealthy countries while losing the benefits of the first choice. In the case of a large country such as Brazil, with a respectable domestic market, the second choice made sense for the capitalist class only during the Cold War, when real fear of communism existed. It now makes sense for rentiers alone. Even the benefits for the financial industry are debatable, because, especially in the case of large retail banks, they depend on an expanding domestic market for growth and already have access to sophisticated managerial technology that will allow them to enormously expand credit volume when interest rates drop. But, probably because of the North's ideological hegemony, the class still includes not just rentiers but businesspeople and active capitalists, who still think in terms of the conventional orthodoxy and would rather align themselves with the northern elites than strike an alliance with Brazil's poor and middle classes and thereby form a national pact. Businesspeople resist forming a national alliance because they feel oppressed by the excessive spending that populist governments engage in to attract votes and benefit the state bureaucracy. Although this class does realize that the absence of a true nation prevents the country from developing, the concept of a national agreement is as yet unclear for them, whereas the temptation to identify with the North remains very strong.

The collapse of the Democratic-Popular Pact from 1987 to 1989 was the cause of the defeat, in the 1989 presidential elections, of Ulysses Guimarães and Mário Covas, the two great nationalist leaders who had emerged during the fight for redemocratization, and the accession to power of the political maverick Fernando Collor, with a neoliberal, or modernizing, program. Of all social classes, industrialists were the most confused by the events of the time. They had been the dominant group since the times of Vargas and the National-Developmentalist Pact; they had survived the coup of 1964 and allied with the military to become the most influential group during the Bureaucratic-Authoritarian Pact;

they had been involved in the movement for redemocratization and again played the role of ruling class in the Democratic-Popular Pact, but now saw themselves evicted from power. Some of the reforms adopted by the subsequent governments, such as quick trade liberalization and, above all, opening the capital account, are anti-industrial policies. Forms of industrial policy that involve incentives or subsidies come under merciless attack and are scaled back. After 1990, for the first time since 1930, industrialists, the Federação das Indústrias do Estado de São Paulo (Federation of Industries of the State of São Paulo, FIESP), and the National Industrial Confederation were outside the walls of power.

In the next section of this chapter I again discuss this new pact, relating it to the Washington Consensus; in the subsequent section, I discuss the need for a national agreement that can serve as the basis for a new political pact that is popular—which means relying on the involvement of workers, in addition to businesspeople in productive sectors—and also national.

The Neoliberal-Dependent Pact and the Washington Consensus

The Neoliberal-Dependent Pact that has been dominant in Brazil since 1990 is a conservative and globalist pact. Because it is conservative, at first it included productive-sector businesspeople. But since the early 2000s they realized that the Washington Consensus is incompatible with economic development, and as development has a direct bearing on their interests, they are in search of an alternative. At the domestic level, this political coalition is made up essentially of rentiers who benefit from the high interest the state pays, financial industry agents who charge commissions from rentiers or are rentiers themselves, and the owners of utilities operating as monopolies or near-monopolies. These groups, and rentiers especially, are not clearly defined. There are large and small rentiers as well as rentiers who are also businesspeople or wage earners. In terms of political action, however, a person either behaves mainly as a rentier or mainly as an active businessperson or member of the professional middle class. On the other hand, because this coalition is globalist, that is, based on a belief that Northern countries have an interest in the development of Southern countries—directly and through their control of institutions such as the IMF and the World Bank—it also relies on the distant but effective participation of the governments and elites in those countries as well as on the more direct participation of the multinationals operating in Brazil. Although rentiers, the financial industry, and the capitalists who have invested in utilities are mainly interested in the high interest rate and high monopolistic prices, wealthy countries and multinationals are interested in the uncompetitive exchange rate, which reduces the country's competitiveness and increases the value of remitted profits, dividends, and royalties. There is nothing surprising about the association of nationals on unequal terms with foreigners, as the co-optation of local elites has always been a favorite strategy of empires. It is based on the strength of the prevailing ideology and on common economic interests. As Paulo Nogueira Batista Jr. (2006, p. 6) notes, "hegemonic nations operate in such a way as to benefit those willing to cooperate with their projects for power."

The liberal and globalist view also finds expression in the belief that the financial markets in Brazil and abroad know best. In fact, markets are institutions whose role is to control and coordinate economic systems, but they are not neutral: they reflect the interests of their participants. Many economists, influenced by the economic liberalism that lies at the root of economics, instead of arguing that wealthy countries know best, prefer to say that it is the markets that do. Markets are excellent coordination mechanisms that allocate resources fairly well, but insofar as they are institutions made up of persons and firms, they are also interested parties: because they are not driven by improved income distribution, they also lack national interest as a criterion. On the other hand, financial markets have become international in the course of globalization, given the great mobility that new technologies have lent to capital. Therefore, the concept of a domestic or national market—which is central to a national view—is foreign to the global and neoliberal view.[3] Thus, as Luís Nassif (2006) writes, "let us assume that the market does have this knowledge and an interest in defending national interests; if an international crisis occurs, it will still leave the country, even if all of its recommendations are followed to the letter."

When the Neoliberal-Dependent Pact became the dominant political coalition in Brazil, the national revolution, that is, the formation of a Brazilian nation-state with the transfer of decisionmaking centers to within the country, was interrupted and the country returned to the semicolonial status such as it had had in the 1822–1930 period. As a semicolony, the nation is weakened by the absence of an agreement among classes, because it lacks the characteristic that Otto Bauer (1907) defined as fundamental—the awareness of a common fate. It will then lack a national development or international competition strategy, and growth will be more difficult, or even impossible. Instead of having a national strategy, the country will submit to a conventional orthodoxy that changes over time. For a century and a half, it was based on the law of comparative advantage. This was how Britain tried to "kick away the ladder" from under the United States and Germany, unsuccessfully, and from under Brazil, successfully until 1930.

Since the 1970s, the policy of growth with foreign savings with an appreciated exchange rate is the modern means by which developed countries try to neutralize competition from the rest of the world. Chang (2002) showed that they have been acting this way since the nineteenth century, based mainly in the law of comparative advantage; now, as I argue in this book, they do it through the policy of growth with foreign savings. Although this conventional orthodoxy has been formulated in wealthy countries that remain strongly nationalistic, it rejects any nationalism on the part of developing countries, equating it with populism.

The Neoliberal-Dependent Pact's ideological instrument for dealing with economic problems is the Washington Consensus or, more specifically, the conventional orthodoxy. Although this orthodoxy is quick to play the "conspiracy theory" card against anyone who identifies the interests that lie behind the economic policy it recommends, it has its own explanation for the class interests that hamper the stability and growth of the Brazilian economy. In its view, economic development fails to occur or the interest rate refuses to fall because populist politicians are reluctant to displease voters and because the state bureaucracy wants to conserve its privileges. The dominant thinking in the Neoliberal-Dependent Pact therefore holds that there is a coalition of politicians and bureaucrats that has captured the state and prevents Brazil's economic development. The state is reduced to its servants or its apparatus and demonized: the state and its bureaucrats are painted as the cause of all evil in Brazil. Although populist politicians do exist and the public wealth is still partly a captive of the bureaucracy, the analysis is biased. State capture is not the prerogative of politicians or the bureaucracy in developing countries. Politicians are always powerful, but few, and always represent the interests of other groups. The state bureaucracy is a strategic subset of the professional or bureaucratic middle class but has had no significant power in Brazil since the military regime collapsed. Under the Democratic-Popular Pact it had no power to wield because it was always accused by the new rulers of having been complicit with the military regime. Thrown out of power, the state bureaucracy was limited to defending its corporate interests, as was the case, for instance, with the Single Regime Act, through which it was able to secure a series of privileges.[4] The Neoliberal-Dependent Pact sees it as the opponent.

At present, if the Neoliberal-Dependent Pact's economic policy were to be believed, one might assume that the state bureaucracy and, more generally, the professional middle class have considerable power. That is not true. The two prevalent parties in this period, PSDB and PT, are both fundamentally supported by the professional and bureaucratic middle class, but they are a mixture of public and private bureaucracy. They have sympathizers among state bureaucrats, but their support base lies in the broad middle class of managers, professors, intellectuals, labor leaders, and association leaders of all kinds. Within the conventionally orthodox ideological framework, the state bureaucracy is the archenemy, a kind of evil angel or a weed that prevents Brazil's development. And it could not be otherwise, given the orthodoxy's neoliberal nature and the fact that its ideas emerged from wealthy countries and the global hegemony they exert. For their dominion to exist, for them to neutralize a developing country's competitiveness, nothing is more strategic than to divide and conquer, nothing is more important than undermining the basic agreement that forms a nation, that is, the agreement between active businesspeople and the state bureaucracy.

The discourse that extols the virtues of reducing the state and criticizes the bureaucracy exists in wealthy countries themselves, but the objective fact is that the state, as measured by the tax burden, has not become smaller since 1980; the pace of growth has dropped, but growth remains, and the national agreement between large corporations and the state bureaucracy is still operative. On the other hand, in developing economies, which serve as "labs" for Northern ideologies and organizations such as the World Bank and the IMF, an ever-tempting possibility is to put the neoliberal rhetoric into practice and, in addition to criticizing state intervention, to undermine the agreement between local business elites and the state bureaucracies. Now, this is the agreement that allows the state to become an instrument for economic development; it is what allows not only industrial policy but the country's entire macroeconomic policy to be considered as supporting domestic enterprise. When workers join this agreement, as they typically do in democracies, the state, in addition to being an instrument for economic growth, becomes an instrument to reduce inequality and increase social cohesiveness.

Insofar as the Washington Consensus is the practical expression of neoliberal ideology, it is the ideology of the market against the state and its bureaucracy. Although new developmentalism wants a strong state and a strong market and sees no contradiction between the two, the Washington Consensus wants to strengthen the market by weakening the state, as if a zero-sum game existed between the two institutions.

Francis Fukuyama (2004), who is above suspicion in this subject, recently admitted this mistake on the part of US policy. The conventional orthodoxy, therefore, since the second half of the twentieth century has played the role laissez-faire played in the preceding century. The state has grown in terms of the tax burden and of the level of market regulation, as a result of the increased dimensions and complexity of modern societies. A strong and relatively large state is a necessary condition for a strong and competitive market. The Washington Consensus is the practical reaction against this growth of the state's apparatus. To be sure, the state also grew for the sake of creating jobs to employ the bureaucracy, but the conventional orthodoxy is not interested in distinguishing legitimate from illegitimate state growth. It is the ideology of the minimalist state, of the night-watchman state, of the state concerned only with domestic and international security, leaving economic coordination, infrastructure investments, and even health and education services to the market. It is the individualistic ideology that assumes that all are equally capable of standing up for their interests. It is, therefore, an ideology of the right wing, of the more powerful, of the wealthier, of the better educated—of the high bourgeoisie and the high bureaucracy. The fact that it is right in its criticism of state inefficiency does not make it acceptable, as this inefficiency is obvious. Its objective is to reduce taxes and direct and indirect real wages by removing the protection given to labor, thereby making firms more competitive in an international market full of developing countries equipped with cheap labor.

The economic policy that has been in force in Brazil since 1990 is that of the Neoliberal-Dependent Pact. The Brazilian state is naturally not completely captive to its members. They reap the most benefits and not only the classic and legitimate benefits a capitalist state assures businesspeople: public order, ensured property, and enforcement of contracts. The main benefit today lies in the interest paid to rentiers. These benefits also include the profits and royalties paid to multinationals, who benefit from the Brazilian domestic market without reciprocity. Sectors excluded from the pact, however, are powerful enough to exact their share. Large manufacturing and services businesses receive subsidized loans from the BNDES; farmers also have subsidized loans from Banco do Brasil; large utilities enjoy monopolistic profits; the middle class has access to free state-sponsored universities; the state bureaucracy relies on a privileged retirement system; and the poor gain from minimum-income programs that have been called *bolsas* (grants) in Brazil: Bolsa Escola, Bolsa Família. But the fact remains that the Brazilian state apparatus operates as a vast income transfer agency. The poor, the main victims of the heavy Brazilian tax burden, get in return only a small share of their contribution, in the form of the *bolsas,* which I see as legitimate. If public expenditures were divided into legitimate expenditures and rents, the captures mentioned above in the form of unreasonable interest rates and subsidies of all kinds must amount to one-third of public spending, as seen in Chapter 6.

The dominant political coalition is naturally the main beneficiary. For it, the strategic institutions to capture are academia and the Central Bank. The capture of academia lies beyond the scope of this book but is essential, as this is the capitalism of knowledge or of technicians, where domination no longer involves force but ideological hegemony. The central domination strategy was to lead the brightest Brazilian students to obtain Ph.D.'s from foreign universities. Sending technicians and scientists in the natural sciences to study in doctorate programs abroad is advisable, but sending Brazil's brightest students to four and five years of graduate economics abroad has been the path to alienation par excellence in economics teaching and research.

This practice also facilitates the capture of the Central Bank by the financial market. As discussed in earlier chapters, the high short-term interest rate present in Brazil can be explained only by this capture. Other causes do exist, in particular the fiscal imbalance, but it has become clear that this imbalance alone, which is largely due to the interest rate itself, is not enough to explain the existing rates. Analysis of the behavior of monetary authorities clearly shows that the Central Bank and the Ministry of Finance, subject as they are to the concepts of the conventional orthodoxy, do not see the interest rate as a problem. The objective of keeping it as low as possible, as the Federal Reserve Bank Act mandates, is completely remote from the Central Bank. The need for the government in general and the Central Bank in particular to reduce the real short-term interest rate to acceptable levels is never even mentioned.

Even though the Neoliberal-Dependent Pact gave the wealthy the privilege of high interest rates, the political power of the poor made itself felt in elections and created the need to raise their income by means of increased social spending and a higher minimum wage. As a consequence, Brazil had income concentration on the very wealthy on the one hand and reduced poverty on the other. But because per capita income grew very little, it is no surprise that the middle class was caught in the gears in the process. Nor is it surprising that this class, whose political weight is usually great because it is an "opinion maker," was swept aside in the 2006 elections, having voted for the defeated candidate, whereas the very rich and the poor cast their votes for the reelection of

Luís Inácio Lula da Silva. No presidential vote has ever been so polarized in Brazil, in terms of income and education, as the 2006 elections, notwithstanding the absence of coherent ideological debate. The winner was the candidate who managed to identify with the poor, not the one with a clear message for the nation, as neither of the two front-runners had such a message to offer. The fact that the middle class, which the economic plan had in a chokehold, lost its political voice cannot, however, be treated lightly. Throughout the entire electoral process, what we saw was a deep crisis of the political system. Although the Neoliberal-Dependent Pact showed its depletion, society was confused and disoriented as to what alternative path to take.

National Agreement

Given the importance of the Neoliberal-Dependent Pact and its intrinsic inability to lead to Brazil's development, the natural question is whether there is a potential alternative coalition with a national character. Although no safe forecast can be made, I believe that Brazilian society already shows sufficient indication that a development-oriented national pact is about to emerge. In other words, the Brazilian nation, after its surrender to hegemonic thinking in the late 1980s, is showing signs that it may be rebuilt—that there is a possibility of a comprehensive national agreement to return its cohesiveness and sense.

These indications are directly related to the failure of the Neoliberal-Dependent Pact since 1994 and, more generally, to the depletion of the Democracy and Justice Cycle that began in 1964. This cycle became depleted not because the goals of liberty and social justice have been achieved but because its central assumption—that economic development was ensured—failed to be borne out or, in other words, because the cycle forgot the concept of nation. Therefore, it is becoming increasingly clear that Brazilian society can advance toward democracy and reduced inequality only if it resumes economic development and, as a result, recovers its status as a nation.

For a nation to exist, a state and a territory are not enough: there must also be the cohesion that only a national agreement can ensure. A national agreement is the basic social contract that gives rise to a nation and keeps it strong and cohesive; it is the comprehensive agreement among a modern society's social classes that allows this society to become a true nation, that is, a society equipped with a state capable of formulating a national development strategy. In this present age of global capitalism, the world's economy is organized along the lines of two competing basic units: firms and nation-states. Conventional economics tends to ignore competition among nations, emphasizing competition among firms, but the two occur simultaneously and relatively independently. Globalization is generalized competition on a planetary level among firms and among nation-states or countries. The economic objective of firms is to make profits and grow, whereas nation-states aim at economic development. Firms prepare for competition by innovating, that is, by accumulating capital and incorporating technical progress in their production, whereas nation-states develop by educating their population, establishing the necessary infrastructure for investment and growth, creating opportunities for profitable investment, maintaining macroeconomic stability, and defining institutions to ensure property and contracts.

Within the democratic framework, not only the state but also the nation must undergo a democratization process, insofar as workers and the new professional middle classes that have been emerging since the twentieth century have become better educated and equipped with additional political power. As a consequence, they share the state's power with the capitalist class. The state ceases to be the expression of a class in order to become the entire society's instrument for collective action or, more accurately, to become the instrument of politically organized society: of civil society or of the nation.

Civil society and nation are similar concepts, but the latter is broader, encompasses more people, and has a clearer economic meaning. A modern society can be politically organized in three ways besides the state: (1) the "people," the universe of citizens with equal rights and equal power: one citizen, one vote; (2) "civil society," where the power of these citizens is proportional to each one's power to command based on his or her organization skills, wealth, and knowledge; and (3) the "nation," which is the same as civil society but aims to include every citizen and has both class and international connotations: it does not exclude domestic conflict but implies a national agreement, an agreement among classes, when it comes to competing internationally and achieving economic development.

In the formative process of national states, the national agreement is, therefore, a necessary condition for the existence of the nation itself. Although the state was authoritarian as an absolutist monarchy or relatively authoritarian under liberal regimes, a national agreement already existed inasmuch as the bourgeoisie enjoyed the solidarity of the remainder of society when it came to defense from a foreign enemy or competing with a foreign adversary. Now, as the state becomes democratic and no longer represents a class so unilaterally, the national agreement gains consistency, and the two fundamental ideologies that presided over its formation—liberalism and nationalism—become dominant. Liberalism and nationalism have always clashed with each other and have been challenged by socialists since the nineteenth century, but as capitalism proved itself more capable of promoting economic development and incorporated a growing number of socialist values and institutions, those two ideologies, even if partly contradictory, remained prevalent. In developed countries, nationalism has become so dominant, shared by every citizen and every class, that it is no longer a distinguishing factor. In such countries, no one has any doubt that the government's role is to defend national labor, knowledge, and capital. It is because nationalism is so strong and tacit that the term *nationalism* could start being used to characterize both the excesses of nationalism, such as those seen in Nazi Germany, and the manifestations in wide sections of peripheral countries that seek real and not merely formal national autonomy, that attempt to free themselves from the yoke of the Washington Consensus.

The developmentalist nationalism of peripheral countries is naturally ill regarded by wealthy countries because of the competitive threat the former countries pose, thanks to their cheap labor and the ease of importing or copying technology. This was already clear in the 1970s, when the emergence of the newly industrializing countries occurred. This gives us two major groups of countries: wealthy countries, whose citizens, joined by their tacit nationalism, no longer need the adjective *nationalist* to distinguish themselves from any of their compatriots, and developing countries. The latter group includes countries that have shaken off dependency, established a national agreement, and adopted a national development strategy—such as Brazil between 1930 and 1980, today's dynamic Asian countries, and Argentina, which appears to have done so after learning its lesson from the deep crisis of 2001. And it includes dependent countries, with no national agreement or development and competition strategy, devoid of a true nation, such as Brazil and Mexico once more since approximately 1990.

In the case of a wealthy country, the national agreement is strong and so is the nation. For its citizens, it would make no sense that the economic policies adopted by the government and inscribed in the state's institutions should be dictated by other, more powerful countries. A small wealthy country may accept the military protection of a stronger country and strike a political alliance with it, but such an alliance never includes economic subordination. On the contrary, it retains an independent and competitive stance in this respect. The case of Japan vis-à-vis the United

States is exemplary. In a developing country, the national agreement is weaker by nature, as the nation divides into nationalists and cosmopolitans and, as a result, becomes fragile and dependent. If the country is not just poor but a medium-development country, as is Brazil, it will then be a competitor, and wealthy countries will naturally act to counter its competitiveness.

The more cohesive a nation, the stronger it will be. Cohesiveness, or, as Émile Durkheim put it, the organic solidarity of its members, is the fundamental positive trait of any social system. A social system—and a nation is nothing if not a special kind of social system—will be strong if it is cohesive; if its members, in spite of the inevitable internal conflicts, stand together when it comes to competing with other nations. A nation's cohesiveness springs from its nationalism or patriotism and is its ability to transform the general understanding of a common fate into a national development strategy. Of course many kinds of patriotism exist, and of course nationalism has on occasion been violent, and even terrible. But just as there are violent, authoritarian, racist forms of nationalism—which can turn into xenophobia—so nationalism can also be democratic, liberal, social, and republican.

The nationalism of today's rich and democratic peoples usually sports these four characteristics. Its citizens are nationalists because they identify politically with the nation, although this doesn't stop them from defending the essential equality of rights for every citizen, to whom they advocate the respect for the rule of law, liberty, social justice, and the need for the civic virtues on the part of citizens and rulers to temper the conflicts inherent to large and complex modern societies. Each individual will assign a different weight to those values—which makes it possible to categorize them as left- or right-leaning, as conservatives or progressives—but all will combine the same values in different ways and all will react indignantly to racism, privilege, and authoritarianism.

Within the framework of globalization, in the early twenty-first century what is the nature of the national agreement that must be struck for Brazil to resume development? This is not about making a list of national priorities. Instead, I will simply introduce the requirements for such an agreement—requirements the citizens of Brazil must accept so that the country can exist and stand strong and cohesive. The first assumption of a national agreement is universal acceptance that the agreement is necessary for the nation's cohesiveness and identity. The second is that the age of globalization is marked by generalized competition among nation-states. The third assumption is that nation-states can successfully compete only if, in addition to achieving reasonable social cohesiveness, they have a clear understanding that they must make their own economic policy decisions, in light of their own judgment rather than of the advice and pressure from wealthy countries. The fourth is that medium-income countries such as Brazil have no choice but to absorb foreign science and technology and to compete internationally: the alternative of closing in on itself implies surrendering in advance. The fifth is that, in their development process, middle-income countries cannot rely on "assistance" or funds from wealthy countries, but must rely on their own ability to save and accumulate capital.

An Alternative Coalition

The clearest sign that an opportunity now exists for the formation of a new national agreement—for an alternative political coalition to the Neoliberal-Dependent Pact—is what is happening to Brazilian industrialists. They were the dominant group in Brazil throughout the national-developmentalist period, played a decisive role in the democratic transition that began in 1977 (when they began to break the agreement they had made with the military), and were again the dominant group in the Democratic-Popular Pact of 1977.

But with the failure of the Cruzado Plan, industrialists became disoriented and disorganized. They realized that the import-substitution model was depleted and that the conventionally orthodox alternative was unacceptable, but did not know where to direct their political activity. For some time, they stood perplexed; organizations such as FIESP and the National Industrial Confederation suddenly saw themselves without a discourse. The neoliberal wind was then blowing with all its might, and industrialists felt themselves at a loss for arguments to counter the new facts. They saw a threat in the trade openness that was needed to make the industrial sector more competitive, when in fact a threat existed only if the opening was too fast, as it was in the end; on the other hand, financial openness, which was a bigger threat, was not regarded as such. This was when the top 30 domestic industrialists founded the Instituto de Estudos para o Desenvolvimento Industrial (Industrial Development Studies Institute; IEDI) to defend Brazilian manufacturing. But, ill-advised at first, without support from competent macroeconomists and political scientists, they failed to realize that the main threat was at the macroeconomic level and from the exchange rate in particular.[5] Instead, they insisted that the government should adopt a "nonselective industrial policy," a clear oxymoron. They were obviously perplexed and confused in the face of the crisis and the changing political pact. After almost 60 years of relative political hegemony (1930–1987), industrialists realized that they were losing power but, faced with the ideological weight of the neoliberal wave, lacked an alternative discourse. As a consequence, many let themselves be carried away by the Washington Consensus and the modernity it promised.

In recent years, however, the failure of the conventionally orthodox economic policy has become clear, and the industrialists realize that they have been left high and dry. So, led by FIESP, IEDI, and the National Industrial Confederation, they have changed their tune.[6] They have engaged better macroeconomic advisers, and their criticism is no longer limited to excessive trade openness and the lack of an industrial policy to target the high interest rate and the appreciated exchange rate. Even so, they remain perplexed, probably because hegemonic thinking weighs heavily on them. They see the problem but hesitate to embrace the solution. Former FIESP president Horácio Piva (2006) said: "We are all astonished, like the rest of society, but no one can come up with a menu of choices capable of getting us out of this impasse." On the other hand, they insist on treating the state and its bureaucracy as adversaries, without realizing that this is a strategy to divide the nation. Paulo Cunha (2006, p. 23), who is probably the most important intellectual leader of Brazil's industrialists, is indignant at the near-stagnation of the Brazilian economy and is a critic of the macroeconomic policy, but he focuses his criticism on the issue of the state's size, arguing that "Brazil is cornered by its state."

An alternative to the current economic policy obviously exists, but in order to realize it one must also be capable of criticizing the Neoliberal-Dependent Pact—which businesspeople are still reluctant to do. Reestablishing the alliance of businesspeople with the state bureaucracy is essential to resuming development, but they do not yet realize this. Although they understand the importance of exchange control, they do not go as far as criticizing the policy of growth with foreign savings; despite their indignation with the interest rate, they continue to blame the fiscal imbalance and the excessive tax burden on political populism and the state bureaucracy's inefficiency and privileges. But they are beginning to realize that what took place in Brazil was a process of capturing the state's wealth, of trespass against citizens' republican rights, which is less beneficial to bureaucrats than to rentiers, the financial industry, and multinationals; that, like the workers and the state bureaucracy, they, and more generally the entire productive business community, are excluded from the existing pact. One of the difficulties they face in understanding the problem is that some of them have become rentiers, either because they sold out to multinationals or because they kept their firms in a dormant state while keeping their accounts in the black through financial income. But this group, though capable of political influence, is a minority. The overwhelming majority of industrialists are now indignant with how the Brazilian economy has been run and with the meager results it has been showing in terms of economic growth.

It is not at all surprising that industrialists as a social class are not completely clear about developments and fail to realize that the current state of affairs can be overcome only if their leaders can take part in a comprehensive national agreement. And that certainly does not prevent them from acting as a national bourgeoisie. Fernando Henrique Cardoso (1964), after interviewing a large number of industrialists, concluded that they were not a national bourgeoisie, that is, a business class committed to the national interest. As the last chapter of his *Empresário Industrial e Desenvolvimento Econômico* clearly shows, he expected the interviewees to show an awareness of Brazil's problems; but in fact they lacked one. Nor should they be expected to have one. Businesspersons are energetic people whose desire for achievement prompts them to take risks and innovate. Their fundamental goals are profit and corporate growth. They do not specialize in ideas and general analyses. In capitalist societies, this role belongs to politicians, the high bureaucracy, and intellectuals. In some cases, businesspersons may also sport traits of these other professions, but these are exceptions that surveys, in their pursuit of generalized findings, cannot discern. Cardoso's book was published in 1964, when businesspersons, threatened by the political radicalism that the 1959 Cuban Revolution had generated, allied with the military and the United States to mount a coup. This then appeared to confirm the book's thesis—a thesis that would later become central to the theory of dependency and the Democracy and Justice Cycle. But this hid an enormous mistake. Of course Brazil lacks an ideal, Bismarckian national bourgeoisie identical or similar to those that existed in rich countries when they made their capitalist revolutions. Brazil, like other Latin American countries, always had "European," and therefore dependent, elites; because its industrial revolution came to pass long after those in central countries, it fell to their ideological hegemony.

But after the 1930s, taking advantage of the crisis that the central system was then experiencing, Brazil managed to stand as a nation—a nation that did not survive the deep crisis of the 1980s and the neoliberal wave. It failed to resist, on the one hand because the crisis was very severe and affected national sovereignty itself as expressed in the country's ability to manage its own currency,[7] and on the other because its elites—not only industrial, but also political and intellectual—are "dependent-national": sometimes, responding to their real interests, the interests of the large economy in which they exist, they are national; at other times, whether for fear of communism as in 1964 or simply because of ideological subordination to a hegemonic center, they are globalist and dependent. They constantly face the dilemma of associating with their people to become a nation or associating with international elites and in practice becoming a colony. Although this might be a real dilemma for a very small country, it is a false one for Brazil. In Brazil, therefore, elites, including businesspeople, experience a constant ambivalence—one that is unknown to the elites in Asian countries, for example. They sometimes identify with a liberal and democratic nationalism, and sometimes become dependent.

But if I had to compare Brazil's industrial and intellectual elites, I would conclude that the former identify better with the nation because their interests are more closely aligned with national interests. In the age of globalization, the uprooting of intellectuals from their national bases is a generalized problem. The domination of foreign academia, and US academia in particular, is overwhelming. This is a result, certainly, of the superior quality of their universities—which is indisputable—but also of simple dependency. One example is scoring under the Capes Qualis system,[8] which serves to evaluate publications by Brazilian researchers. Under this system, papers published in good foreign reviews get two or three times the score given for publications in good domestic academic reviews. The argument for this is that "it is harder to publish in international reviews"—which is true. But what Brazilian academia is accomplishing with this practice is to subject the standards of accreditation of its scientific production to determination by foreign universities. This would be a reasonable thing to do with physics, biology, or mathematics reviews; but with the social sciences— for economics, for political science—it is a sign of severe ideological subordination.

Industrialists also have problems of national self-affirmation and self-esteem, but nothing compared with what academia suffers. Even among intellectuals, though, a rediscovery of the nation and of national identity is beginning. But concern with cultural identity alone will not suffice; the national political identity, which is something different, also has to be addressed. For example, Brazil has a stronger cultural identity than Canada, but Canada's political identity—the people's awareness that the government exists to defend domestic labor, knowledge, and capital—is much stronger.

Another important sign has been the change in attitudes by the press. The media, like the state, reflect the correlation of forces within a society. After the fall of the Berlin Wall, which in Brazil coincided with the hyperinflation of February 1990 (when the month's inflation was over 50 percent), neoliberalism and the US hegemony became absolute and the Brazilian press reflected this. The conventional orthodoxy was regarded as the only responsible economic policy path. After 2002, however, as society changed, so did the media. Newspapers started to shed more light on the brutal weight of the interest expenditure on the public budget and on the economic policy's puny results in terms of growth; at the same time, they began to publish new-developmentalist arguments more often.

The circumstances are therefore far from ideal, but conditions do exist for Brazilians to informally strike a new national agreement, for the formation of a new economic development–oriented political coalition. The basis will have to be formed by national industrialists because Brazil's economic development still depends on a fundamental level on the growth of their firms. But a distinction must be made between transformation industrialists, who are now in crisis, and those connected with agribusiness and mining, which are prospering under the effects of the Dutch disease. The former are natural members of this coalition; for the latter, this will depend on their stance concerning the issue of the exchange rate. They all have an interest in a depreciated exchange rate, but an appreciated rate like the one prevailing in Brazil since 2005 makes agribusiness and mining quite profitable. This is why we often see the economists who represent them denying the existence of the Dutch disease in Brazil, arguing that the trade surplus remains high (which was perfectly compatible with the disease before 2007, the point at which export growth calmed down while imports soared and the trade surplus diminished) or that industrial exports remain high (exports from agribusiness, mines, and plants that are quickly turning into *maquilas* are also perfectly compatible with the Dutch disease). They fear taxes on exports, although such taxes would not harm them because they would either accompany foreign exchange depreciation or not make any sense. Politically, however, the agribusiness and mining sectors are so far undecided, aligning now with the conventional orthodoxy, now with other industrialists.

In addition to the dissatisfaction of transformation industrialists, there is growing discontent among the professional middle class and workers and a growing concern among intellectuals with the problem of the nation. The middle classes see their own hardship, the reduced opportunities available to their children, and the transformation of Brazil into an emigrant country, where increasing numbers of middle-class youth can find employment only abroad. The professional middle class, however large and heterogeneous, will always be a strategic partner; it now includes the managerial, technical, and intellectual cadres that make up a nation's knowledge capital. Workers, in turn, who bear the brunt of the troubles and already endure chronically high unemployment and almost stagnant wages, should naturally become part of a national development–oriented agreement. Certain sectors will stay away from the agreement or see their current power reduced. I refer, in particular, to the rentiers who thrive on high interest rates, the members of the financial industry, and the operators of monopolistic utilities. The financial industry, however, will continue to play a decisive role in the domestic economy, and its members would soon become part of the national agreement.

The most strategic understanding to be had among participants is that between businesspeople and the state's bureaucrats and politicians. This is the agreement that Brazil now sorely lacks, insofar as businesspeople have let themselves be influenced by the North and have accepted the neoliberal thesis that the source of all of the country's problems lies in the bureaucracy. Now, even if this bureaucracy, like any social group, defends interests that do not always coincide with more general ones, the fact of the matter is that it plays a strategic role within the state apparatus, just as businesspeople play a strategic role in the accumulation and production process. On the other hand, we know that the state is a nation's instrument par excellence for collective action and that it is the duty of politicians (elected bureaucrats) to lead this state with advice from career bureaucrats. Therefore, a national agreement and the definition of a national development strategy are possible only if businesspeople and state bureaucrats overcome their differences and mistrust. The great development Brazil experienced from the 1930s to the 1970s was possible only because this basic agreement was in place.

Achieving a national agreement will mean that its participants will be able to use the state as an instrument for collective action in pursuit of their political objectives. To this end, they will have to be willing to face the agreement's adversaries. A need for such an agreement is denied by neoliberals, who claim any development strategy is unnecessary; by the hard right and the hard left; and by globalist elites that have fallen to co-optation by wealthy countries. Under the empires of old, domination took place by force and the cooperation of local elites; under the hegemonic system, force has been largely replaced with soft power, the immense ideological power of US academia, cinema, and pop music, so that the co-optation of local elites is compounded by the submission of broad segments of Brazilian society, held in thrall by the scientific, technological, and cultural superiority of wealthy countries. In this process, because hegemonic countries are complex democracies, one can always rely on assistance from many of their citizens, who are aware that we do all live in the same world and that cooperation must often take precedence over competition.

Notes

1. I discuss Brazil's political coalitions since 1930 extensively in Bresser-Pereira (2003).

2. These included cattle raisers such as Getúlio Vargas himself, for example.

3. The fact that the domestic market is a fundamental reason for productive-sector businesspeople to be nationalist does not mean that we should return to the import-substitution model. It just means that the domestic market is a national asset that can and should be negotiated: this is what is done in foreign trade, with countries opening their markets reciprocally and multilaterally to others. But this is not the case with direct investment, where the opened markets in developing countries are not met with reciprocity in wealthy countries.

4. This law was amended, with the removal of the privileges, when I was minister of federal administration and state reform from 1995 to 1998.

5. I remember, in the first three years of the 1990s, when I attended the meetings of FIESP's Higher Economy Council, pointing out the problem to other members. I said: "You are resisting trade openness, which is inevitable; it just needs better management; but you fail to realize that the main risk lies in the exchange rate, which will probably appreciate with the end of high inflation, which will come sooner or later." In 2001, when I was invited to dinner with IEDI officials, the first thing their leader, Paulo Cunha, did was remind me of that remark.

6. The 2004 election of Paulo Skaff as president of FIESP marked this change. Industrialists have since then adopted a clearer position on changes in macroeconomic policy, taking advantage of the criticism that since 2002 has been gaining momentum and becoming consistent among economists.

7. As Belluzzo and Almeida (2002, p. 17) note, "this crisis . . . was above all a sovereignty crisis of the state, threatened in one of its fundamental prerogatives, managing its money. Managing the money means, first and foremost, preserving the unity of its three functions—unit of account, medium of exchange and store of value—and preventing other assets (foreign currency, public or private securities, private merchandise) from taking over any or all of these functions."

8. The Capes Qualis system is the Ministry of Education's Higher Learning Bureau.

11

New Developmentalism

I hope I have shown clearly in the preceding chapters why the macroeconomic policy that the conventional orthodoxy proposes and practices is incompatible with Brazil's economic development. This policy is the fruit of a political coalition where some partners, headquartered abroad, are mainly interested in neutralizing the country's ability to compete internationally, and other partners are interested in securing immediate benefits domestically. Still, a question remains: might there be an alternative economic policy? The basic thesis of the conventional orthodoxy is that there is not. The only viable alternatives are itself, on the one hand, and economic populism and the return of inflation, on the other; a choice between the logic of domination and that of chaos. Such a choice is naturally fear-inducing. Therefore, by building a frightening straw man, the global hegemony from the North imposes itself on peripheral societies and keeps them hostage to fear. All dominant groups use fear as an instrument of domination. In the past, under authoritarian regimes it was straightforward fear of the police apparatus and of political repression. Today, in democratic regimes, fear is generated in a more sophisticated manner: it is no longer fear of the state but of a certain entity that is partly true, and partly shadow. In the United States, for example, domination works through the fear of terrorism. In Brazil, it works through the fear of inflation.

In this final chapter I show that there is an alternative—the new-developmentalist alternative. An alternative that stands as a third discourse between that of the conventional orthodoxy, which is antinational, and that of the old left's economic populism. This third discourse is essentially nationalist and identified with national interests but is a democratic, liberal, social, and republican nationalism. A third discourse that knows that, in the age of globalization, the most comprehensive principle is that of generalized rivalry among nation-states through their firms but also knows that the openness of all markets and the vigorous competition that characterizes it imply greater interdependency and require increased cooperation, particularly in the process of defining international rules or institutions to regulate this competition.

New developmentalism is the name given to a national development strategy that arises as a natural solution to the lasting quasi stagnation of the Brazilian economy and, at the same time, is the set of diagnoses, policies, and institutions that must act as the basis for the formulation of such a strategy. What is a national development strategy? It is more than just ideology: it is a set of institutions and policies, of diagnoses and values geared toward international competition and economic development as it informally involves all of society or a large portion of it. How can it do this? As is typical of institutions, it gives all a route to follow, provides general guidance to be noted. Furthermore, although it does not assume a conflict-free society, it involves a reasonable unity when it comes to competing internationally, and it always considers the actions of other adversaries or competitors. It is not, however, a national development plan, because it is not formal, because it lacks a document that accurately defines objectives and policies, because the agreement among social classes inherent in it has neither text nor signatures. A national development strategy motivates individual behavior not only through individual interests but also through competition with other nations. Its leadership is the responsibility of the government and of the more active members of civil society. Its fundamental instrument is the state itself, given the state's ability to set and implement rules and policies with its administrative and financial capabilities. The result, from the moment a great national agreement is struck and society starts loosely, but effectively, sharing methods and objectives, is accelerated development—a long period during which the country experiences high growth rates in per capita income and living standards.

A national development strategy implies a set of variables, both real and institutional, that are fundamental to economic development. An increase in the nation's capacity for savings and investment; the way technical progress is incorporated into production; human capital development; the increased national social cohesiveness that results in social capital or in a stronger and more democratic civil society; a macroeconomic policy that ensures the financial health of the state and the state-nation, leading to domestic and foreign indebtedness levels within conservative limits—all these are constituents of a national development strategy. In this process, institutions, instead of simple one-size-fits-all abstractions, are regarded and conceived of concretely and historically. A national development strategy will gain meaning and power when its institutions—whether short-term ones I call policies or public policies or the relatively permanent ones (institutions proper)—respond to society's needs, when they are compatible with the economy's endowment of production factors or, in broader terms, with the elements that make up society at its structural level.

As a national strategy, new developmentalism is the means by which middle-income countries in the early twenty-first century seek to offset the neutralizing strategies of competing countries and gradually catch up—converge on their income levels. Like old developmentalism, it is not an economic theory but a competition strategy based mainly on classical economics, on Keynesian macroeconomics, and on development economics. It is the set of ideas that enables developing nations to reject the economic reforms and policy proposals of and pressures from rich countries, such as fully open capital accounts and growth with foreign savings, insofar as these proposals are a neoimperialist attempt to prevent their development. It is the practical means by which businesspeople, government bureaucrats, workers, and intellectuals may stand together as a nation and promote economic development. I do not include poor countries as part of new developmentalism, not because they have no need for a national development strategy but because, having yet to attain primitive accumulation and industrial revolution, the challenges they face and the strategies they need are different.

But is not new developmentalism also an ideology, like the Washington Consensus and the bureaucratic-populist discourse? Yes and no. Yes, because every national strategy implies an ideology—a set of ideas and values geared toward political action. No, because unlike the Washington Consensus, which is merely a foreign proposal, new developmentalism will make sense only if based on a domestic consensus and therefore capable of standing as a true national development strategy. Full consensus is impossible, but one that joins together the businesspeople in the productive sector, workers, government bureaucrats, and middle-class professionals—a national agreement, therefore—is now in its formative stages, taking advantage of the failure of the Washington Consensus. This emerging consensus regards globalization as neither a blessing nor a curse, but a system of intense competition among national states through their firms. It understands that, in this competition, it is fundamental to strengthen the state fiscally, administratively, and politically and, at the same time, to provide domestic firms with the conditions to be competitive in the world. It acknowledges, as Argentina has already done after the crisis that hit it in 2001, that development is prevented, in the short run, by an exceedingly high short-term basic interest rate set by the Central Bank that pushes up the long-term interest rate, uncoupling it from Brazil's sovereign risk. It assumes that, in order to achieve development, the investment rate must increase, and the state must make a contribution through positive public savings, the result of contained expenditures. Finally, and more generally, the new developmentalism that is emerging as a national development strategy is based on the conviction that development, in addition to being prevented by the absence of the concept of nation, is also hampered by income concentration, which, besides being unfair, keeps Brazilian society highly heterogeneous, thereby making it more difficult to legitimize institutions and avoid populism.

Old and New Developmentalism Compared

The developmentalism of the 1950s and the new developmentalism differ in terms of two intervening variables. On the one hand, new historical facts changed world capitalism, which moved from its 30 golden years to the more competitive and conservative times of globalization. On the other hand, medium-development countries such as Brazil changed their own development stages, industrialized, and became internationally competitive in the manufacturing sector and are no longer characterized by infant industries and incomplete capitalist structures.

The main change at the international level was from the capitalism of the golden years (1945–1975), when the welfare state was built and Keynesianism reigned while development economics (of Arthur Lewis, Ragnar Nurkse, Celso Furtado, Raúl Prebisch, and Gunnar Myrdal) prevailed as a theory and a practice of economic development, to the neoliberal capitalism of globalization, where growth rates are lower and competition among nation-states is far fiercer.[1] In the golden years, medium-development countries still posed no threat to rich nations. Since the 1970s, however, with the emergence of the newly industrializing countries and, since the 1990s, with the emergence of China, the competition of these countries has greatly increased: the threat their cheap labor poses to rich nations is clearer than ever. At that time, rich nations, and the United States in particular, in need of allies for the Cold War, were far more generous; today, only the poorest African countries can expect some generosity—but even they must be wary, because the treatment that rich nations and the World Bank afford them and the help, or alleged help, they receive are often perverse. The main difference at the national level has to do with the fact that Brazil in the 1950s was completing its capitalist revolution, evolving from a country where surpluses were appropriated by landowners and the state to one that realizes itself through the market. At that time, industry was in its infancy; it is now mature. The growth model was based on import substitution, which was effective in establishing the industrial bases of Latin American countries but which should have been abandoned after the crisis of the 1960s: countries should have begun reducing protection and moved in the direction of an export-led model. They did not do so, however, until the crisis of the 1980s forced them to, often hurriedly and without planning. This 20-year delay was one of the main distortions the developmentalism of the 1950s suffered.

As I sum up in Table 11.1, new developmentalism assumes that middle-income countries have already overcome the infant-industry stage and requires them to be competitive in all industries to which they dedicate themselves; it further requires some industries to be especially competitive in order to export. New developmentalism rejects the 1950s old developmentalist pessimism toward exports. Like any strategy of development, it does not propose to base its growth on the export of low value-added agricultural products, instead laying odds on the possibility of developing countries' exporting manufactured or high value-added goods, and holds this strategy as central. The experience since the 1970s clearly shows that this export pessimism was one of the great theoretical blunders of development economics. Even in the late 1960s, Latin American countries should have begun a decisive transition from the import-substitution to the export-led model, as did South Korea and Thailand. In Latin America, Chile was the first to make this transition

Table 11.1 Old and New Developmentalism Compared

Old Developmentalism	New Developmentalism
State plays a leading role in terms of forced savings and investment in firms.	State has a subsidiary, but important, role in terms of forced savings and investment in firms.
Protectionist and pessimistic	Export-led and realistic
A certain complacency toward inflation	No complacency toward inflation

and, as a result, its development is often cited as an example of a successful neoliberal strategy. In fact, neoliberalism was fully implemented in Chile only between 1973 and 1981 and ended with a major balance-of-payment crisis in 1982.[2] The export-led model is not specifically neoliberal because, strictly speaking and among other factors, the neoclassical economics that lies behind this ideology has no room for development strategies. Dynamic Asian countries, which adopted a developmentalist strategy beginning in the 1950s, could already export manufactured goods in the 1960s and, at least since the 1970s, can be considered new developmentalist countries.

The export-led model has two great advantages over its import-substituting counterpart. First, industries are not restricted to the domestic marketplace. This is important for small countries but also crucial to a country with a relatively large domestic market, such as Brazil. Second, if a country chooses to adopt this strategy, the economic authorities, making industrial policy on behalf of their industries, will be able to count on an efficiency criterion: only firms efficient enough to make exports will benefit from industrial policy. In the case of the import-substitution model, very inefficient firms may be enjoying protection; under the export-led model, the chances of this happening are substantially smaller. The fact that the strategy new developmentalism represents is not protectionist does not mean that countries should be willing to accept indiscriminate openness. They should pragmatically bargain for mutual openness within the domain of the WTO and local trade agreements. And, mainly, it does not mean that the country should renounce industrial policies. The space for these has been reduced by the highly unfavorable agreements of the WTO's Uruguay Round, but room still exists for such policies, which, considered strategically and in terms of future competitive advantages, may provide an important edge as long as the supported firms are successful (Wade 2003; Chang 2006).

New developmentalism rejects the mistaken notion of growth based mainly on public demand and deficits that became popular in Latin America in the 1960s. This was one of the most severe distortions that developmentalism suffered at the hands of its populist followers. The theoretical base of this national development strategy lies in Keynesian macroeconomics and in development economics, which, in turn, rests chiefly on classical economics. John Maynard Keynes pointed out the importance of aggregate demand and legitimized resorting to fiscal deficits in the presence of a recession. He did not, however, advocate chronic budget deficits. His assumption was that a fiscally balanced national economy might, for a brief period of time, relinquish equilibrium to reestablish employment levels.[3] The notable economists who formulated the developmentalist strategy, such as Furtado, Raúl Prebisch, and Ignácio Rangel, were Keynesians and understood that managing aggregate demand was an important tool in promoting development. But—unlike their less distinctive copycats—they never stood for the economic populism of chronic deficits. When Celso Furtado proposed the Triennial Plan of 1963 as a counter against the severe crisis of the early 1960s, those second-rate followers accused him of "having taken a turn to orthodoxy." In fact, what Furtado believed in, and new developmentalism firmly defends, was fiscal balance. New developmentalism defends it not for its "orthodoxy" but because the state is a nation's instrument par excellence for collective action. If the state is so strategically important, its apparatus must be strong, sound, and capable, and, for these very reasons, its finances must be in balance. And more, its debt must be small and with long maturities. The worst thing that can happen to a state as a law-constitutional system is to lose authority, and, as an organization, is to become hostage to creditors, be they domestic or foreign. Foreign creditors are particularly dangerous because they can leave the country with their capital at any time. Domestic ones, however, turn into rentiers and, with the support of the financial system, may impose disastrous economic policies on the country, as has been the case in Brazil.

The third and final difference between the developmentalism of the 1950s and new developmentalism can be found in the state's role in promoting forced savings and investing in the economic infrastructure. Both forms of developmentalism cast the state in a leading role in ensuring the proper operation of the market and providing general conditions for capital accumulation, such as education, health, and transportation as well as communications and energy infrastructures. In addition, however, under the developmentalism of the 1950s, the state played a crucial role in promoting forced savings, thereby contributing to countries' primitive accumulation process; furthermore, it made direct investments in infrastructure and heavy industry where the investments required were too massive for the private sector's savings to finance alone.

This has changed since the 1980s. For new developmentalism, the state still can and must promote forced savings and invest in certain strategic industries, but the national private sector now has the resources and managerial ability to generate a sizable portion of the investments needed. The new developmentalism rejects the neoliberal thesis that "the state no longer has resources" because whether the state has resources depends on how its finances are managed. But new developmentalism understands that, in all sectors where reasonable competition exists, the state must not be an investor but should concentrate instead on defending and ensuring competition. Even after these have been excluded, there are many investments left to the state, financed by public savings rather than debt.

Finally, in new developmentalism there is a concern with the protection of the environment or with sustainable development that did not exist under old developmentalism. This is not surprising, because the environment became a central world problem only after the United Nations 1972 Stockholm Conference. The contradictions between economic growth and sustainable development are smaller than many suppose, but they exist. Thus, a constant and creative compromise between the two objectives is required. As Ignacy Sachs (2008, p. 252), whose contributions on sustained development are well-known, remarks: "It is unthinkable to stop economic growth while so many poor exist."

In sum, and again, reflecting the different stage that medium-development countries have reached, new developmentalism regards the market as a more efficient institution, one more capable of coordinating the economic system, than did the old developmentalist economists, although the new attitude is far from the irrational faith in the market of the Washington Consensus.

New Developmentalism and the Conventional Orthodoxy

Let us now examine the differences between new developmentalism and the conventional orthodoxy. The first, and most general, difference between these two is, as referred to in the final paragraph of the foregoing section, that the Washington Consensus is market-fundamentalist, believing that "in the beginning there was the market," an entity that provides optimal coordination if left to its own devices. New developmentalism, in turn, regards the market as an extraordinarily efficient institution when it comes to coordinating economic system but acknowledges its limitations. Factor allocation is the task the market performs best, but even in this area it has its limitations. Incentives to invest and innovate are wanting. And, at the level of income distribution, the market is a completely unsatisfactory mechanism, as it privileges the strongest and most capable. The conventional orthodoxy does acknowledge the market's shortcomings but argues that they are better than the state's attempts to correct them; new developmentalism, however, rejects this pessimism about the capacity for collective action and yearns for a strong state, not at the cost of the market but in order for the market to be strong. If humanity is capable of building institutions, including the market itself, to regulate human actions, there is no reason why humanity should not be able to strengthen the state as an apparatus or organization—making its rule more legitimate, its finances sounder, and its management more efficient—and to strengthen the state as a rule of law, making its institutions ever more closely aligned with social needs. This is precisely what politics and democracy are for.

As one of the pillars of new developmentalism is classical economics, which is essentially a theory of the "wealth of nations" (Adam Smith) or of "capital accumulation and the rate of profit" (Karl Marx), besides the macroeconomic prices (principally the profit rate, the interest rate, and the exchange rate), social structures and institutions are fundamental to it. In addition, as new developmentalism embraces a historical perspective of development, the institutionalist teachings of the German historical school, the US institutionalism of the early twentieth century, and the 1940s and 1950s development economics are essential elements of its vision of development.[4] Institutions are, therefore, fundamental, and reforming them is a constant need: in our complex, dynamic societies, regulation of economic activities and the market must be constantly reviewed. New developmentalism is, therefore, reformist. The conventional orthodoxy, on the other hand, based as it is on the neoclassical theory, has only recently become aware of the importance of institutions, with the emergence of the "new institutionalism."

Unlike historical institutionalism, which, at the level of economic development, regards precapitalist institutions and the distortions of capitalism as obstacles to development and tries to develop institutions to actively promote it, the new institutionalism's proposal is overly simplistic: all institutions need to do is ensure property rights and contracts or, more broadly, the proper operation of the markets, and given this the markets themselves will automatically promote development. In the neoliberal jargon found, for example, in *The Economist,* a government is economically good if it is "reformist"—where "reformist" means making market-oriented reforms. For new developmentalism, a government is economically good as far as it is "developmentalist"—if it promotes development and income redistribution via the adoption of economic policies and institutional reforms oriented, as far as possible, toward the market, but often correcting the market's automatic actions. Put another way, a government is "developmentalist" if it can rely on a national development strategy, for this set of institutions and economic policies aimed at the proper operation of the markets and at development is no more or less than such a strategy. For the Washington Consensus, institutions must be almost exclusively limited to constitutional norms; for new developmentalism, economic policies and, more broadly, economic and monetary policy regimes are institutions that require constant reform and adjustment within the framework of a more general strategy. Besides relatively permanent institutions, industrial policies are needed. They do not stand as a fundamental difference between new developmentalism and the conventional orthodoxy, because new developmentalism uses industrial policy more moderately, topically, and strategically, where the firm in need of support indicates that it has or will have the ability to compete internationally: an industrial policy that can be mistaken for protectionism is not acceptable.

New developmentalism and the Washington Consensus have many institutional reforms in common. But their objectives often differ. Take, for example, the public management reform. New developmentalism advocates it because it longs for a more capable and efficient state; the Washington Consensus does so because it sees an opportunity to reduce the tax burden. For new developmentalism this may be a desirable consequence, but this is a different matter. The tax burden is a political issue that depends chiefly on the functions democratic societies assign the state and, second, on the efficiency of public services. In other cases, it is a matter of quantity. New developmentalism favors trade liberalization but is not radical about it, knowing how to use international talks to secure reciprocal advantages, since the world markets are far from being free. In other cases, it is a matter of emphasis: both new developmentalism and the Washington Consensus favor more flexible labor markets, but new developmentalism, based mainly on experience in northern Europe, does not take flexibility for lack of protection, whereas the conventional orthodoxy renders labor more flexible in order to make working conditions precarious and to help push down wages.

In order to draw a comparison between new developmentalism and the conventional orthodoxy, we can distinguish between development strategies and macroeconomic stability–oriented ones, although the two kinds are closely related. We have seen that there can be no development without stability. Let us then begin with a comparison of the macroeconomic policies summarized in Table 11.2. Both assume a need for macroeconomic stability, but the conventional orthodoxy understands this as control over public debt and inflation, whereas new developmentalism further ties stability to interest and exchange rates capable of ensuring the intertemporal balance of states' public accounts and of nation-states' foreign accounts.

Table 11.2 Macroeconomic Policies Compared

Conventional Orthodoxy	New Developmentalism
1. Fiscal adjustment for primary surplus	1. Fiscal adjustment for positive public savings
2. Single Central Bank mandate: inflation	2. Threefold Central Bank mandate: inflation, foreign exchange, and employment
3. One Central Bank instrument: interest rate	3. Two Central Bank instruments: interest rate and purchase of reserves to control capital inflows
4. Endogenous short-term interest rate: high	4. Exogenous short-term interest rate: may be low
5. Floating and endogenous exchange rate	5. Floating, but managed, exchange rate

The conventionally orthodox approach can be summarized as follows: In order to ensure macroeconomic stability the country must maintain a primary surplus that keeps the public debt–to–GDP ratio at a level
acceptable to creditors; the Central Bank must have a single purpose—
to fight inflation—as it has only one instrument, the short-term interest
rate; given the fiscal disequilibrium, this rate—which, despite being the
single instrument, is essentially endogenous (that is, set by the market)—must be high to keep inflation in check; the exchange rate, too, is
endogenous and its equilibrium will be ensured by the market.

New developmentalism offers materially different proposals: the
goal of fiscal adjustment is not just primary surplus but positive public
savings, implying not only reduced current expenditures but also reduced interest rates; the purpose of the Central Bank, in consultation
with the Ministry of Finance, is threefold: to control inflation, to keep
the exchange rate at a level compatible with a stable balance of payments, and to provide the needed stimulus to export-oriented investments. The Ministry of Finance and the Central Bank, therefore, on
defining the foreign exchange policy, must also consider the employment level and profitable investment opportunities; and they do not
have just a single instrument to rely on (the interest rate that the conventional orthodoxy contradictorily considers endogenous) but several,
such as levying modest and flexible taxes on the goods that give rise to
the Dutch disease, engaging in reserves purchases, and if this is not sufficient, establishing controls over capital inflows to offset the tendency
of the exchange rate to overappreciation that exists in mid-development
countries. The interest rate is an instrument to fight inflation but can be
much lower than the conventional orthodoxy assumes; the exchange

rate must be allowed to float but must also be managed—there is no such thing as a completely free exchange rate.

Now compare the economic development strategies summarized in Table 11.3. The conventionally orthodox approach (it is no longer fitting to call it a strategy) is based on the need for institutional reforms to reduce the state and strengthen the market; it casts the state in a minimal role as regards investments and industrial policy and sees no role for the nation—the concept is absent; it fails to prioritize any economic sector—leaving it to the market; it proposes open capital accounts and a policy of growth with foreign savings. New developmentalism, in turn, wants institutional reforms that, in addition to strengthening the market, strengthen the state—but a state with a capable apparatus and institutions equipped with legitimacy to serve as instruments of society. New developmentalism also regards the nation, that is, the national society that shares beliefs and demonstrates solidarity when it comes to competing internationally, as the fundamental player in development; it understands that the fundamental institution for development is not just ensuring property rights and contracts but the presence of a national development strategy to encourage businesspeople to invest. The new-developmentalist strategy prioritizes economic industries with high value added per capita—that is, those that are technology- or knowledge-intensive; and it understands that it is not just possible, but necessary, to grow with domestic savings, as was the case in every country that has experienced development—the policy of growth with foreign savings is one more factor causing an appreciation of the exchange rate that should be avoided at all costs: a competitive exchange rate is a requirement for growth.

Table 11.3 Development Strategies Compared

Conventional Orthodoxy	New Developmentalism
1. Reforms to reduce the state and strengthen the market	1. Reforms to strengthen the state and the market
2. Minimal state role in investment and industrial policy	2. Moderate state role in investment and industrial policy
3. No role for the nation: assurance of property rights and contracts is enough	3. National competition strategy considered essential to development
4. No sector prioritized—leave it to the market	4. Prioritized exports and per capita value added
5. Fund investment with foreign savings	5. Growth with domestic investment and savings
6. Open capital accounts and no exchange controls	6. Control capital accounts as needed

The items in these two tables have been discussed in previous chapters. Still, the two tables not only shed light on the criticism of the conventional orthodoxy but also demonstrate that a new-developmentalist alternative exists that, more than being compatible with macroeconomic stability, is in fact its only assurance. On the other hand, it is worth noting that, since the 1960s, the conventional economic policy has revolved around the recommendation of growth with foreign savings, which I have examined in Chapter 4. This is typically a development macroeconomics problem because, although classical economics assigns little importance to the exchange rate, limiting its scope to short-term problems, it has a powerful medium-term effect on investments and growth. Before, the IMF was concerned with the exchange rate, which appreciated during populist cycles, causing balance-of-payment crises (Canitrot 1991 [1975]), prompting the IMF to demand exchange rate devaluation in addition to fiscal adjustment. After the 1990s, however, the IMF forgot current account deficits (they were foreign savings, after all) and exchange rate depreciation. The twin-deficits hypothesis exempted it from concern with the current account deficit: all it had to worry about was the primary surplus. For some time its preferred discourse had to do with exchange anchors and dollarization; after the failure of this strategy in Mexico, Brazil, and, mainly, Argentina, the IMF turned to free-floating exchange rates as the panacea for all foreign exchange problems. New developmentalism is strongly critical of this view and wants control not only over the state's public accounts (budget deficit) but also over the nation's total accounts (current account). It does not merely want the state to have little debt and to report positive public savings; it also wants the nation-state to have foreign accounts capable of ensuring its safety and national autonomy. It does not want merely a managed interest rate but also a managed exchange rate, even if within the framework of a floating exchange rate regime that it refers to not as "dirty," as the conventional orthodoxy has it, but as "managed."

Reduced Interest Rate

At the level of macroeconomic policy, the main tasks at hand are completing the fiscal adjustment, lowering the interest rate, raising the exchange rate, and reducing the volatility of these two rates; intermediate objectives are to increase public savings and the economy's investment rate; the final objective is growth with stability. Reducing the interest rate is the crucial task the Brazilian economy now faces. It would not make sense to map out an alternative economic policy in this book, but there is a need for greater detail on how to lower the interest rate. The conventional orthodoxy, despite its claim that the short-term interest rate is the only instrument available to the Central Bank, also argues that it is impossible to bring the rate to a level below 8 percent in real terms per year. This is a mistake. In order to escape from the pitfall of high short-term interest rates and an appreciated exchange rate, we need a strategy similar to the one used in 1993 and 1994 to end high and inertial inflation. The decision is not that of the chairman of the Central Bank alone, or of the finance minister, but mainly of the president, because it will involve the entire government and have the nation's support as its main foundation. In addition to changing economic policy, there will be a need to set in motion several reforms with an immediate impact on inflation and on the interest rate. The goal is to reduce the short-term interest rate, which is set by the Central Bank, to an average of 3 percent in real terms, with deviations of a real 2 percent to 4 percent plus or minus (in countries with stable currencies, this deviation is around 1 percent in real terms). The long-term interest rate, in turn, must be set by the market (and not by the Central Bank) and draw close to the international interest rate defined by the US Treasury, plus Brazil's sovereign risk, plus any forecast depreciation of the real— given the current levels of these parameters, it should therefore be at around 5 percent a year in real terms.

To attain these objectives, the simplest and most important reform is to decouple the short-term interest rate from the rate on Brazilian Treasury bills, eliminating their indexation to the Selic rate. We will then resume a practice common to every Brazilian monetary policy: the interest rate the Central Bank sets to make its policy accrues to bank reserves, not public debt. This practice is unique—it is a *jabuticaba,*[5] as Mario Henrique Simonsen used to say in reference to uniquely Brazilian and perverse practices—and is the leading institutional explanation for the fact that Brazil's basic interest rate is, by far, the world's highest. This change should be accompanied by the deindexation of utilities' prices: not by breaking contracts, but by eliminating indexation at the time of contract renewal and by discussing deindexation in the course of any contract revision. After deindexation, a contract's prices may be adjusted annually or biannually by the past rate of inflation along with other variables, chief among which is productivity gains. On the other hand, Congress must approve a reform to prevent the government from entering into or regulating any agreement that includes an indexation clause. In the process of hoisting the short-term interest rate out of its current pitfall, authorities will have to reduce expenditures and, possibly, generate a surplus; they will have to redouble their fiscal adjustment efforts. With such an adjustment, the government will not only provide a signal that it rejects populism in any form but also control possible inflationary processes arising from a potential demand shock due to the lower interest rate. Interest rates will fall, therefore, while fiscal adjustment keeps aggregate demand in check. In this process, there is no reason to fear a default on public debt caused by domestic creditors unhappy with lower interest rates. No such danger exists, as the interest rate being reduced is the one applicable to bank reserves, whose only possible return on capital is the basic interest rate. Even so, however, there will be a need to anticipate increased inflation as a result of the exchange rate depreciation caused by the dropping interest rate. This temporary increase in inflation cannot be avoided and is incompatible with the inflation targeting policy—or, at least, with inflation targeting used simply to manage this policy instead of changing the regime.

With a reformed financial system, the government will no longer define the interest rate on its debt. That decision will be made by the market, as is the case in market economies. This is a curious—not to say pathetic—fact. The financial industry will be able to continue trying to "force" the Central Bank to maintain rates at the current levels but will not succeed in the presence of a clear separation between short-term and long-term interest rates, the demise of the crutch that LFTs represent, and the strong fiscal adjustment of the transition. The Washington Consensus, which claims to love the market, rejects it in this case. The Central Bank will influence the long-term interest rate with its decisions on the short-term rate. Given Brazil's still-high foreign indebtedness level, it is the country's sovereign risk that determines the long-term rate. As this risk plus the US Treasury's rate are at a substantially lower level than the Selic, a lower interest rate on the Brazilian Treasury's bills will tend to make itself felt within a relatively short period.

The government must not rely on the market alone, however, and on its decision to lower the short-term interest rate, decoupling it from federal securities: it must also do its homework at the fiscal end, implementing a harsh adjustment program with zero nominal budget deficit as its goal. Since this deficit is at around 3 percent of GDP and interest expenditure is close to 8 percent of GDP, and since it would be reasonable to expect this expenditure to drop by half, an adjustment would not be necessary in theory. But this would be a mistake: a silly arithmetical error. Reducing public current expenditures is crucial at the macroeconomic level to prevent an acceleration of inflation by reason of demand pressures and to signal to the market that there is no reason to raise Brazil's sovereign risk. With demand under control, there is no reason to expect inflation to accelerate, except for a modest and temporary increase due to the exchange rate depreciation caused by the lower interest rate. On the other hand, there is no reason to speak of suspended debt rollover, as the basic interest rate that is being lowered is the one that pertains to bank reserves and for which there is no alternative except the overnight or base rates. But, from a strictly public-accounts viewpoint, a fiscal adjustment with a marked reduction of current expenditures is essential to increase the state's savings and investment. Lower interest rates are not being pursued just to end in a capture of the public wealth: the core objective is to increase public investment, to stimulate private investment and, with a capital accumulation rate in excess of 25 percent, to resume growth.

The reduced interest rate strategy implies, therefore, temporarily higher inflation as a result of exchange rate depreciation: "temporarily" because the Brazilian economy is no longer indexed. With inertial inflation, any inflationary shock implied a new inflation level. Now, despite the presence of indexed utilities—something that must be eliminated—indexation is marginal. In the absence of inflation-accelerating and inflation-sustaining factors, inflation will fall back. Clearly, thus, the inflation targeting policy is incompatible with the regime change that a lowered interest rate strategy implies. In normal times, when not in a pitfall of high interest, a country may follow to the letter an inflation targeting model such as the one Brazil's Central Bank uses. To get out of a perverse equilibrium, however, an inflation targeting policy is counterproductive.

The pitfall of interest rates may be overcome with strict control over public expenditures while steadfastly reducing the short-term interest rate, which at such a time will no longer weigh on Brazil's public debt but only on bank reserves. The risk that such steps would raise inflation to dangerously high levels is very small, and the risk of leading to balance-of-payment disequilibrium is nonexistent, as the lower rates would drive down the exchange rate. The risk of domestic creditors' refusing to finance the public debt is also zero, as they would be compensated at a market-based rate, that is, the long-term interest rate. The risk of the financial industry's refusing to accept the short-term interest rate is likewise zero, as it has no alternative choice but to invest its funds in the short term. As for the risk that foreign investors would refuse to refinance the debt, this is not a real issue, as the interest rate that accrues to them (the long-term rate) is not being reduced; only the short-term interest rate is, and this, when it is no longer the indexer for public bills, might cease to be called Selic.

Reduction of the interest rate will be complemented by exchange rate depreciation and a drop in the great volatility that characterizes both of these rates. As Paula (2006, p. 20) points out, in a context defined by a floating exchange rate regime in coexistence with an inflation targeting regime under conditions of capital account liberalization, there is a strong relationship between monetary policy and exchange rate policy: excessive exchange rate volatility leads to trouble managing the macroeconomic policy, in addition to having a negative effect on investment decisions. A macroeconomic policy resulting in reduced exchange rate and interest rate volatility will have a positive effect both on economic growth—as investment and production decisions are stimulated by the improved economic environment and by the macroeconomic policy itself and the current and prospective behavior of aggregate demand due to the reduced uncertainty affecting decisionmakers—and on continued price stability, given the important role the exchange rate plays in creating inflationary pressures in the Brazilian economy.

Reduced interest rate volatility will be achieved only with fiscal discipline and a competent monetary policy that has a moderate and stable interest rate as a permanent objective. Reduced exchange rate volatility, in turn, will be achieved only insofar as the country rejects the policy of growth with foreign savings, has no chronic current account deficits, and can rely on sizable international reserves. There is no reason to imagine that Brazil and other developing countries are condemned to permanent structural foreign disequilibrium. This was a thesis of old developmentalism that, interestingly, the conventional orthodoxy embraced but that new developmentalism rejects, based not only on the lack of logical grounds for the argument but also (and mainly) on the fact that dynamic Asian countries empirically show that it is false. Owing to the tendency toward exchange rate overappreciation and the policy of growth with foreign savings, balance-of-payment crises are frequent in these countries but can be easily avoided as long as the governments are determined. Exchange rate administration is to be done structurally by repudiating the policy of growth with foreign savings and the accumulation of international reserves. The wise advice the conventional orthodoxy has to give with regard to the inconvenience of excessive reserves may, naturally, be disregarded, as also can be the contradictory thesis that the exchange rate cannot be managed. We have seen that the first way of managing it is through buying and sterilizing reserves. For as long as the cost of this purchase is prohibitive because of high interest, however, the alternative of capital controls must be taken into consideration.

Finally, governmental authorities must constantly keep in mind that the purpose of such policies is to bring about economic growth and, therefore, lower unemployment and decreased social inequality. Monetary policy rules must be seen as decisionmaking guidelines rather than strict norms. As regards unemployment specifically, the connection between this variable and monetary policy is of great importance. Contrary to what certain conventional theorists propose, monetary policy usually has positive and lasting effects on real interest rates and, as a consequence, on economic activity and unemployment. In other words, it has an influence on unemployment rates, more so than the conventional orthodoxy is willing to admit.

A National Development Strategy

The Brazilian economy has been nearly stagnant since 1980, but we are not forever chained to the reasoning that presided over this situation. Although Brazilian society adopted the conventional orthodoxy because of its inability to act as a nation, this inability is not inescapable. In this book, emphasis has been placed on macroeconomic policy. The root cause of quasi stagnation was defined as the lack of macroeconomic stability, as expressed in interest and exchange rates that do not ensure intertemporally balanced public and foreign accounts. The proposed changes were designed to restore macroeconomic equilibrium. But this is not to say that successfully changing the macroeconomic policy is enough for the country to resume growth. Other steps will always be needed. Institutional reforms must continue to reduce inequality, to align the real country with the formal country, and to strengthen the nation and its institutions—the state and the market.

Institutional reforms and public policies implemented according to national criteria will make up a national strategy for economic development. The Washington Consensus argues that institutions and the protection of property rights and of contracts in particular are crucial to promoting economic growth. No doubt exists as to the relevance of these two specific institutions, but what really causes a country to grow, to change its economic and social structure, to improve living standards, and to make institutions themselves more legitimate, is a national development strategy. The age of global capitalism is a period in time when empires have lost their purpose and legitimacy, and nation-states span the entire globe. It is a period in which the basic community unit is still the family, but the basic unit of the world market has become the internationally competitive firm and that of the world political system has become the nation-state or country. Under globalization, therefore, nation-states, although more interdependent, became much more economically strategic. The world in which we live is organized into nation-states that compete (and cooperate) with one another. Their interdependency springs both from competition and from their cooperation in establishing the rules of competition itself. Although their great rivalries still exist, these are no longer solved through wars but rather through international norms or agreements to regulate competition.

The basic guideline for the review of a country's institutional structure is to reward productive activities and to punish predatory ones, such as monopolies, market cornering, rent-seeking, and corruption. Accelerated economic development can take place only in institutional environments where talents and resources are channeled toward wealth production, rather than predatory activities that appropriate whatever wealth is produced. On the other hand, for the market to be an efficient production mechanism, transaction costs—which are extraordinarily high in Brazil—must drop. In addition to decisive steps in terms of competition regulation, the legal system must be reformed to ensure contract enforcement and effectiveness. It is particularly important to reform the civil and criminal procedural codes so as to expedite legal decisions while at the same time implementing and improving the alternative dispute resolution system. These policies, by the way, will be effective only if the institutional environment can effectively apply stimuli and penalties in the appropriate direction.

Under the pressure from the North's ideologies, it has become inappropriate to speak of social classes, but these remain as relevant as ever. Development now depends on a major informal alliance among businesspeople in the real sector, public-sector and private-sector technicians, and workers—the holders, therefore, of the three fundamental factors for economic development: capital and enterprise, technical and organizational knowledge, and labor. A nation is built only in the presence of such an agreement: an agreement that does not prevent internal conflict but still ensures the basic solidarity a nation requires.

The desired development, which is possible from the moment true macroeconomic stability is recovered, must involve all of society and will imply neutralizing the trend of the exchange rate to overappreciate and reducing interest—offsetting the corresponding decrease of the share of interest income with an increased share of profits and wages.

An essential element of the new national development strategy is the construction of a mass consumption society. The idea has been present in Brazilian thinking since the 1970s, when we criticized the income-concentrating model the military regime had adopted. The alternative to income concentration from the middle class up that characterized the "industrialized underdevelopment model" (Bresser-Pereira 1977) was an economy at once export-led and oriented toward mass consumption and, therefore, toward a gradual deconcentration of income.

The creation of a mass consumption society enables matching growth with redistribution in a society where inequality is not simply a matter of social injustice: it is a major obstacle to economic development. It is an opportunity for a country characterized by high income-concentration levels. Even firms making or marketing consumer goods have already realized this, and in recent years, one of their main challenges has been to reach the lower social classes. A policy of creating a mass consumption society does not contradict an export policy except in the very short term, because the latter requires a competitive exchange rate, and the unavoidable initial depreciation implies reduced wages. In the medium run, however, a continued policy of income redistribution and the constitution of a mass consumption society are compatible with resumed growth only if combined with an export-led policy that sets efficiency parameters for the production of tradable goods. As João Paulo de Almeida Magalhães (2006, p. 195) points out, "in isolation, either of the two strategies has little chance of success, and they naturally complement one another. Success of the export-oriented policy will immediately determine rapid GDP growth, which will enable the redistribution policy; this, in turn, will consolidate the gains obtained from the greater multiplier effect of exports on the domestic market."

All of these changes should take place under the aegis of a new political coalition, with businesspeople in the productive sector as central players, politicians and senior bureaucrats as helmsmen, and new developmentalism as the national development strategy to be followed. Can new developmentalism become hegemonic in Brazil as developmentalism was in the past? The failure of the conventional proposal makes me confident that, indeed, it can. We have seen that, by following rich countries' prescriptions, all kinds of reforms and adjustments were made, but Latin America failed to develop. In Mexico, which fully and formally embraced all of the North's recommendations by associating itself with the United States under NAFTA, the economy has been semistagnant ever since. Chile has been used as an example of the Washington Consensus, but it is a small country, and its policies are closer to new developmentalism than to the conventional orthodoxy.[6] The crisis Argentina faced in 2001 was a turning point: the requiem mass for the conventional orthodoxy or the Washington Consensus because no country so faithfully adopted its precepts and no president dedicated himself more earnestly to confidence building than Carlos Menem. Since the crisis, Argentina under President Néstor Kirschner and former minister of finance Roberto Lavagna has begun to establish itself as a concrete experiment in new developmentalism. It is becoming increasingly clear that Argentina has learned from the painful experience of such faithful acceptance of the conventionally orthodox recommendations. As Lavagna (2006), after summarizing his economic policy, said in an interview to a Brazilian newpaper:

> We had to reject all of the IMF's prescriptions: we rejected the idea of compensating the banking system en masse for the devaluation, we rejected the notion that accelerated inflation might serve to liquidate the financial system's liabilities, and we rejected the idea of mandating an exchange of bills for depositors' funds; we also rejected tax reforms or the idea that fiscal surplus might be achieved by working on the side of expenditures alone.

The representatives of the Washington Consensus try to compare Argentina with Venezuela or Bolivia, denouncing "mere populism" in all three countries, but this makes no sense. Argentina is a country whose development and political maturity levels are far above those of the other two. The conventional orthodoxy accuses the Kirschner administration of causing inflation rates of 11 percent a year and of implementing some controls over prices. In this respect, Brazil fares better. But Argentina's public expenditures are under control, interest rates are very low, and notwithstanding the IMF's brutal pressure, the exchange rate is kept competitive, and major export goods pay a tax to prevent Dutch disease. As a consequence, Argentina has been reporting average growth rates three times as high as those of Brazil. The argument that this is "but a recovery of previous production levels" has been refuted, as those levels have been surpassed. In fact, Argentina is showing the way and is living proof of the emptiness of potential GDP calculations with which the conventional orthodoxy seeks to justify Brazil's low growth rates. As soon as Brazil attempts to extricate itself from the macroeconomic hole into which it has fallen, its growth rates will be as surprisingly high as Argentina's are today.

On the other hand, new-developmentalist thinking, in addition to counting among its ranks notorious and active development economics macroeconomists, is being renewed by new economists graduating from

Brazilian doctoral programs. In Argentina and Chile, too, eminent economists exist who identify themselves with this strategy. Still, the problem of ideological hegemony remains unsolved. Latin American countries will resume sustained development only if their economists, businesspeople, and state bureaucrats recall the successful experience of the old developmentalism, criticize the distortions it endured at the hands of populism in the 1980s, and are capable of taking a step forward. They have already criticized the mistakes made and realized that new historical facts make this criticism outdated. They now need to accept that the national revolution that was then taking place, with old developmentalism as the national strategy, was interrupted by the deep crisis of the 1980s and by the neoliberal ideological wave from the North. They need an in-depth diagnosis of the quasi stagnation that the conventional orthodoxy has caused. They need to take a careful look at the national development strategy of dynamic Asian countries. They need to take part in the great collective national endeavor that is the formulation of new developmentalism—the new national development strategy for their countries.

I understand that this process of raising awareness is fully under way. Latin America's development has always been a "national-dependent" development because the region's elites were constantly immersed in conflict and ambiguity, now affirming themselves as a nation, now yielding to foreign ideological hegemony. There is, however, a cyclic element to this process, and clear indications exist that the time of neoliberalism and the conventional orthodoxy has gone and that new prospects are opening up for Brazil and Latin America. The great challenge Latin American countries faced in the 1980s was to reestablish democracy; in the meantime, they failed to rediscover the road to development. They failed because they chose to reform the state without taking the nation into account; because, in the necessary process of giving the market more space in the coordination of the economy, they ended up weakening the state. In the 2000s, the great challenge facing Brazil is rebuilding its nation; only then can it conclude the state's reform; rely on a strong, democratic state; and compete successfully within the framework of global capitalism.

Notes

1. In the 2000s, strong growth has resumed, but the main cause has been growth in China and India.
2. See Diaz-Alejandro (1981); Ffrench-Davis (2003).

3. See Bresser-Pereira and Dall'Acqua (1991).

4. The German historical school is the school of Gustav Schmoller, Otto Rank, Max Weber, and, along a different path, Friedrich List; the US institutionalist school is the school of Thorstein Veblen, Wesley Mitchell, and John R. Commons.

5. Jabuticaba (*Myrcia cauliflora*) is also known as Brazilian grape. It is a fruit-bearing tree of the myrtle family that is native to Brazil and not found elsewhere.

6. Chile took a perilous step toward the conventional orthodoxy by signing a bilateral agreement with the United States in 2005 and, in this treaty, renouncing any control over the exchange rate. The treaty may lead to a "Mexicanization" of Chile, that is, lead it into quasi stagnation as severe as Brazil's or even more severe. The term *Mexicanization* was used by Ilan Goldfajn (2006), an economist associated with the conventional orthodoxy, to designate a country on its way to quasi stagnation. This is significant because no country in Latin America yielded more broadly and officially to the conventional orthodoxy than Mexico did when it became part of the North Atlantic Free Trade Zone in the early 1990s.

Acronyms

BNDES	Banco Nacional de Desenvolvimento Econômico e Social (National Economic and Social Development Bank)
CAGED	Cadastro Geral de Empregados and Desempregados (General Roll of the Employed and Unemployed)
COPOM	Conselho de Política Monetária (Monetary Policy Council)
CPI	consumer price index
ECLAC	Economic Commission for Latin America and Caribe
EMBI+	Emerging Markets Bond Index Plus
FGV	Fundação Getúlio Vargas
FIESP	Federation of Industries of the State of São Paulo
Funcex	Fundação Centros de Estudos de Comércio Exterior (Center of Studies of Exterior Commerce)
GDP	gross domestic product
IBGE	Instituto Brasileiro de Geografia e Estatística (Brazilian Institute of Geography and Statistics)
IEDI	Instituto de Estudos para o Desenvolvimento Industrial (Industrial Development Studies Institute)
IGP	Índice Geral de Preços (General Price Index)
IMF	International Monetary Fund
INEP	Instituto Nacional de Estudos e Pesquisas (National Institute for Studies and Educational Research
INSS	Instituto Nacional do Seguro Social (Social Security National Institute)
IPCA	Índice de Preços ao Consumidor Amplo (Extended Consumer Price Index)

IPEA	Instituto de Pesquisa Econômica Aplicada (Institute for Applied Economic Research)
ISEB	Instituto Superior de Estudos Brasileiros (Superior Institute of Brazilian Studies)
LFTs	Letras Financeiras do Tesouro (Treasury Financial Bonds)
MDCI	Ministry of Development, Industry, and Commerce
MITI	Ministry of International Trade and Industry (Japan)
NAFTA	North American Free Trade Agreement
NAIRU	nonaccelerating inflation rate of unemployment
OECD	Organization for Economic Cooperation and Development
OPEC	Organization of Petroleum Exporting Counties
PMDB	Partido do Movimento Democrático Brasileiro (Brazilian Democratic Movement Party)
PNAD	Pesquisa Nacional por Amostra de Domicílios (National Household Survey)
PPP	purchasing power parity
PSDB	Partido da Social Democracia Brasileira (Brazilian Social Democracy Party)
PT	Partido dos Trabalhadores (Labor Party)
Selic	Sistema Especial de Liquidação e de Custódia (Special System of Liquidation and Custody)
SUS	Sistema Único de Saúde (Unified Health System)
TJLP	*taxa de juros de longo prazo* (long-term interest rate)
TV-NAIRU	time varying NAIRU
URV	Unidade Real de Valor (Real Value Unit)
WTO	World Trade Organization

References

Afonso, José Roberto, Erika A. Amorim, and Geraldo Biasoto Jr. (2005) "Fiscal Space and Public Sector Investments in Infrastructure: A Brazilian Case Study." IPEA Discussion Paper, 1141, Brasília.

Aglietta, Michel, and Vladimir Borgy (2005) "L'Heritage de Greenspan: Le Triomphe de la politique discrétionnaire." [Greenspan's Heritage: The Triumph of Political Discretion]. *Bulletin du Cepii* 251, December: 1–4.

Albert, Michel (1991) *Capitalisme contre capitalisme*. Paris: Éditions du Seuil.

Alem, Ana Claudia, José Roberto Mendonça de Barros, and Fábio Giambiagi (2002) "Bases para uma política industrial moderna" [Basis for a Modern Industrial Policy]. Rio de Janeiro: Fourteenth Fórum Nacional, May.

Almeida, Mansueto, Fábio Giambiagi, and Samuel Pessoa (2006) "Expansão e dilemas no controle do gasto público federal" [Expansion and Dilemmas in the Control of Federal Public Expenditures]. *Boletim de Conjuntura do IPEA* 73, June: 89–98.

Alves, Antonio J., Fernando Ferrari Filho, and Luiz Fernando de Paula (2004) "Crise cambial, instabilidade financeira, e reforma do sistema monetário" [Exchange Crisis, Financial Instability, and Reform of the Monetary System]. In Fernando Ferrari Filho and Luiz Fernando de Paula (eds.), *Globalização financeira* [Financial Globalization]. Petrópolis: Editora Vozes, pp. 369–461.

Amsden, Alice H. (1989) *Asia's Next Giant*. Oxford: Oxford University Press.

Arestis, Philip, Gabriel Palma, and Malcolm Sawyer (eds.) (1997) *Post Keynesian Economics and the History of Economics: Essays in Honour of Geoff Harcourt*. London: Routledge.

Arestis, Philip, Luiz Fernando de Paula, and Fernando Ferrari Filho (2006) "Inflation Targeting in Emerging Countries: The Case of Brazil." Available at http://paginas.terra.com.br/educacao/luizfpaula.

Arestis, Philip, and Malcolm Sawyer (2004) *Re-examining Monetary and Fiscal Policy for the 21st Century*. Cheltenham: E. Elgar Press.

Arestis, Philip, and Thanos Skouras (eds.) (1985) *Post Keynesian Economic Theory.* Armonk, NY: M. E. Sharpe.

Arida, Persio (2002) "Por uma moeda plenamente conversível" [For a Fully Convertible Currency]. *Valor Econômico,* November 12.

———— (2003) "Speech on Receiving *The Economist* Prize of 2003." São Paulo, August 13.

———— (2004) "Aspectos macroeconômicos da conversibilidade: Uma discussão do caso brasileiro" [Macroeconomic Aspects of Convertibility: A Discussion of the Brazilian Case]. Photocopy, June 26.

Arida, Persio, Edmar Lisboa Bacha, and André Lara Resende (2005) "Credit, Interest, and Jurisdictional Uncertainty: Conjectures on the Case of Brazil." In F. Giavazzi, I. Goldfjan, and S. Herrera (eds.), *Inflation Targeting, Debt, and the Brazilian Experience, 1999 to 2003.* Cambridge, MA: MIT Press.

Arida, Persio, and André Lara Resende (1985 [1984]) "Inertial Inflation and Monetary Reform." In John Williamson (ed.), *Inflation and Indexation: Argentina, Brazil, and Israel.* Washington, DC: Institute for International Economics.

Bacha, Edmar L. (2002) "Comments to 'A Strategy of Development with Stability.'" Letter dated January 6. Available at www.bresserpereira.org.br.

Baland, Jean-Marie, and Patrick François (2000) "Rent-seeking and Resource Booms." *Journal of Development Economics* 61 (3): pp. 527–542.

Baldwin, Richard (2006) "The Great Unbundling(s)." Finland Economic Council Discussion Paper, September. Available at www.tinyurl.com/2ol2n8.

Ball, Laurence (2000) "Policy Rules and External Shocks." National Bureau of Economic Research Working Paper 7910, Cambridge, MA, September.

Ball, Laurence, and Niamh Sheridan (2003) "Does Inflation Targeting Matter?" National Bureau of Economic Research Working Paper 9577, Cambridge, MA, March.

Barbosa, Fernando de Holanda (1996) "Política monetária: Instrumentos, objetivos, e a experiência brasileira" [Monetary Policy: Instruments, Objectives, and the Brazilian Experience]. In R. R. Sawaya (ed.), *O Plano Real e a política econômica brasileira* [The Real Plan and the Brazilian Political Economy]. São Paulo: Educ, pp. 79–103.

———— (2006) "The Contagion Effect of Public Debt on Monetary Policy: The Brazilian Experience." *Brazilian Journal of Political Economy* 26 (2): pp. 231–238.

Barro, Robert J., and David B. Gordon (1983) "Rules, Discretion, and Reputation in a Model of Monetary Policy." *Journal of Monetary Economics* 12 (1): pp. 101–121. Barros, Ricardo Paes de, Mirela de Carvalho, Samuel Franco, and Rosane Mendonça (2006) "Uma análise das principais causas da queda recente na desigualdade de renda brasileira" [An Analysis of the Main Causes of the Recent Decrease in the Brazilian Income Inequality]. IPEA Discussion Paper 1203, Brasília, August.

Barros, Ricardo Paes de, Samir Cury, and Gabriel Ulyssea (2007) "A desigualdade da renda no Brasil encontra-se subestimada?" [Is Income Inequality Underestimated in Brazil?]. Photocopy.

Batista, Paulo Nogueira, Jr. (2008) "Nacionalismo e desenvolvimento" [Nationalism and Development]. In Luiz Carlos Bresser-Pereira (ed.), *Nação, Cambio, e Desenvolvimento* [Nation, Exchange, and Development]. Rio de Janeiro: Editora FGV, pp. 25–34.

Bauer, Otto (1979 [1907]) *La questión de la Nacionalidad y la socialdemocracia.* México: Siglo Veintiuno Editores.

——— (1996 [1924]) "The Nation." In Gopal Balakrishnan (ed.), *Mapping the Nation.* London: Verso, pp. 39–77.

Bauman, Ricardo (2006) "Dilemas e perspectivas das exportações brasileiras" [Dilemmas and Perspectives on Brazilian Exports]. In Luiz Carlos Bresser-Pereira (ed.), *Economia brasileira na encruzilhada* [Brazilian Economy at the Crossroads]. Rio de Janeiro: Editora da Fundação Getúlio Vargas, pp. 137–162.

Belluzzo, Luiz Gonzaga de Mello, and Júlio Gomes de Almeida (2002) *Depois da queda* [After the Fall]. Rio de Janeiro: Civilização Brasileira.

Berglund, Gunnar, and Matias Vernengo (2006) *The Means to Prosperity: Fiscal Policy Reconsidered.* London: Routledge.

Berr, Eric, and François Combarnous (2007) "The False Promises of the (Second) Washington Consensus: Evidences from Latin America and the Caribbean (1990–2003)." *Brazilian Journal of Political Economy* 27 (4): pp. 525–545.

Bevilaqua, Afonso (2006) "BC reforçou economia" [Central Bank Strengthened the Economy]. Interview, *Valor Econômico,* July 6.

Bhaduri, Amit, and Joseph Steindl (1985) "The Rise of Monetarism as a Social Doctrine." In Philip Arestis and Thanos Skouras (eds.), *Post Keynesian Economic Theory.* Sussex: Wheatsheaf, pp. 24–56.

Bicalho, Aurélio (2005) "Teste de sustentabilidade e ajuste fiscal do Brasil pós-Real" [Test of Sustainability and Fiscal Adjustment in Brazil Post-Real]. Ph.D. diss., Escola de Pós-Graduação em Economia da Fundação Getúlio Vargas, Rio de Janeiro.

Bielschowsky, Ricardo (2006) "Consumo deve ser base para desenvolvimento" [Consumption Must Be a Base for Development]. Interview, *Valor Econômico,* December 20.

Blanchard, Olivier J. (2005) "Fiscal Dominance and Inflation Targeting: Lessons from Brazil." In F. Giavazzi, I. Goldfjan, and S. Herrera (eds.), *Inflation Targeting, Debt, and the Brazilian Experience, 1999 to 2003.* Cambridge, MA: MIT Press, pp. 49–80.

Blanchard, Olivier J., and Francesco Giavazzi (2004) "Improving the SGP Through a Proper Accounting of Public Investment." Centre for Economic Policy Research Discussion Paper 4220, London.

Blinder, Alan S. (1999) *Central Banks in Theory and Practice.* Cambridge, MA: MIT Press.

——— (2006) "Offshoring: The Next Industrial Revolution?" *Foreign Affairs* 85 (2): pp. 113–128.

Blinder, Alan S., and Ricardo Reis (2005) "Understanding the Greenspan Standard." Paper presented at the Federal Reserve Bank of Kansas City

Symposium, "The Greenspan Era: Lessons for the Future," Jackson Hole, Wyoming, August 15–17.

Bofinger, Peter (2001) *Monetary Policy.* Oxford: Oxford University Press.

Bofinger, Peter, Eric Mayer, and Timo Wollmershäuser (2002) "The BMW Model: Simple Macroeconomics for Closed and Open Economies—A Requiem for the IS/LM-AS/AD and the Mundell-Fleming Model." Würzburg University Economic Paper 35, October. Available at www.wifak .uni-wuerzburg.de/vwl1/wepdownload/abstract35.htm.

Bogdanski, Joel, Alexander A. Tombini, and Sérgio R. Werlang (2000) "Implementing Inflation Target in Brazil." Banco Central do Brasil Discussion Paper 1, Brasília.

Bresser-Pereira, Luiz Carlos (1977) *Estado e subdesenvolvimento industrializado* [State and Industrialized Underdevelopment]. São Paulo: Editora Brasiliense.

―――― (1991a [1990]) "A crise da América Latina: Consenso de Washington ou crise fiscal?" [Crisis in Latin America: Washington Consensus or Fiscal Crisis?]. *Pesquisa e Planejamento Econômico* 21 (1) (April): 3–23. Lecture in the annual congress of the Brazilian National Association of Post-Graduate Economics Courses. Brasília, December 1990.

―――― (ed.) (1991b) *Populismo econômico* [Economic Populism]. São Paulo: Editora Nobel.

―――― (1992) *A crise do estado* [The Crisis of the State]. São Paulo: Editora Nobel.

―――― (1994) "A economia e a política do Plano Real" [The Economy and the Real Plan Policy]. *Brazilian Journal of Political Economy* 14 (4): pp. 129–148.

―――― (1996a) "A inflação decifrada" [Inflation Deciphered]. *Brazilian Journal of Political Economy* 16 (3): pp. 20–35.

―――― (1996b) *Economic Crisis and State Reform in Brazil.* Boulder: Lynne Rienner Publishers.

―――― (2001a [1999]) "Incompetência e *confidence building* por trás de 20 años de quase-estagnação da América Latina" [Incompetence and Confidence Building After 20 Years of Quasi-stagnation in Latin America]. *Brazilian Journal of Political Economy* 21 (1): pp. 141–166. Paper presented to a seminar at the Centre for Brazilian Studies of Oxford University, December 1999.

―――― (2001b) "A fragilidade que nasce da dependência da poupança externa" [The Fragility That Comes from Foreign Savings Dependency]. *Valor 1000,* special edition of *Valor Econômico,* September.

―――― (2002a) "Financiamento para o subdesenvolvimento: O Brasil e o segundo Consenso de Washington" [Financing for Underdevelopment: Brazil and the Second Washington Consensus]. In Ana Célia Castro (ed.), *Desenvolvimento em debate: Painéis do desenvolvimento brasileiro I* [Development in Debate: Panels of the Brazilian Development I], vol. 2. Rio de Janeiro: Mauad/BNDES, pp. 359–398.

―――― (2002b) "Citizenship and Res Publica: The Emergence of Republican Rights." *Citizenship Studies* 6 (2): pp. 145–164.

—— (2003) *Desenvolvimento e Crise no Brasil: 1930–2003.* [Development and Crisis in Brazil: 1930–2003]. 5th ed. São Paulo: Editora 34.

—— (2004a) *Democracy and Public Management Reform: Building the Republican State.* Oxford: Oxford University Press.

—— (2004b) "Brazil's Quasi-stagnation and the Growth *cum* Foreign Savings Strategy." *International Journal of Political Economy* 32 (4): pp. 76–102.

—— (2005a) "Capitalismo dos técnicos e democracia" [Professionals' Capitalism and Democracy]. *Revista Brasileira de Ciências Sociais* 20 (59): pp. 133–148.

—— (2005b) "Do ISEB e da Cepal à teoria da dependência" [From ECLAC and ISEB to Dependency Theory]. In Caio Navarro de Toledo (ed.), *Intelectuais e política no Brasil: A experiência do ISEB* [Intellectuals and Politics in Brazil: The ISEB Experience]. Rio de Janeiro: Editora Revan, pp. 201–232.

—— (2005c). "Macroeconomia pós–plano Real: as relações básicas" [Macroeconomics Post–Real Plan: The Basic Relations]. In João Sicsú, Luiz Fernando de Paula, and Renaut Michel (eds.), *Novo desenvolvimentismo: Um projeto nacional de crescimento com eqüidade social* [New Developmentalism: A National Project for Growth with Social Equity]. Barueri: Editora Manole and Fundação Konrad Adenauer, pp. 3–47.

—— (2005d) "The Two Methods of Economics." Paper presented to Fifteenth Annual Conference of the European Association for Evolutionary Political Economy, Maastricht, November 7–10, 2003. Revised in 2005. Available at www.bresserpereira.org.br.

—— (2006a) "Estratégia nacional de desenvolvimento" [National Development Strategy]. *Brazilian Journal of Political Economy* 26 (2): pp. 203–230.

—— (ed.) (2006b) *Economia brasileira na encruzilhada* [Brazilian Economy at the Crossroads]. Rio de Janeiro: Editora da Fundação Getúlio Vargas.

—— (2007) *Macroeconomia da Estagnação* [Macroeconomics of Stagnation]. São Paulo: Editora 34.

—— (2008) "Dutch Disease and Its Neutralization: A Ricardian Approach." *Brazilian Journal of Political Economy* 28 (1): pp. 47–71.

Bresser-Pereira, Luiz Carlos, and Fernando Dall'Acqua (1991) "Economic Populism x Keynes: Reinterpreting Budget Deficit in Latin America." *Journal of Post Keynesian Economics* 14 (1): pp. 29–38.

Bresser-Pereira, Luiz Carlos, and Paulo Gala (2008) "Foreign Savings, Insufficiency of Demand, and Low Growth." *Journal of Post Keynesian Economics* 30 (3) (Spring): 315–334.

Bresser-Pereira, Luiz Carlos, and Nelson Marconi (1991) "Hyperinflation and Stabilization in Brazil: The First Collor Plan." In P. Davidson and J. Kregel, *Economic Problems of the 1990s.* London: Edward Elgar. Paper first presented to the Second International Post Keynesian Workshop, Knoxville, Tennessee, June 1990.

—— (2002) "Uma estratégia de desenvolvimento com estabilidade" [A Strategy of Development with Stability]. *Brazilian Journal of Political Economy* 22 (3): pp. 146–177.

———— (2003) "Crescimento econômico com poupança externa?" [Economic Growth with Foreign Savings?]. *Brazilian Journal of Political Economy* 22 (2): pp. 3–27.

———— (2008) "Existe doença holandesa no Brasil?" [Does the Dutch Disease Exist in Brazil?]. Paper presented in Getúlio Vargas Foundation's Fourth Economic Forum, São Paulo, September 2007.

Bresser-Pereira, Luiz Carlos, and Yoshiaki Nakano (1987) *The Theory of Inertial Inflation*. Boulder: Lynne Rienner Publishers.

Bresser-Pereira, Luiz Carlos, and Carmen A. Varela (2004) "The Second Washington Consensus and Latin America's Quasi-stagnation." *Journal of Post Keynesian Economics* 27 (2): pp. 231–250.

Bruno, Miguel (2006) "Lucro, acumulação de capital e crescimento econômico sob finanças liberalizadas: O caso brasileiro" [Profit, Capital Accumulation, and Economic Growth Under Liberalized Finance: The Brazilian Case]. In Luiz Fernando de Paula, Léo da Rocha Ferreira, and Milton de Assis (eds.), *Perspectivas para a economia brasileira: Inserção internacional e políticas públicas* [Perspectives for the Brazilian Economy: International Insertion and Public Policies]. Rio de Janeiro: Editora UERJ, pp. 91–116.

Câmara Netto, Alcino, and Matias Vernengo (2004) "Fiscal Policy and Washington Consensus: A Post Keynesian Perspective." *Journal of Post Keynesian Economics* 27 (2): pp. 333–343.

Canitrot, Adolfo (1991 [1975]) "A experiência populista de redistribuição de renda" [The Populist Experience of Income Redistribution]. In Luiz Carlos Bresser-Pereira (ed.), *Populismo económico* [Economic Populism]. São Paulo: Editora Nobel, pp. 11–36.

Cardoso, Fernando Henrique (1964) *Empresário industrial e desenvolvimento econômico* [Industrial Entrepreneur and Economic Development]. São Paulo: Difusão Européia do.

Cardoso, Fernando Henrique, and Enzo Faletto (1970 [1969]) *Dependência e desenvolvimento na América Latina* [Dependence and Development in Latin America]. Rio de Janeiro: Zahar Editores. First published in Spanish in 1969.

Carvalho, Fernando Cardim de (1992) *Mr. Keynes and the Post Keynesians.* Cheltenham: Edward Elgar Press.

———— (2005) "O sistema financeiro brasileiro: A modernização necessária" [The Brazilian Financial System: The Necessary Modernization]. In João Sicsú, Luiz Fernando de Paula, and Renaut Michel (eds.), *Novo desenvolvimentismo: Um projeto nacional de crescimento com eqüidade social* [New Developmentalism: A National Project for Growth with Social Equity]. Barueri: Editora Manole and Fundação Konrad Adenauer, pp. 329–346.

Carvalho, Fernando Cardim de, and João Sicsú (2006) "Controvérsias recentes sobre controles de capitais" [Recent Debate on Capital Controls]. In João Sicsú and Fernando Ferrari Filho (eds.), *Câmbio e controle de capitais: Avaliando a eficiênia de modelos macroeconômicos* [Exchange and Capital Control: Evaluating the Efficiency of Maroeconomic Models]. Rio de Janeiro: Editora Elsevier, pp. 1–29.

Cepeda, Vera (2004) "Roberto Simonsen e a formação da ideologia industrial no Brasil: Limites e impasses" [Robert Simonsen and the Formation of the Industrial Ideology in Brazil: Limits and Dilemmas]. Ph.D. diss., Political Science Department, São Paulo University.

Chang, Ha-Joon (2002) *Kicking Away the Ladder.* London: Anthem Press.

—— (2006) "Policy Space in Historical Perspective, with a Special Reference to Trade and Industrial Policies." *Economic and Political Weekly* 41 (7) (February): pp. 18–24.

—— (ed.) (2003) *Rethinking Development Economics.* London: Anthem Press.

Chatterji, Monojit, and Simon Price (1988) "Unions, Dutch Disease, and Unemployment." *Oxford Economic Papers* 40 (2) (June): pp. 302–321.

Chenery, Hollys, and Michael Bruno (1962) "Development Alternatives in an Open Economy: The Case of Israel." *Economic Journal* 72 (March): pp. 79–103.

Chick, Victoria (2004) "On Open Systems." *Brazilian Journal of Political Economy* 24 (1): pp. 3–16.

Cline, William R., and Sidney Weintraub (eds.) (1981) *Economic Stabilization in Developing Countries.* Washington, DC: Brookings Institution.

Coase, Ronald H. (1937) "The Nature of the Firm." *Econômica* 4 (16): pp. 386–405.

—— (1988) *The Firm, the Market, and the Law.* Chicago: University of Chicago Press.

Consad (Conselho Nacional de Secretários de Estado de Administração) (2006) *Avanços e perspectivas da gestão pública nos estados* [Progress and Perspectives of Public Management in the States]. São Paulo: Fundap.

Corden, W. M. (1984) "Booming Sector and Dutch Disease Economics: Survey and Consolidation." *Oxford Economic Papers* 36 (3): pp. 359–380.

Corden, W. M., and J. P. Neary (1982) "Booming Sector and De-industrialization in a Small Open Economy." *Economic Journal* 92 (368): pp. 825–848.

Coutinho, Luciano, and Luiz Gonzaga de Mello Belluzzo (2004) "'Financeirização' da riqueza, inflação de ativos, e decisão de gastos em economias abertas" ["Financerization" of Wealth, Inflation of Assets, and Decision on Expenditures in Open Economies]. In Fernando Ferrari Filho and Luiz Fernando de Paula (eds.), *Globalização financeira* [Financial Globalization]. Petrópolis: Editora Vozes, pp. 59–77.

Cunha, Paulo (2006) "Dissecando a integral do erro" [Analyzing the Error's Essence]. In Luiz Carlos Bresser-Pereira (ed.), *Economia brasileira na encruzilhada* [Brazilian Economy at the Crossroads]. Rio de Janeiro: Editora da Fundação Getúlio Vargas, pp. 11–23.

Damasceno, Aderbal Oliveira (2008) "Liberalização da conta de capitais e crescimento econômico: Evidências de dados em painel para a América Latina" [Capital Account Liberalization and Economic Growth: Evidence from Data in Latin American Panel]. *Brazilian Journal of Political Economy* 28 (4): pp. 595–611.

Delfim Netto, Antonio (2005) "Equilíbrio fiscal e eficiência privada" [Fiscal Equilibrium and Private Efficiency]. *Valor Econômico,* June 21.

—— (2006) "Política econômica e crescimento" [Economic Policy and Growth]. In Luiz Carlos Bresser-Pereira (ed.), *Economia brasileira na encruilhada*

[Brazilian Economy at the Crossroads]. Rio de Janeiro: Editora da Fundação Getúlio Vargas, pp. 83–96.

Diaz-Alejandro, Carlos (1991 [1981]) "Southern Cone Stabilization Plans." In Bresser-Pereira (ed.), *Populismo econômico* [Economic Populism]. São Paulo: Editora Nobel.

Dow, Sheila C. (1996) *The Methodology of Macroeconomic Thought.* Cheltenham: Edward Elgar.

Emmott, Bill (1999) "Freedom's Journey—A Survey of the 20th Century." *The Economist,* September 11.

Esping-Andersen, Gøsta (1990) *The Three Worlds of Welfare Capitalism.* Princeton, NJ: Princeton University Press.

Fajnzylber, P., N. Loyaza, and C. Alderón (2004) "Economic Growth in Latin America and Caribbean." World Bank Working Paper 265, Washington, DC, June.

Favero, Carlo A., and Francesco Giavazzi (2005) "Inflation Targeting and Debt: Lessons from Brazil." In F. Giavazzi, Ilan Goldfjan, and Santiago Herrera (eds.), *Inflation Targeting, Debt, and the Brazilian Experience, 1999 to 2003.* Cambridge, MA: MIT Press.

Ferrari Filho, Fernando, and Luiz Fernando de Paula (eds.) (2004) *Globalização financeira* [Financial Globalization]. Petrópolis: Editora Vozes.

Ferrari Filho, Fernando, Frederico Jayme Jr., Gilberto Tadeu Lima, José Luís Oreiro, and Luiz Fernando de Paula (2005) "Uma avaliação crítica da proposta de conversibilidade plena do real" [A Critical Evaluation of the Proposal for Currency Convertibility of the Real]. *Brazilian Journal of Political Economy* 25 (1): pp. 133–151.

Ferreira, João Marcelo Grossi, Jolanda E. Ygosse Baptista, and Samuel de Abreu Pessoa (2006) "Why Did the Brazilian Investment Ratio Not Recover After Inflation Stabilization? An Econometric Study on the Culprits." Banco Itaú, EESP/FGV, EPGR/FGV, unpublished manuscript, December.

Ferrer, Aldo (2004) *La densidad nacional* [The National Density]. Buenos Aires: Capital Intelectual.

Ffrench-Davis, Ricardo (2003) *Entre el neo-liberalismo y el crecimiento con equidad* [Between Neoliberalism and Growth with Equity]. 3rd ed. Santiago do Chile: J. C. Sáes Editor.

Figueiredo, Luiz Fernando, Pedro Fachada, and Sergio Goldestein (2002) "Monetary Policy in Brazil: Remarks on the Inflation Targeting Regime, Public Debt Management, and Open Market Operations." Banco Central do Brasil Discussion Paper 37, Brasília.

Frenkel, Roberto (2003) "Globalización y crisis financieras en América Latina" [Globalization and Financial Crisis in Latin America]. *Brazilian Journal of Political Economy* 23 (3): pp. 94–111.

Friedman, Thomas (2000) *The Lexus and the Olive Tree.* 2nd ed. New York: Random House.

Fukuyama, Francis (2004) *State-Building: Governance and World Order in the 21st Century.* Ithaca, NY: Cornell University Press.

Furtado, Celso (1966) *Subdesenvolvimento e estagnação na América Latina* [Underdevelopment and Stagnation in Latin America]. Rio de Janeiro: Editora Civilização Brasileira.

Gala, Paulo (2006) "Taxa de câmbio e macroeconomia do desenvolvimento" [Exchange Rate and the Macroeconomics of Development]. Ph.D. diss., Escola de Economia de São Paulo, Fundação Getúlio Vargas.

Galbraith, James (1997) "Time to Ditch the NAIRU." *Journal of Economic Perspectives* 11 (1): pp. 93–108.

Galbraith, John Kenneth (1958) *The Affluent Society.* Boston: Houghton Mifflin.

Garcia, Márcio (2004) "Brazil in the 20th Century: How to Escape the Interest Rate Trap." Photocopy. PUC, Department of Economics, Rio de Janeiro.

Gellner, Ernest (1983) *Nations and Nationalism.* Ithaca, NY: Cornell University Press.

——— (1996 [1993]) "The Coming of Nationalism and Its Interpretation: The Myths of Nation and Class." In Gopal Balakrishnan and B. Anderson (eds.), *Mapping the Nation.* London: Verso, pp. 98–145.

Gerschenkron, Alexander (1962) *Economic Backwardness in Historical Perspective: A Book of Essays.* New York: Praeger.

Godoi, Alexandra Strommer de Farias (2007) "O milagre irlandês como exemplo da adoção de uma estratégia nacional de desenvolvimento" [The Irish Miracle as an Example of the Adoption of a National Development Strategy]. *Brazilian Journal of Political Economy* 27 (4): pp. 546–566.

Goldfajn, Ilan (2006) "A 'mexicanização' da economia brasileira" [The "Mexicanization" of the Brazilian Economy]. *O Estado de S. Paulo,* September 5.

Goodin, Robert E., Bruce Headey, Ruud Muffels, and Henk-Jan Dirven (1999) *The Real Worlds of Welfare Capitalism.* Cambridge: Cambridge University Press.

Grossmann, Gene, and Esteban Rossi-Hansberg (2007) "The Rise of Offshoring: It's Not Wine for Cloth Anymore." In *The New Economic Geography: Effects and Policy Implications.* Federal Reserve Bank of Kansas City.

Gwartney, James, and Robert Lawson (1999) *Economic Freedom of the World 1998/1999—Interim Report.* Washington, DC: Free the World and The Fraser Institute.

Haddad, Claudio (2003) "Vendendo ilusão" [Selling Illusion]. *Valor Econômico,* December 5.

Hall, Peter A., and David Soskice (2001a) "An Introduction to Varieties of Capitalism." In Peter A. Hall and David Soskice (eds.), *Varieties of Capitalism.* Oxford: Oxford University Press, pp. 1–70.

——— (eds.) (2001b) *Varieties of Capitalism.* Oxford: Oxford University Press.

Harberger, Arnold C. (1996) "Fiscal Deficit and the Inflation Process." In Manuel Guitian and Robert Mundell, *Inflation and Growth in China.* Washington, DC: IMF, pp. 46–75.

Holland, Marcio (2006a) "Monetary and Exchange Rate Policy in Brazil After Inflation Targeting." In *Proceedings of the International Conference on Policy Modeling,* vol. 1. Berkeley: University of California, pp. 1–20.

——— (2006b) "Por que as taxas de juros reais de curto prazo são tão elevadas no Brasil?" [Why Are Real Short-term Exchange Rates So High in Brazil?]. Photocopy.

Holland, Marcio, Fernando M. Gonçalves, and Andrei D. Spacov (2005) "Can Jurisdictional Uncertainty and Capital Control Explain the High Level of Real Interest Rates in Brazil? Evidence from Panel Data." *Atas do 33° Encontro*

Nacional de Economia da ANPEC—Associação Nacional dos Centros de Pós-Graduação em Economia [Proceedings of the 33rd National Meeting of Economics of the National Association of Graduate Centers in Economics], Natal, December 8–10.

Huber, Evelyne (ed.) (2002) *Models of Capitalism: Lessons for Latin America.* University Park: Pennsylvania State University Press.

IEDI (Instituto de Estudos para o Desenvolvimento Industrial) (2006) "O comércio exterior brasileiro no primeiro semestre de 2006" [Brazilian Foreign Trade in the First Semester of 2006]. São Paulo: IEDI.

—— (2007a) *A balança comercial da indústria de transformação por intensidade tecnológica em 2006* [The International Commercial Balance of the Brazilian Manufacturing Industry in 2006 According to Technological Intensity]. São Paulo: IEDI.

—— (2007b) "A ironia da produção industrial: Apreciação cambial e porosidade da cadeia produtiva deterioram o saldo comercial onde a produção mais cresce" [The Irony of Industrial Production: Exchange Appreciation and Porosity of the Productive Chain Deteriorate the Commercial Balance Where the Production Principally Grows]. *Carta IEDI* 248 (February): pp. 1–4.

Johnson, Chalmers (1982) *MITI and the Japanese Miracle.* Stanford: Stanford University Press.

Kakwani, Nanak, Marcelo Neri, and Hyun H. Son (2006) "Linkages Between Pro-growth, Social Programmes, and Labour Market: The Recent Brazilian Experience." United Nations Development Programme, International Poverty Center Working Paper 26, August.

Kregel, Jan (1994–1995) "The Viability of Economic Policy and the Priorities of Economic Policy." *Journal of Post Keynesian Economics* 17 (2): pp. 261–277.

—— (2004) "Riscos e implicações da globalização financeira para a autonomia de políticas nacionais" [Risks and Implications of Financial Globalization for National Policies Autonomy]. In Fernando Ferrari Filho and Luiz Fernando de Paula (eds.), *Globalização financeira* [Financial Globalization]. Petrópolis: Editora Vozes, pp. 31–58.

—— (2006) "Prefácio" [Preface]. In João Sicsú and Fernando Ferrari Filho (eds.), *Câmbio e controle de capitais: Avaliando a eficiência de modelos macroeconômicos* [Exchange and Capitol Control: Evaluating the Efficiency of Macroeconomic Models]. Rio de Janeiro: Editora Elsevier, pp. ix–xiii.

Kydland, Finn E., and Edward C. Prescott (1977) "Rules Rather Than Discretion: The Inconsistency of Optimal Plans." *Journal of Political Economy* 85: pp. 473–492.

Larsen, Erling R. (2004) "Escaping the Resource Curse and the Dutch Disease: When and Why Norway Caught Up with and Forged Ahead of Its Neighbors." Statistics Norway, Research Department Discussion Paper 377, May.

Lavagna, Roberto (2006) "Tivemos de rejeitar a receita do FMI" [We Had to Reject the IMF's Recipe]. Interview, *Folha de S. Paulo,* July 30.

Le Heron, Edwin (2003) "A New Consensus on Monetary Policy?" *Brazilian Journal of Political Economy* 23 (4): pp. 3–27.

Le Heron, Edwin, and Emmanuel Carré (2006) "Credibility Versus Confidence in Monetary Policy." In R. Wray and M. Forstater (eds.), *Money, Financial Instability, and Stabilization Policy.* Cheltenham: Elgar Press, pp. 58–84.

Lewis, Arthur W. (1958 [1954]) "Economic Development with Unlimited Supply of Labor." In A. N. Agarwala and S. P. Singh (eds.), *The Economics of Underdevelopment.* New York: Oxford University Press, pp. 400–449.

List, Friedrich (1999 [1846]) *National System of Political Economy.* Roseville, CA: Dry Bones Press.

Lopes, Francisco L. (2002) "A proposta Bresser-Nakano para o futuro da política econômica" [The Bresser-Nakano Proposal for the Future of Economic Policy]. *Macrométrica* 25 (January). Available at www.bresserpereira.org.br.

Lucas, Fábio (2002) *Expressões da identidade brasileira* [Expressions of the Brazilian Identity]. São Paulo: Editora da PUC.

Magalhães, João Paulo de Almeida (2006) "Nova estratégia de desenvolvimento para o Brasil: Um enfoque de longo prazo" [New Development Strategy for Brazil: A Long-term Vision]. *Brazilian Journal of Political Economy* 26 (2): pp. 186–202.

Mankiw, N. Gregory (2006). "The Macroeconomist as Scientist and Engineer." *Journal of Economic Perspectives* 20 (4) (Fall): 29–46.

MARE (Ministério da Administração Federal e Reforma do Estado) (1995) *Plano Diretor* [White Paper on the Reform of the State Apparatus]. Brasília: Imprensa Nacional. English version available at www.bresserpereira.org.br.

Markwald, Ricardo, and Fernando J. Ribeiro (2006) "O surto exportador brasileiro no período 2002–04" [The Brazilian Export Boom in the Period 2002–2004]. In Luiz Carlos Bresser-Pereira (ed.), *Economia brasileira na encruzilhada* [Brazilian Economy at the Crossroads]. Rio de Janeiro: Editora da Fundação Getúlio Vargas, pp. 193–226.

Marques, Rosa Maria (1997) *A proteção social e o mundo do trabalho* [Social Protection and the World of Work]. São Paulo: Editora Bienal.

McCombie, John S. L. (1997) "Empirics of Balance-of-Payments Constrained Growth." *Journal of Post-Keynesian Economics* 19 (3): pp. 345–375.

McCombie, John S. L., and Anthony P. Thirlwall (1994) *Economic Growth and the Balance-of-Payments Constraint.* London: St. Martin's Press.

McKinnon, Ronald (1973) *Money and Capital in Economic Development.* Washington, DC: Brookings Institution.

Mendes, Marcos (ed.) (2006) *Gasto público eficiente* [Efficient Public Expenditure]. Rio de Janeiro: Topbooks.

Minella, A., P. S. Freitas, I. Goldfajn, and M. K. Muinhos (2003) "Inflation Targeting in Brazil: Constructing Credibility Under Exchange Rate Volatility." *Journal of International Money and Finance* 22 (7): pp. 1015–1040.

Muinhos, Marcelo K., and Márcio Nakane (2006) "Comparing Equilibrium Interest Rates: Different Approaches to Measure the Brazilian Rates." Banco Central do Brasil, Discussion Paper 101, Brasília, March.

Nakano, Yoshiaki (2002) "Modelo IS-MP" [IS-MP Model]. Escola de Economia de São Paulo da Fundação Getúlio Vargas, October.

———— (2006a) "Fundamentos para a independência do Banco Central" [Basis for the Independence of the Central Bank]. *Valor Econômico,* October 24.

———— (2006b) "A queda do risco—Brasil e a taxa interna de juros" [The Decrease of Risk—Brazil and the Domestic Interest Rate]. *Valor Econômico,* February 14.

Nassif, André (2008) "Há evidências de desindustrialização no Brasil?" [Is There Evidence of Deindustrialization in Brazil?]. *Revista de Economia Política* 28 (1): pp. 72–97.

Nassif, Luís (2003) "Preparando o segundo tempo" [Preparing the Second Round]. *Folha de S. Paulo,* August 2.

———— (2006) "O mercado comanda" [The Market Commands]. *Nassif on Line,* September 18. Available at http://luisnassifonline.blog.uol.com.br.

National Confederation of Industry (2006) "Crescimento: A visão da indústria" [Growth: Industry's Point of View]. Photocopy. Brasília.

Nayyar, Deepak (2003) "Globalization and Development." In Ha-Joon Chang (ed.), *Rethinking Development Economics.* London: Anthem Press, pp. 61–82.

North, Douglass C. (1990) *Institutions, Institutional Change, and Economic Performance.* Cambridge: Cambridge University Press.

Nunberg, Barbara, and John Nellis (1995) "Civil Service Reform and the World Bank." World Bank Discussion Paper 161.

Nye, Joseph S. (2002) *The Paradox of American Power: Why the World's Only Superpower Can't Go It Alone.* Oxford: Oxford University Press.

Ocampo, José Antonio (2003) "Development and the Global Order." In Ha-Joon Chang (ed.), *Rethinking Development Economics.* London: Anthem Press, pp. 83–104.

———— (ed.) (2005) *Beyond Reforms: Structural Dynamics and Macroeconomic Vulnerability.* Stanford, CA: Stanford University Press and World Bank.

Ono, Fábio Hideki, Guilherme Jonas Costa da Silva, José Luís Oreiro, and Luiz Fernando de Paula (2005) "Conversibilidade da conta de capital, taxa de juros, e crescimento econômico: Uma avaliação empírica da proposta de plena conversibilidade do real" [Capital Account Convertibility, Interest Rates, and Economic Growth: An Empirical Evaluation of the Real's Total Convertibility]. *Revista de Economia Contemporânea* 9 (2): pp. 231–262.

Oomes, Nienke, and Katerina Kalcheva (2007) "Diagnosing Dutch Disease: Does Russia Have the Symptoms?" IMF Working Paper 07/102, April.

Oreiro, José Luís (2006) "Uma nota sobre os diferentes conceitos de taxa de juros de equilíbrio e os dilemas da política econômica no Brasil" [A Note on Different Concepts of Equilibrium Interest Rate and the Dilemmas of Economic Policy in Brazil]. *Boletim Economia & Tecnologia* 6 (Centro de Pesquisas Econômicas of the Federal University of Paraná), July–September: pp. 17–20.

Oreiro, José Luís, Luciano Nakabashi, and Breno Lemos (2007) "Por que o Brasil cresce pouco?" [Why Does Brazil Grow So Insufficiently?]. *Valor Econômico,* March 19.

Oreiro, José Luís, Luiz Fernando de Paula, and Guilherme J. C. da Silva (2004) "Por uma moeda parcialmente conversível: Uma crítica a Arida e Bacha"

[For a Partially Convertible Currency: A Critique of Arida and Bacha]. *Brazilian Journal of Political Economy* 24 (2): pp. 223–237.

Oreiro, José Luís, Luiz Fernando de Paula, Fábio Hideki Ono, and Guilherme Jonas Costa da Silva (2006) "Determinantes macroeconômicos do *spread* bancário no Brasil: Teoria e evidência recente" [Macroeconomic Determinants of the Banking Spread in Brazil: Theory and Recent Evidence]. *Revista de Economia Aplicada* 10 (4): pp. 609–634.

Palma, Gabriel (2005) "Four Sources of 'De-industrialization' and a New Concept of Dutch Disease." In José Antonio Ocampo (ed.), *Beyond Reforms: Structural Dynamics and Macroeconomic Vulnerability*. Stanford, CA: Stanford University Press and World Bank, pp. 71–116.

Pasinetti, Luigi (1997) "The Social Burden of High Interest Rates." In Philip Arestis, Gabriel Palma, and Malcolm Sawyer (eds.), *Post Keynesian Economics and the History of Economics: Essays in Honour of Geoff Harcourt*, pp. 149–156.

Pastore, Affonso Celso, and Cristina Pinotti (2006) "O câmbio no Brasil e no Chile" [Exchange Rate in Brazil and Chile]. *Valor Econômico,* September 11.

Paula, Luiz Fernando de (2003) "Controle de capitais: Lições para o Brasil" [Capital Controls: Lessons for Brazil]. In R. Benecke and R. Nascimento (eds.), *Opções de política econômica para o Brasil* [Options of Economic Policy for Brazil]. Rio de Janeiro: Fundação Konrad Adenauer, pp. 445–465.

——— (2008) "Uma nova política macroeconômica: Algumas proposições a partir de uma visão novo-desenvolvimentista" [A New Macroeconomic Policy: Some Propositions from a New-Developmentalist Viewpoint]. In Luiz Carlos Bresser-Pereira (ed.), *Nação, cambio, e desenvolvimento* [Nation, Exchange, and Development]. Rio de Janeiro: Editora FGV, pp. 95–134.

Pereira, Edgard Antonio (2008 [2007]) "Doença holandesa e falha no desenvolvimento econômico" [Dutch Disease and Failure in Economic Development]. Paper presented in Getulio Vargas Foundation's Fourth Economic Forum, São Paulo, September 2007. Forthcoming in Luiz Carlos Bresser-Pereira (ed.), *Doença Holandesa e indústria* [Dutch Disease and Industry]. Rio de Janeiro: Editora da Fundação Getúlio Vargas.

Pires, Manoel Carlos de Castro (2006) "Uma avaliação da poupança em conta corrente do governo" [An Evaluation of Savings in the Government Current Account]. *Economia & Tecnologia* (Centro de Pesquisas Econômicas of the Federal University of Paraná) 5, April–June: pp. 69–77.

Piva, Horácio Lafer (2006) "Crise política atrapalha próximo governo" [Political Crisis Upsets Next Government]. Interview, *Folha de S. Paulo*, September 25.

Porcile, Gabriel, and Gilberto Tadeu Lima (2006) "Tipo de cambio, empleo y crecimiento en un modelo con restricción externa." *Investigación Económica* 67 (257): pp. 63–89.

Prasad, Eswar, Ken Rogoff, Shang-Jin Wey, and Ayhan Khose (2003) "Effects of Financial Globalization on Developing Countries." IMF Occasional Paper 220, Washington, DC.

Prebisch, Raúl (1963) *Hacia una dinámica del desarrollo llatinoamericano* [Toward a Dynamic of Latin American Development]. México: Fondo de Cultura Económica.

Rama, Martin (1999) "Public Sector Downsizing: An Introduction." *World Bank Economic Review* 13 (1): pp. 1–22.

Rangel, Ignácio M. (1963) *A inflação brasileira* [The Brazilian Inflation]. Rio de Janeiro: Tempo Brasileiro.

——— (1985) "Recessão, inflação, e dívida externa" [Recession, Inflation, and External Debt]. *Brazilian Journal of Political Economy* 5 (3): pp. 5–25.

Razin, Ofair, and Susan M. Collins (1997) "Exchange Rate Misalignment and Growth." National Bureau of Economic Research Working Paper 6147, Cambridge, MA, September.

Renan, Ernest (1993 [1882]) *Qu'est-ce qu'une nation?* [What Is a Nation?]. Paris: Pocket/Agora.

Rodrik, Dani (1998) "Who Needs Capital-Account Convertibility?" In Stanley Fischer et al., *Should IMF Pursue Capital-Account Convertibility?* Essays in International Finance no. 207. Princeton: Princeton University Press, pp. 55–65.

——— (1999) *The New Global Economy and Developing Countries: Making Openness Work*. Washington, DC: Overseas Development Council; Baltimore: Johns Hopkins University Press.

——— (2007) *One Economics, Many Recipes*. Princeton, NJ: Princeton University Press.

Rogoff, Kenneth (1985) "The Optimal Degree of Commitment to an Intermediate Monetary Target." *Quarterly Journal of Economics* 100 (4): pp. 1169–1189.

Rosenstein-Rodan, Paul (1943) "Problems of Industrialization in Eastern Europe and South-Eastern Europe." *Economic Journal* 53, June: pp. 202–211.

Sachs, Ignacy (2008) *La Troisième rive* [The Third Margin]. Paris: Bourin Éditeur.

Sachs, J. D. (1989) "Social Conflict and Populist Policies in Latin America." National Bureau of Economic Research, Working Paper no. 2897, March.

Sachs, J. D., and Andrew M. Warner (1999) "The Big Push, Natural Resource Booms, and Growth." *Journal of Development Economics* 59 (1): pp. 43–76.

——— (2001) "The Curse of Natural Resources." *European Economic Review* 45 (4–6): pp. 827–838.

Said, Edward W. (2003 [1978]) *Orientalism*. London: Penguin Books.

Sala-i-Martin, Xavier, and Arvind Subramanian (2003) "Addressing the Natural Resource Curse: An Illustration from Nigeria." National Bureau of Economic Research Working Paper 9084, Cambridge, MA, June.

Schwarz, Roberto (1973) "As idéias for a do lugar" [The Ideas out of Order]. *Estudos Cebrap* 3, January: pp. 149–162.

Shaw, Edward (1973) *Financial Deepening in Economic Development*. Oxford: Oxford University Press.

Sicsú, João, and Fernando Ferrari Filho (eds.) (2006) *Câmbio e controle de capitais: Avaliando a eficiência de modelos macroeconômicos* [Exchange and Capital Control: Evaluating the Efficiency of Macroeconomic Models]. Rio de Janeiro: Editora Elsevier.

Sicsú, João, Luiz Fernando de Paula, and Renaut Michel (eds.) (2005) *Novo desenvolvimentismo: Um projeto nacional de crescimento com eqüidade social* [New Developmentalism: A National Project for Growth with Social Equity]. Barueri: Editora Manole and Fundação Konrad Adenauer.

Silva, Alexandre M. Angelo da, and Manoel C. de Castro Pires (2006) "Dívida pública, poupança em conta corrente, e superávit primário: Uma análise de sustentabilidade" [Public Debt, Current Account Savings, and Primary Surplus: An Analysis of Sustainability]. IPEA Discussion Paper 1196, Brasília, June.

Soares, Sergei (2006) "Distribuição de renda no Brasil de 1976 a 2004" [Income Distribution in Brazil from 1976 to 2004]. Photocopy.

Stephens, John D. (2002) "European Welfare State Regimes: Configurations, Outcomes, Transformations," In Evelyne Huber (ed.), *Models of Capitalism: Lessons for Latin America.* University Park: Pennsylvania State University Press, pp. 303–338.

Suplicy, Eduardo Matarazzo (2003) "Renda básica: A resposta está sendo soprada pelo vento" [Basic Income: The Answer Is Blowing in the Wind]. *Brazilian Journal of Political Economy* 23 (3): pp. 47–62.

Svensson, Lars O. (1998) "Inflation Targeting as a Monetary Policy Rule." National Bureau of Economic Research Working Paper 6790, Cambridge, MA.

Taylor, John B. (1993) "Discretion Versus Policy Rules in Practice." Carnegie-Rochester Series on Public Policies 39: pp. 195–214.

Taylor, Lance (2004) *Reconstructing Macroeconomics.* Cambridge: Cambridge University Press.

Toledo, Caio Navarro de (ed.) (2005) *Intelectuais e política no Brasil: A experiência do ISEB* [Intellectuals and Politics in Brazil: The Experience of ISEB]. Rio de Janeiro: Editora Revan.

Torvik, R. (2001) "Learning by Doing and the Dutch Disease." *European Economic Review* 45: pp. 285–306.

Trevisan, Claudia (2006) *China: O renascimento do império.* [China: The Rebirth of the Empire]. São Paulo: Editora Planeta.

Unafisco/Delegacia Sindical de São Paulo (2006) "Execução orçamentária do Brasil—de FHC a Lula" [Budget Execution of Brazil—from FHC to Lula]. Photocopy.

Wade, Robert (1990) *Governing the Market.* Princeton, NJ: Princeton University Press.

—— (2003) "What Strategies Are Viable for Developing Countries Today? The World Trade Organization and the Shrinking of 'Development Space.'" *Review of International Political Economy* 10 (4) (November): 621–644.

Werlang, Sérgio (2006) "A meta para a inflação de 2008 e a taxa de juros" [Inflation Target for 2008 and the Interest Rate]. *Valor Econômico*, July 10.

Williamson, John (1990) "What Washington Means by Policy Reform." In John Williamson (ed.), *Latin American Adjustment: How Much Has Happened?* Washington, DC: Institute for International Economics, pp. 7–38.

Williamson, Oliver E. (1985) *The Economic Institutions of Capitalism.* New York: The Free Press.

Woo-Cummings, Meredith (ed.) (1999) *The Developmental State*. Ithaca, NY: Cornell University Press, pp. 32–60.

Zochun, Maria Helena (ed.) (2006) "Simplificando o Brasil: Tributação e gastos públicos" [Simplifying Brazil: Taxation and Public Expenditures]. *Cadernos Fecomercio de Economia* 11 (April): pp. 1–44.

Index

About the Book

After the 1994 Real Plan ended fourteen years of high inflation in Brazil, the country's economy was expected—mistakenly—to grow quickly. Luiz Carlos Bresser-Pereira discusses Brazil's economic trajectory from the mid-1990s to the present Lula administration, critically appraising the neoliberal reforms that have curtailed growth and proposing a national development strategy geared toward effective competition in the global marketplace.

Luiz Carlos Bresser-Pereira is professor emeritus of politics and economics at the Getúlio Vargas Foundation. In addition to his long academic career, he has served as Brazil's minister of finance, minister of federal administration and state reform, and minister of science and technology, and also as secretary of the government of the state of São Paulo.